Big Data and Democracy

Big Data and Democracy

Edited by
KEVIN MACNISH AND
JAI GALLIOTT

EDINBURGH
University Press

Edinburgh University Press is one of the leading university presses in the UK. We publish academic books and journals in our selected subject areas across the humanities and social sciences, combining cutting-edge scholarship with high editorial and production values to produce academic works of lasting importance. For more information visit our website: edinburghuniversitypress.com

Edinburgh University Press Ltd
The Tun – Holyrood Road, 12(2f) Jackson's Entry, Edinburgh EH8 8PJ

First published in hardback by Edinburgh University Press 2020

Typeset in 10/13 Giovanni by
IDSUK (DataConnection) Ltd

A CIP record for this book is available from the British Library

ISBN 978 1 4744 6352 2 (hardback)
ISBN 978 1 4744 6353 9 (paperback)
ISBN 978 1 4744 6354 6 (webready PDF)
ISBN 978 1 4744 6355 3 (epub)

CONTENTS

CONTRIBUTORS

Ramón Alvarado is an Assistant Professor of Philosophy and Data Ethics at the University of Oregon. His research focuses on the epistemic and ethical implications of the use of computers and computational methods in science and society.

Thorsten Brønholt conducts research in the Department of Political Science, University of Copenhagen, a school known for its heavy focus on methodologies. He is also a trained project manager. As both an internal and an external consultant, he has designed and carried out several large ($n > 6,000$) quantitative surveys for the Municipality of Copenhagen.

Massimiliano (Max) Cappuccio is Deputy Director of the Values in Defence and Security Technology group. He also holds a secondary affiliation with UAE University. His research in embodied cognitive science and social cognition theory attempts to combine enactive and extended approaches to the mind. As a cognitive philosopher, his research on cognitive processes and intelligent systems is interdisciplinary, and aims to integrate phenomenological analyses, empirical experimentation and synthetic modelling.

David Douglas researches with the Department of Philosophy and is ethics adviser within the Centre for Telematics and Information Technology (CTIT) at the University of Twente, the Netherlands.

Carl Fox is Lecturer in the IDEA Centre at the University of Leeds. He holds a strong interest in the ethics of the media, in particular the relationship between legitimacy and stability in the public sphere. He is currently a co-investigator on an AHRC-funded project examining media regulation and the role of codes of ethics for the press in ten European countries.

Jai Galliott leads the Values in Defence and Security Technology Group within the University of New South Wales at the Australian Defence Force Academy. He is a former Royal Australian Navy officer and Australian Army Research Fellow, and Visiting Fellow at the Centre for Technology and Global Affairs at the University of Oxford.

Philip Garnett is Lecturer in the York Cross-Disciplinary Centre for Systems Analysis & School of Management at the University of York. He is interested in systems theory, complex systems theory, and network analysis techniques that allow us to understand organisations and how they operate. His research is broadly focused on modelling organisational structure and interactions between organisations and their environment, and understanding the flow of information through organisations.

Stephanie Gauttier is a Marie Curie Postdoctoral Fellow at the University of Twente. She has published widely on the use of technological enhancements and wearable technologies in medicine and the workplace. Her current research, sponsored by the Marie Curie IF fellowship looks at how the concept of human enhancement can be translated to organisations, partly by looking at how human enhancement technologies can impact workflow management and the ethical issues this raises.

Sarah M. Hughes is an ESRC-funded Research Fellow in the Department of Geography at the University of Durham. Her current research focuses upon conceptualisations of resistance within the UK asylum system.

David Kinkead teaches in the Department of Philosophy at the University of Queensland.

Wulf Loh researches in the Department of Philosophy at the University of Stuttgart.

Björn Lundgren is researcher in the Division of Philosophy at the Royal Institute of Technology (KTH), Stockholm, Sweden.

Kevin Macnish is Assistant Professor in Ethics and IT at the University of Twente. His research is in the ethics of surveillance, security and technology, and he has published a book and a number of articles on surveillance ethics.

John MacWillie researches at California State University, East Bay, California (CSUEB) with expertise in artificial intelligence, history of science and philosophy of science.

Tim McFarland is a Research Fellow in the Values in Defence and Security Technology group within the School of Engineering and Information Technology of the University of New South Wales at the Australian Defence

Force Academy. His current work is on the social, legal and ethical questions arising from the emergence of new military and security technologies, and their implications for the design and use of military systems.

Steve McKinlay is Senior Lecturer in Computing and Research Coordinator at the Wellington Institute of Technology.

Kieron O'Hara is Associate Professor in Electronics and Computer Science at the University of Southampton, partly supported by the EPSRC project SOCIAM.

Joe Saunders is an Assistant Professor in Philosophy at Durham University, UK. He is the co-editor, with Carl Fox, of *Media Ethics, Free Speech, and the Requirements of Democracy* (2019).

Tom Sorell is Professor of Politics and Philosophy and Head of the Interdisciplinary Ethics Research Group in PAIS. He was an RCUK Global Uncertainties Leadership Fellow (2013–16). Previously, he was John Ferguson Professor of Global Ethics and Director of the Centre for the Study of Global Ethics, University of Birmingham.

Harald Stelzer is Professor of Political Philosophy and Head of the Section Political Philosophy at the University of Graz, Austria. His main research interests are in the problems and opportunities of the normative evaluation of political courses of action under special consideration of uncertainty and risks in regard to emerging technologies.

Anne Suphan is a post-doctoral researcher at Hohenheim University, Germany. She received her PhD in Organization Studies and Cultural Theory from the University of St. Gallen, Switzerland. Her research interests include social media, digital divide, digital sociology and visual research methods.

Hristina Veljanova is researcher at the Section Political Philosophy at the University of Graz. She is also pursuing her PhD on designing for values in autonomous vehicles at the University of Graz. Her research interests lie in the areas of philosophy and ethics of technology, machine ethics, robot ethics, moral philosophy and justice theories.

Christopher Zirnig is a researcher in the Institute of Law and Social Sciences at the University of Hohenheim.

An Introduction to Big Data and Democracy

Kevin Macnish and Jai Galliott

Over the past decade, political systems across Europe, Asia and North America have been challenged by events including large waves of immigration, a resurgence of economic protectionism and the rise of a pernicious brand of nationalism. Established politicians have adapted their rhetoric and processes in ways that risk alienating the population bases they serve, while populist politicians promising easy solutions have gained significant traction with the electorate. Yet in the coming decade, the greatest challenge to face democracies will be to develop new capabilities and protections that allow for the appropriate management and exploitation of big data. We use the term 'big data' to mean the exponentially increasing amount of digital information being created by new information technologies (such as mobile Internet, cloud storage, social networking and the 'Internet of Things' that has come to include everything from polling machines to sex toys), as well as the advanced analytics used to process that data. Big data yields not simply a quantitative increase in information, but a qualitative change in how we create new knowledge and understand the world, bringing with it a host of ethical questions. These data-related information technologies have already begun to revolutionise commerce and science, transforming the economy and acting as enablers for other game-changing technology trends, from next-generation genomics to energy exploration.

Despite this, the impact of big data on democracy has only recently come under the microscope. This is not altogether surprising. The term 'big data' entered general public consciousness early in 2012 when an article by Charles Duhigg in the *New York Times* reported on a US superstore identifying a teenage girl as pregnant before she had told her father (Duhigg 2012). The early public focus on the impact of big data thus fell on retail opportunities and threats to civic and individual values such as privacy. In the UK at least, the Care.Data fiasco of 2014, in which the government announced that all data collected on patients in the UK would be entered into a single database without seeking consent, turned attention to medical applications (Knapton 2016). This was reinforced, again in the UK, with the Google DeepMind/ Royal Free Trust hospitals case the same year, in which a private company was being passed sensitive medical information by a public institution (Powles and Hodson 2017; Hern 2017; Suleyman and King 2017).

In September 2016, the CEO of Cambridge Analytica, Alexander Nix, gave a presentation at the annual Concordia Summit in New York City. His presentation, 'The Power of Big Data and Psychographics', described his approach to audience targeting and data modelling, and explained how, when combined with psychological profiling, this would 'enhance' elections and disrupt conventional marketing (Concordia 2016). Proceeding to discuss how his company had assisted the unsuccessful bid of US Senator Ted Cruz for the Republican Party nomination for the 2016 US Presidential election, Nix explained that his company had developed a model to 'predict the personality of every single adult in the United States of America' based on 'hundreds and hundreds of thousands' of responses by Americans to a survey. The purpose of this model was to tailor political messages to target individuals with certain personality traits. As Nix explained, 'today communication is becoming ever increasingly targeted. It's being individualised for every single person in this room . . . [Y]ou'll only receive adverts that not only are on the products and services, or in the case of elections, issues that you care about most, but that have been nuanced in order to reflect the way you see the world' (Concordia 2016).

While Cambridge Analytica would later close after intense scrutiny as to how they had acquired data via a personality test app that an independent researcher had deployed on Facebook (Solon and Laughland 2018), the techniques Nix described demonstrate the possibilities with regard to political messaging on offer thanks to the combination of social media and big data analytics. Facebook in particular faces what some are calling an 'existential crisis' over revelations that its user data fell into the hands of the Trump campaign (Byers 2018). Whether the attacks on the social media giant are justified, the fact is that the Obama campaign also employed big data analytic techniques on Facebook data in 2012. Indeed, the re-election campaign for President Barack Obama in the 2012 US Presidential election was seen as innovative precisely for its use of social media and big data analytics (O'Neil 2016: 188–93). However, the reaction from the pundits and press in 2012 was somewhat different, with articles titled 'Obama, Facebook and the Power of Friendship: the 2012 Data Election' (Pilkington and Michel 2012) and 'How Obama's Team Used Big Data to Rally Voters' (Issenberg 2012). The Obama campaign encouraged supporters to download an Obama 2012 Facebook app that, when activated, let the campaign collect Facebook data both on users and their friends. The campaign later boasted that more than a million people had downloaded the app, which, given an average friend-list size of 190, means that as many as 190 million had at least some of their Facebook data vacuumed up by the Obama campaign without their explicit knowledge or consent (Leetaru 2018). While the use of data analytics was prevalent by both the Obama campaign and the Trump campaign, a significant factor in the meantime has been the rise of people accessing news articles via social media, and the associated rise of 'fake news' stories and websites.

In the same year as Trump won the US presidential elections, in the UK the Leave campaign in the European Referendum similarly boasted success, with the official Leave campaign, Vote Leave, proclaiming that big data had played the pivotal role (Cummings 2016). Even more remarkable, is that few people realised that this technology, the collection, aggregation and application of big data, was being utilised during the referendum. It was later revealed that Cambridge Analytica provided initial help and guidance to the Leave.EU campaign, which then went on to develop its own artificial intelligence analysis methodology (Ram 2018). The 2017 elections in Germany were subsequently shrouded in anxiety, some stemming from concerns about the role of big data. Fake accounts and social bots, filter bubbles and echo chambers, foreign propaganda machineries and campaign micro-targeting called the neutrality, inclusiveness and permeability of Germany's digital public spheres into question (Essif 2017; Kruschinski and Haller 2017).

Big data has meant that political organisations now have the tools to identify issues important to specific individuals, determine how to present their case in the most effective way for those individuals, and the means to communicate their message directly to them. In many ways, this is ideal for the democratic process: if I as a citizen do not care about military spending, why waste my time with advertising about that? Tell me what your party will do to social welfare spending. Big data allows you to know that I care for social welfare and not the military, and allows your party to reach me directly. At the same time, your party can inform a soldier that her job is secure if you should gain power.

The potential downside of this is the result of the soldier and I seeing different messages. Political discourse thus risks becoming a private (typically one-way) conversation between the speaker and the targeted audience. Yet this has always been true: from voting in ancient Athens to politicians door-stepping voters today, those seeking election could fine-tune their message to individual voters. Likewise, political advertising is hardly new, with some advertisements appealing to some voters and other advertising appealing to different voters. Different posters may go up in different parts of the same city or country depending on the demographic being reached. Is there really anything new in what has been happening with big data in democratic processes?

The chapters in this volume propose several areas of concern which have arisen in recent years in relation to big data and democracy, and which can be conceived as fundamentally novel. These range from trust in automated systems operating on the basis of big data to the aforementioned individualisation of political messaging. In the case of the latter, the substantive change in the nature of advertising is that whereas a variety of political posters may have been used, as posters these were in the public space and available for examination by all citizens, even if they were more likely to be seen by only a sub-set. Individuated political advertising on social media micro-targets the message to a sub-set without the opportunity of others seeing what is being sent.

Any attempt at making political discourse private risks undermining the public discussion of political views and identities. These risks are further exacerbated by the proliferation of echo chambers and filter bubbles, as social media contributes to reinforcing our own prejudices while shielding us from the values, thoughts and feelings of others. As discussed in several chapters of this volume, a stable democracy requires a shared identity and political culture to prevent it fracturing into separate political communities. This in turn necessitates some common communication network for political messages to be transmitted, understood and evaluated by citizens. Without neutral, inclusive and open public spheres, the aggregation of individual interests or beliefs about the common good risks distortion, the control of political institutions loses effectiveness, and the civic commitments of citizens may deteriorate as trust declines.

We are currently in the middle of a technological disruption that will transform the way society is organised and may go on to impact the freedoms of citizens if we do not immediately investigate the challenges posed by big data. The effectiveness of these technologies and techniques appears to have reached new heights, with the digital upheaval in full swing and showing no signs of slowing. The quantity of data we produce doubles every year, so that in 2016 we produced as much processable data as in the history of humankind up to 2015. Every minute we produce hundreds of thousands of Google searches and Facebook posts. Each of these contains information that reveal how we think and feel. The things around us, from clothing to cars to kettles, are increasingly connected to the Internet. It is estimated that in 10 years' time there will be 150 billion networked measuring sensors, twenty times more than the number of people on Earth. Then, the amount of data will double every 12 hours.

At the same time, the challenges to democratic society presented by data analytics are not limited to the party-political process. The Snowden revelations included claims that vast quantities of internet data were being collected by the US, UK and other intelligence agencies with the purported goal of uncovering patterns of behaviour which might indicate military or security threats. Artificial intelligence based on assessments of large data sets is increasingly being tested for parole boards and in predictive policing, leading to concerns that people may soon be apprehended for 'pre-crime'. Furthermore, while many in society have a degree of control over at least some of the data they share, others who rely on welfare do not and must share openly with the state to receive support (Macnish 2017). This volume investigates the phenomenon that is big data and provides a much-needed critical exploration of the extent to which the exponentially increasing amount of digital information available to political actors is transforming the shaping of societies through the democratic process and questions whether are there reasonable democratic limits that can be placed on the employment of big data depending on the collection, storage, processing or use of that data.

The book is divided into four parts. Part One looks at the relationship that exists between citizens and data. In the first chapter, Kieron O'Hara applies a Weberian analysis to developments in big data. He argues that just as Weber noted a move from the pre-modern to the modern with the advent of bureaucracy, so we are now entering a time of digital modernity. The focus in digital modernity is less the present (what is happening now) as the subjunctive (what could happen), governed by data. This, he argues, gives data a central role in governing for both good and ill.

In his chapter, Carl Fox argues that citizens deserve 'opacity respect' in which the state refrains from peering into citizens' lives to determine their capacities, for good or ill. Governments should assume that we are rational agents, barring certain obvious exceptions such as infants and people who are mentally incapacitated, in the same way that we assume this of each other. To dig deeper, without permission, is to undermine human dignity and that which renders us equal as humans, thereby forming a foundation of the democratic ideology.

Kevin Macnish and Stephanie Gauttier take a different angle on the question of democratic implications of data by looking at the concept of ownership of personal data. This has been suggested as a way of giving citizens control of 'their' data and is assumed in European law. However, Macnish and Gauttier argue that there are, at best, only weak philosophical grounds on which to base this claim, and that the consequences of viewing our relationship with the data that describe us in terms of ownership may turn out to be highly undesirable. Instead, they argue that control should be based around custody of data and the potential for harm.

Tom Sorell turns our attention to two state (police) uses of big data that have elicited concern: the creation of DNA databases and the use of past data to predict future crimes and criminals. In response to the former, Sorell argues that there is nothing intrinsically wrong with large-scale, indiscriminate databases of DNA profiles. These do not constitute an invasion of privacy, and nor do they necessarily render an entire population suspect, although he accepts that in the current climate they may be interpreted that way. As regards predictive policing, Sorell's argument is that these uses are more concerning, basing future decisions on past information that may no longer be pertinent and could well be discriminatory.

Part Two turns to look at political advertising, a point of reference in Fox's chapter, and the centre of attention for Joe Saunders. What is it about the micro-targeting of political advertising, asks Saunders, that is so wrong? His response is that, like dog-whistle politics, sending different advertising to different targets can obscure the open public discussion of policy that is critical to the democratic process. As such, parties (and individuals) that win power through such means find themselves with no democratic mandate to govern.

This discussion is followed by a chapter on Twitter and electoral bias by Wulf Loh, Anne Suphan and Christopher Zirnig. Here the authors introduce Habermasian criteria for the functioning of a healthy democracy and apply research from the use of Twitter during the most recent German general election to describe the influence (or lack thereof) of social media on the electoral process. In particular, the authors highlight what they call a social media divide.

In his chapter, Thorsten Brønholt introduces the concept of gated communities of the digitised mind. These draw on the notions of echo chambers and filter bubbles to suggest that there are regions for at least some of us that function in the same way as a gated community in which we mix only with those least likely to challenge our views. He supports this argument with original analysis of fifteen Danish politicians which summarises the results from semi-structured interviews with the respondents, and an analysis of their personal Facebook and Twitter feeds, as well as identical Google searches on their private devices.

In the final chapter of this section, Dave Kinkead and David Douglas draw on the history of democracies to see how big data and its use with social media sites introduces new challenges to the contemporary market-place of ideas. They note that traditionally one could narrowcast a tailored message with some impunity, but limited effect, while broadcasts (with larger impact) were open to examination by the public. Micro-targeted political advertising now allows for the narrowcast message to be tweaked and directed on a scale never before seen.

Part Three looks at more technical issues relating to big data. John Mac-Willie's chapter develops an ontological understanding of the infrastructure underlying big data applications through an historical overview of developments in information communications technology since the 1950s. This leads him to conclude that big data is a fundamentally new object in the world, bringing with it key issues of richness and complexity in computer networks.

In his chapter, Steve McKinlay argues that the use of big data algorithms introduces a key problem in terms of epistemic opacity. Opacity in various forms is an issue that many authors identify as posing problems for democratic functioning and accountability. In McKinlay's case, the argument focuses on the impact that epistemic opacity has on our ability to trust non-human agents. He holds that while the outputs of big data-derived decisions can be significant for citizens, where we do not have the ability to understand how these decisions were made we cannot ultimately trust the decider. Decisions based on mere probability are not, he argues, sufficiently grounded for democratic systems and risk harming citizens.

Ramón Alvarado also looks at issues of opacity, but whereas McKinlay argues that the core challenges to arise from this are those relating to trust, Alvarado turns his attention elsewhere. Following a detailed examination of different kinds of opacity, he raises the problem of 'many hands' (where to attribute responsibility in complex systems), error assessment and path complexity. In the process, he successfully offers the reader a demystified understanding of how big data computational methods function and suggests ways in which opacity threatens fundamental elements of the democratic process.

Finally in this section, Tim McFarland, Jai Galliott and Massimiliano Cappuccio consider the use of big data in military contexts. They draw on three paradoxes raised by Neil Richards and Jonathan King to examine particular challenges facing the military. These are the transparency paradox, the need for the collection and use of data to be as transparent as possible while being collected and used for national security or military purposes which themselves require secrecy; the identity paradox, which recognises that while big data reflects the identity and behaviour of those whose data is used, so too can it be used to alter those identities and behaviours; and the power paradox, highlighting the increased power gained through big data coupled with the risks of using those data in a largely unregulated environment.

The fourth and final section of the book takes up the implications for trust in society raised by McKinlay (above). The first chapter in this section, by Björn Lundgren, looks at the meaning and role of anonymity, which is often threatened when data sets are agglomerated in big data practices, leading to de-anonymisation. He argues that there are a number of key values threatened by the de-anonymisation, but that the concept of anonymity is not sufficient given what is really at stake. Instead, he holds that what is really under threat is our ability to be anonymous, which he characterises as a reasonable control over what we communicate.

Philip Garnett and Sarah Hughes then turn their attention to the role of big data in accessing information from public inquiries. Looking in particular at the Chelsea Manning court martial in the US and the Leveson Inquiry in the UK, they argue that the manner in which information pertaining to inquiries is made public is, at best, unsatisfactory. They propose a variety of means to make this information more accessible and hence more transparent to the public through employing big data techniques.

Finally, Harald Stelzer and Hristina Veljanova argue in their chapter for a new ethical compass with which to approach big data concerns. They identify key ethical concerns which often arise in cases regarding big data and then provide a framework through which we might approach these concerns such that we can have a degree of certainty that we have not overlooked ethical worries.

Our hope is that this volume will present a rigorous yet accessible source of original research of interest to anyone considering questions pertaining to the philosophy of big data, especially as it pertains to questions surrounding democracy, the democratic process and the role of modern forms of social media. These are clearly pressing issues facing contemporary democracies, and the chapters herein provide much-needed clarity in understanding and challenging those issues.

References

Byers, D., 'Facebook Is Facing an Existential Crisis', *CNNMoney*, 19 March 2018, available at: https://money.cnn.com/2018/03/19/technology/business/facebook-data-privacy-crisis/index.html, last accessed 5 May 2019.

Concordia, 'Cambridge Analytica: the Power of Big Data and Psychographics', *Youtube*, 2016, available at: https://www.youtube.com/watch?v=n8Dd5aVXLCc, last accessed 20 July 2019.

Cummings, D., 'On the Referendum #20: the Campaign, Physics and Data Science – Vote Leave's "Voter Intention Collection System" (VICS) Now Available for All', *Dominic Cummings's Blog*, 29 October 2016, available at: https://dominiccummings.com/2016/10/29/on-the-referendum-20-the-campaign-physics-and-data-science-vote-leaves-voter-intention-collection-system-vics-now-available-for-all, last accessed 20 July 2019.

Duhigg, C., 'How Companies Learn Your Secrets', *New York Times*, 16 February 2012, available at: http://www.nytimes.com/2012/02/19/magazine/shopping-habits.html, last accessed 20 July 2019.

Essif, A., 'CDU, SPD and Greens Use Big Data to Target Bundestag Voters', *DW.COM*, 26 August 2017, available at: https://www.dw.com/en/cdu-spd-and-greens-use-big-data-to-target-bundestag-voters/a-40244410, last accessed 20 July 2019.

Hern, A., 'Google DeepMind 1.6m Patient Record Deal "Inappropriate"', *The Guardian*, 16 May 2017, available at: http://www.theguardian.com/technology/2017/may/16/google-deepmind-16m-patient-record-deal-inappropriate-data-guardian-royal-free, last accessed 20 July 2019.

Issenberg, S., 'How Obama's Team Used Big Data to Rally Voters', *MIT Technology Review*, 19 December 2012, available at: https://www.technologyreview.com/s/509026/how-obamas-team-used-big-data-to-rally-voters, last accessed 20 July 2019.

Knapton, Sarah, 'How the NHS Got It so Wrong with Care.Data', *The Telegraph*, 7 July 2016, available at: http://www.telegraph.co.uk/science/2016/07/07/how-the-nhs-got-it-so-wrong-with-caredata, last accessed 20 July 2019.

Kruschinski, S. and A. Haller, 'Restrictions on Data-Driven Political Micro-Targeting in Germany', *Internet Policy Review* 6(4) (2017), available at: https://policyreview.info/articles/analysis/restrictions-data-driven-political-micro-targeting-germany, last accessed 20 July 2019.

Leetaru, K., 'Why Are We Only Now Talking about Facebook and Elections?' *Forbes*, 19 March 2018, available at: https://www.forbes.com/sites/kalevleetaru/2018/03/19/why-are-we-only-now-talking-about-facebook-and-elections, last accessed 20 July 2019.

Macnish, K., *The Ethics of Surveillance: An Introduction* (London: Routledge, 2017).

O'Neil, C., *Weapons of Math Destruction: How Big Data Increases Inequality and Threatens Democracy* (London: Penguin, 2016).

Pilkington, E. and A. Michel, 'Obama, Facebook and the Power of Friendship: the 2012 Data Election', *The Guardian*, 17 February 2012, available at: https://www.theguardian.com/world/2012/feb/17/obama-digital-data-machine-facebook-election, last accessed 20 July 2019.

Powles, J. and H. Hodson, 'Google DeepMind and Healthcare in an Age of Algorithms', *Health and Technology* 7(4) (2017): 351–67.

Ram, A., 'Leave.EU Accused of Data Misuse during Brexit Campaign', *Financial Times*, 17 April 2018, available at: https://www.ft.com/content/fdf8f2ba-4243-11e8-803a-295c97e6fd0b, last accessed 20 July 2019.

Solon, O. and O. Laughland, 'Cambridge Analytica Closing after Facebook Data Harvesting Scandal', The Guardian, 2 May 2018, available at: https://www.theguardian.com/uk-news/2018/may/02/cambridge-analytica-closing-down-after-facebook-row-reports-say, last accessed 27 January 2020.

Suleyman, M. and D. King, 'The Information Commissioner, the Royal Free, and What We've Learned', *DeepMind Blog*, 3 July 2017, available at: https://deepmind.com/blog/ico-royal-free, last accessed 20 July 2019.

Part One

ONE

Big Data, Consequentialism and Privacy

Kieron O'Hara

Introduction: Big Data and Government

In this chapter, I consider the use of data in order to alter people's choices, along the lines of the 'nudge' philosophy of Richard Thaler and Cass Sunstein (2008). Although this technique of opinion management is part of the toolbox of both the private and public sectors, the greater powers of the public sector to compel citizens mean that its legitimacy is all the more important. In this chapter, I concentrate on whether government is justified in using data in this context to drive policy to produce good outcomes for citizens.

Data can be used together with understanding of behavioural psychology to alter the choices that people make. Information can be provided about choices, but presented in such a way that people are more likely to act, such as putting red/amber/green traffic light warnings about calorie counts in fast food restaurants. Feedback is also derived from data, either to suggest what social norms are, or to provide immediate feedback on behaviour. Gamification is another common tactic, with leaderboards, points or other affirmations reinforcing positive behaviour (Halpern 2015).

I want to consider the status of democratic (or benignly paternalistic) governments attempting to improve the lot of their citizens using the data dividend informed by behavioural psychology. Such an approach is distinct from (a) laissez-faire libertarianism; (b) informed liberalism, whereby citizens are furnished with information about their choices, and then have to make their own decisions; and (c) paternalism, where government legislates to make what it considers desirable behaviour compulsory, or to make what it considers undesirable behaviour illegal.

Because data collection about individuals is now virtually invisible, and because data informs many of our choices, our behaviour is increasingly influenced by data, or by the application of data by interested parties, and it is unsurprising that governments are sometimes keen to get in on the act. A covert paternalistic philosophy that avoids (the appearance of) coercion called *nudging* (Thaler and Sunstein 2008), is particularly effective in the data world – since the data simultaneously furnishes the means of (a) understanding the heuristics and biases characteristic of populations; (b) assessing whether citizens' performance, choices or well-being are acceptable compared with standards set by government or experts; and (c) providing feedback. Technology amplifies the effect of the nudge, because it is networked, pervasive and dynamically updated (Yeung 2017). Modernising governments, such as that of David Cameron in the UK (2010–16), have invested resources in the development of units for implementing policy based on the nudge philosophy (Halpern 2015).

In this chapter I explore the ethical implications of these developments, as modernity develops the characteristics of a specifically *digital* modernity. We will focus on privacy interests as affected by the use of data by democratic governments.

Big Data as a Game Changer

Governments have always generated and used data for managing populations and delivering services to ensure their continued legitimacy. Administrative systems create data-flows as a byproduct of their work, which then suggest new problems and pressing priorities. These data-driven problem statements serve two purposes: first, they drive new initiatives from the administration; while, secondly, they directly furnish arguments that more resources should be given by government and, ultimately, taxpayers, to address them.

The data technologies involved range in effectiveness and convenience, and provide measurements and properties of citizens, foreigners, companies, institutions and the environment. Schools, hospitals and police forces have a series of interactions with citizens in particular contexts (education, crime, illness), from which data can be gleaned. The remits of other types of institution, such as statistical authorities or mapping agencies, begins with the gathering of information, justified by the assumption that it will enable rational management of certain aspects of a nation. This appeals politically because of three promises. First, government will be more effective; given a problem, sufficient data will enable the problem to be solved. Secondly, government will be cheaper; resources can be concentrated where they are needed, which we can identify with the right data. Thirdly, government will be more legitimate; it can focus on solving problems, rather than blindly interfering and blundering through civil society. Security is a particular concern for governments, and data seems to shine a light into precisely the covert activities that are perceived as threats to security (Coles-Kemp et al. 2018).

Big data is revolutionary because it provides a rich, real-time picture of the world – albeit not necessarily an accurate one. Much of the literature of big data focuses on its properties *qua* data object of quantification – the so-called 3 Vs of large volume, high velocity and diverse variety. These mean that learning algorithms have a lot of material to work with that is produced in real-time. Statistics itself has had to adapt, because we are moving from the analysis of static datasets to the need to cope with streaming data being produced all the time. Yet the promise of big data goes beyond the 3 Vs (Kitchin 2014). Partly this is because of the technologies to which it is linked. The World Wide Web is an information space that has become a default interface between all sorts of interlocutors, such as business-to-business, government-to-citizen, consumer-to-consumer, and so on. The data therefore cover as wide a section of society as a government might wish. They cover entire populations, in a wide range of their interactions and solitary pursuits. They gather information about what people actually think or what they are interested in, not what they tell surveys (Stephens-Davidowitz 2017); they also cover more intimate situations, such as searches for particular pornographic content. And if these interactions are online, more aspects of them can be captured as data. The grain-size of capture is very fine. Furthermore, the data will typically allow linking of disparate databases. This allows researchers to isolate demographic groups and perform rapid randomised controlled experiments over large populations. Machine learning analysis techniques have kept pace with the growth of data, so that very weak signals can be found even in very noisy data (with immediate statistical significance because of the nearly 100 per cent sample size).

From Modernity to Digital Modernity

The spread of digital technology is an important driver for narratives of modernisation and modernity. Modernity is a feature of certain types of narrative that describe a contrast to pre-modern, unsophisticated or irrational/traditional culture. Such narratives may be descriptive, cataloguing trends and events; *teleological*, describing a set of inevitable outcomes; or normative, stating a desirable goal to which we should work. Such narratives do not exist in pure form, but act as guidelines that shape policymakers' (and others') thinking (O'Hara 2018).

When a consensus across government, business, the arts and the media persists, these narratives are hard to resist. Many have represented these developments as leading to discontinuities in human history (Kurzweil 2005; Brynjolfsson and McAfee 2014; Barrat 2015; Schwab 2016), in which the technology itself will actively reshape the lives of people and the futures of nations and businesses (Schmidt and Cohen 2013).

Modernity is a relative term – a society or culture is less modern than another (a) where tradition and geography are stronger influences than rationalism and abstraction, (b) which are exclusive rather than inclusive, and (c) where social structures are imposed hierarchies as opposed to contractual networks. Digital technology accelerates modernisation processes, and we can speak of digital modernity as an extension of modernity (O'Hara 2018).

The role of big data within modernisation narratives is perhaps most clearly seen in the centre/periphery theory, which contrasts being at the centre of things, where value is created, to being peripheral (Shils 1975). At the periphery we find rural areas and the developing world. These contrast to major cities, clusters of creativity and industry where innovation happens (Formica 2017). Modernity shrinks space (Harvey 1990), as modernisation marginalises the periphery and privileges the centre, where clusters flourish. Within a cluster, acquaintance is not rationed by geography, so we can develop links with many others, creating richer networks. Connections are not accidental or imposed, as in the sparsely-populated periphery. In the centre, connections are rational and transactional.

How is this transformed into digital modernity by ubiquitous digital technology? The term 'cyberspace' was popularised by William Gibson's science-fiction novel *Neuromancer*, as a term for the compression of space via quantification to produce greater intelligence:

> Cyberspace. A consensual hallucination experienced daily by billions of legitimate operators, in every nation, by children being taught mathematical concepts . . . A graphic representation of data abstracted from the banks of every computer in the human system. Unthinkable complexity. Lines of light ranged in the nonspace of the mind, clusters and constellations of data. Like city lights, receding . . . (Gibson 1984: 69)

Rational connection increases, because data is searchable and we can find the connections we want, rather than be presented with those that are available (O'Hara 2018). Cyberspace is populated by avatars, digital doubles made up of increasingly rich data (Parkinson et al. 2017). Records of our transactions, communications and measurements of our own well-being abound.

Smart cities are a response to the technical, material, social and organisational problems associated with modernism's push towards urban growth, to improve quality of life and provide a competitive and sustainable city (Shapiro 2006; Batty et al. 2012). The smart city is awash with citizen-aware intelligent environments and user-centric services, such as smart homes and smart buildings, smart energy, and smart health and well-being, which between them will improve efficiency, lower resource consumption and promote quality of life. The city achieves an online presence, and the transformation of the citizen into avatar is perfected. Policy depends now on the state of the person's data, not of the flesh and blood human.

The Subjunctive World

The result is a transformation in the 'tense' of our (public) lives. For a pre-modern community, actions, preferences and norms are given and traditional – they are eternal. A reason for action is that 'this is what we have always done', a hallmark of the pre-modern. The results are in many ways arbitrary, legible to those within the society, and odd and irrational-looking from the outside.

The tense of modernity, on the other hand, is the present. Modernity is built around choice and autonomy – free markets, free association and democracy. What counts is what I want now. Legibility is provided not by familiar practice, but by principles, which mean that practices are understood by a wider range of people.

Digital modernity changes the tense once more, from the present to the subjunctive. The ideal choice or action in this narrative is the choice that I would have made, if only I had enough information to calculate utility accurately. Modernity was a compromise. Our data infrastructure now provides so much information that ideal can be calculated. The infrastructure itself can create a world around me that will make the ideal choice evident to me. I can be nudged into making the 'right' decision, or the 'correct' choice can be recommended to me. In a less free society the emphasis is on social acceptability; the citizen's ideal here is the actions he or she would have performed in order to maximise social cohesion, if only he or she had enough information.

Hence, digital modernity brings us into a subjunctive world, in which we are presented with the possibility of not only the rational reconstruction of society, but also the means of discovery and satisfaction of human needs, wants and desires, all from the new sources of data (O'Hara 2018).

The Meta-ethics of Machine Learning

When we try to understand data-driven government in terms not of Enlight-enment modernity, but of digital modernity, we make four important observations. First, the understanding of behaviour, responses and out-comes represented by the data is, in Bernard Williams' terms, 'thin' rather than 'thick' (Williams 2005: 46). Although, by its very comprehensiveness, the picture that big data paints is rich, its expressivity is based on semantics with low descriptive content, and not on concepts resting on a strong set of shared understandings. Legibility is wide, not deep, because the concepts represented in the data are intended to be actionable for a large number of heterogeneous agents.

Secondly, the reasoning involved to produce recommendations tailored to individuals is optimised for a digitally modern bureaucracy. A modern bureaucracy is generally seen as a set of systematic processes and ordered hierarchies that are rational, efficient and objective. Under digital moder-nity, many of these hierarchies are undermined by the low-friction flow of information, to produce more agile network structures and platforms. Rather than hoarding data in silos, digital bureaucracy tries to exploit data serendipitously, and tries to enhance its value by promoting abundance.

Thirdly, the reasoning is generalised and statistical, and its justification consequentialist. Big data cannot determine what anyone actually does. It deals with probabilities. Machine learning finds signals across populations, such as the discovery, based on Facebook data in the 2010 US mid-term elections, that a 2.2 per cent increase occurred in voting among people who received positive messages about voting in addition to the profile pictures of half a dozen Facebook friends who had clicked an 'I voted' button.

Fourthly, many of our interests are group interests. One identifies with many groups and we often think collectively in these contexts. They are meaningful to us. However, they are not the segments or categories used in machine learning. Indeed, some of the more recent well-known categories or archetypes based on socio-economic variables or attitudes, such as 'soccer moms' or 'Basildon Man', are understandable but not interesting in our daily lives. However, the segmentation of the population performed with big data is actually based on past behavioural choices, grouping together people who have made the same purchases, travelled the same journeys, retweeted similar tweets and so on.

One of the major criticisms of consequentialism is that the innocent suffer with the guilty; the example often given is that if a known crimi-nal has gone on the run, the government might punish his family, with a similar, or possibly more powerful, deterrent effect on future potential criminals. This is unfair to the innocent wife or children, but the social consequences are benign. It is possible for consequentialists to escape this argument with various refinements to their theories, but big data will inevitably produce injustices, because it is based on objective calculation with firm, arbitrary thresholds.

The ethical acceptability of the systems depends on two assumptions within a consequentialist framework. First, the law of large numbers entails acceptance that in a number of cases, individual injustices might occur. This is inevitable in a large population. On this big data version of Bentham's hedonic calculus, these minor (to the system) injustices are outweighed by the greater good. Secondly, the system is objective, unlike one where personal acquaintance and a rich set of shared understandings determine outcomes; objective systems are fairer and more inclusive than the alternative. Hence, ethical argument about big data is inevitably focused on its gross consequences.

Yet calculating the consequences of the operation of big data techniques is not easy. When the techniques are used covertly, as it is alleged in certain contested elections such as the UK Brexit referendum and the US Presidential election of 2016, it is hard to quantify what effects they have had. So small are the effects that it is unclear whether the results of either of these two elections were actually changed, but equally so close were they that it cannot be ruled out either. The effect has been to poison politics, as aggrieved losers now feel swindled out of their result. If the effect were determined to be real and significant, and if the outcomes of either of these elections were changed, the original winners would doubtless feel aggrieved, because nobody was actually coerced into voting as they did. There is a danger that the use of data allied to consequentialism, despite its advantages for public policymaking, may undercut its own legitimacy and that of the managerial political class that espouse it (Osborne 2007; Richards 2017).

In the subjunctive world, judgements are far more provisional than might appear. One phenomenon that is rarely taken into account is the reflexivity of human interaction. We behave and act, and data is gathered up to a point t_1. At t_2 an algorithm is applied to the data, to make predictions about a point in the future, t_3. This assumes that t_3 is like t_1 in the relevant respects of our behaviour. The data available at t_1 are comprehensive, and laws of large numbers apply. However, there is an extra component to the epistemological context of t_3 that was not around at t_1, which is the prediction made at t_2. That will change attitudes, either of governments about their citizens, or of the citizens themselves. In this way, the prediction, far from narrowing down the space of options, opens up new possibilities, which are not often considered in the narrative of the subjunctive world.

Governments in Digital Modernity

Digital governments are assumed to produce better decisions (Eggers et al. 2017); this also implicitly suggests that a government in possession of the data is in a better position to make decisions about societies rather than the people directly involved. It has been suggested that, on a Rawlsian frame-work, the advantage of nudging is that it could help to curb behaviour that is incompatible with the duty of civility, and therefore help to support a liberal pluralism (Stevens forthcoming). How does this stand ethically?

There are many uses for data informed by behavioural psychology whose ethical bona fides seem secure. For example, a lot of nudging deals with setting defaults. In many choices we have to make, there has to be some default – for instance, a pension scheme has either to be opt-in or opt-out. Secondly, nudging involves rigorous testing of messaging in communica-tions, again hard to argue with. For instance, the behavioural psychology part of a communications programme might involve experiments with dif-ferent messages, different accompanying images, personalised letters versus impersonal ones, to see which communications elicit a better response. A third type of example is to avert serious and obvious harms, like the white lines down the centre of the road which nudge drivers into not cutting cor-ners. Most importantly, a final type of use of behavioural psychology is the testing of policy using randomised control trials, a kind of systematic incremental empirical testing of the efficacy of policy (Halpern 2015: 291), which is entirely sensible.

These are the quick wins of nudging, and most applications of the phi-losophy are in this uncontroversial space. Having said that, it should be pointed out that the idea of Thaler and Steve Hilton that this is 'about bring-ing in new ways of thinking that could roll back the state while extending choice and freedom for citizens in subtle and empowering ways' (Halpern 2015: 51) seems obviously incorrect. The state may need less machinery, but its influence grows, choice is pared down, citizens are no freer and it remains to be seen how being persuaded to do something by a more power-ful agent who holds a load of data about you is 'empowering'. The goal of action is decided by someone else, not you. Even in the apparently straight-forward case of defaults, a complex type of choice could be nudged using smart defaults personalised to the particular individual, so that the default option could be different for people of different ages, sexuality, income or whatever (Halpern 2015: 307).

Even more problematic is the type of case where people's preferences are manipulated. The profusion of data means that the individual is measur-able and, via feedback, is perfectible. In the cyberspace of digital modernity, imperfection is to a large extent policed by the digital citizenry (Ronson 2015). However, governments are also keen to set standards and targets, and to take these pressures to conform and improve out of private hands.

In his account of civil society and the evolution of the European state, Michael Oakeshott (1975) produced an account of two ideas of the state: as *societas* and as *universitas*. *Societas* is a neutral state, which creates an arena in which civil association can take place, a kind of level playing-field. *Universitas* is an idea of the state as a more active, compulsory corporate entity with its own purposes and goals, to which it can and will suborn its citizens. The latter is a notion of the state with managers, not rulers, role-performers, not subjects, instrumental rules, not responsibilities. *Universitas* tends to develop a problem-solving ethos, often social challenges which are hard to solve, which then can increase the size of the state as it commandeers ever-more resources to address them. Oakeshott does not explicitly associate these two conceptions of the state with pre-modernity and modernity, although they map onto these social conditions.

Oakeshott was not very concerned with digital technology. However, in thinking of the development of *universitas*, he did consider a type of state that can be associated with digital modernity. He writes of the state as 'an association of invalids, all victims of the same disease and incorporated in seeking relief from their common ailment; and the office of government is a remedial engagement. Rulers are *therapeutae*, the directors of a sanatorium from which no patient may discharge himself by a choice of his own' (1975: 308).

This line of thinking had few takers in 1975, when the state had a whole set of different problems to solve. However, his notion of the *therapeutic state* comes into its own in the condition of digital modernity, where the idea of 'disease' or 'negative well-being' can now be defined using the copious data available. Whereas a modern, 'enlightened' state takes the unenlightened nature of its citizens as the pretext for intervention in social life, the therapeutic state diagnoses its citizens empirically as afflicted and in need of treatment.

Privacy under Digital Modernity

In this section I look more closely at how the subjunctive world of digital modernity contrasts with pre-modernity and modernity by focusing on privacy. Privacy has many aspects, but to illustrate the contrast I will look specifically at association, decision-making and archiving. Association concerns the people that we encounter, particularly in intimate contexts, and privacy in this context means a level of control over our freedom of association. Decision-making can take place in a private space, and express more or less authentic choices. Archiving concerns the records kept of our lives: how complete are the records, and how accessible to others are they?

Pre-modern association is often imposed. One's friends are people who happen to be of the same age in the geographical spot in which one finds oneself. Association in modernity is more often chosen. One travels to find education and work, and in these situations over which traditional societies have relatively less control, one finds one's friends. With digital modernity, association ceases to be a simple choice, but one selects from lists of the recommended. An app will tell one which people are potential friends, which potential lovers or sexual partners, and which valuable for one's career.

With respect to decision-making, pre-modern societies rely on practice and tradition. We do this (this way) because we always have, and we do not necessarily have a good reason why. Modernity is characterised by individual choice; democracy lets us choose our leaders, while free markets let us exchange whatever we have for whatever we want. In digital modernity, the world is crafted so that the choices we might want to make are anticipated and placed in salient contexts, while those we might regret are hidden. The world is personalised to reduce the risk and effort of choosing.

With respect to records, pre-modern societies rely on memory to keep the past, augmented by ceremonies, memorials and other markers. The modern world rested on the archive, efficiently curated by stakeholders, based on their own interests, with access controls for outsiders. These archives are replaced in digital modernity with large-scale open searchable information spaces, the World Wide Web most obviously. We cannot rule out any piece of information being knowable somewhere, and it is hard if not impossible to halt information flow.

Against this background, we can map the evolution of privacy. In a premodern society, privacy as such is null; one is subject to access or direction from all sorts of authority figures and those in geographical co-location. However, much of this access is arbitrary, depending on, for example, the selectivity of memory or the reach of the state, so one is not completely open to scrutiny; one may as a matter of fact have plenty of privacy, but few rights to it. The key pre-modern concept, then, is *obscurity*. Modernity brings the development of private spaces, and mechanisms both technological and legal for their defence. Privacy makes its appearance as a principled ideal.

Under digital modernity, privacy is being superseded by personalisation, the creation of an individual world in which one is embedded, and that is to an extent unique to oneself. But privacy is inimical to this personalised world, because the personalisation will be more effective the more is known about one.

There have been many arguments about whether big data will be helpful for the individual, or alternatively a system of surveillance. This is misleading, because in order to be helpful to an individual, a system based on big data *must* be one of total surveillance, at least in terms of a panoptic understanding of the life it wishes to help. If it is not, it cannot be helpful (or indeed harmful, for that matter). In digital modernity, these concepts cannot be separated so easily.

Privacy and Respect for the Person

In the subjunctive world the calculation of what the agent would have preferred had he or she been omniscient is outsourced to external agencies, including government. When government makes this calculation, it implicitly defines both the rich subjunctive world, and the set of choices that citizens 'ought' to make. From the 'unalienable right' in the American Declaration of Independence to the pursuit of happiness, the subjunctive world moves not to allow the citizen to pursue happiness is his or her own way, but rather to supply that happiness itself.

It is sometimes argued that there is an economic aspect to many of these decisions, particularly when it comes to healthcare. Governments are entitled to nudge smokers, drinkers, the obese and the indolent away from their bad habits because their collective health problems in later life will cost taxpayers, as well as employers and insurance companies, a great deal of money. The underlying assumption is true, and a relevant consideration. However, it is also the case that the financial case is secondary to the moral judgement that ruining one's own health is a personal failure from which government is entitled to protect you; if the moral judgement were not prior, then the financial case would not be taken into account.

It is worth pointing out that terms like 'Orwellian', 'Big Brother' and 'Panopticon' (from Bentham's prison design) are often misused. The Bentham/Orwell model has five characteristics, only one of which is shared with digital surveillance. The shared characteristic is that the individual is always visible. The differences with today's big data surveillance are fourfold. First, in the Panopticon, one is not always watched. Secondly, one does not know when one is the object of attention. Thirdly, the infrastructure is attached to a code of sanctions backed by severe violence. Fourthly, and often overlooked, the point of the model is to create a system under which human-of-human surveillance will scale; as there are presumably more telescreens than humans in Airstrip One, round-the-clock surveillance would require the services of over half the population. The Bentham/Orwell model, however, needs only a fraction of that, because of the incentives for self-censorship (this is why the violence is so essential to the scheme). The model is irrelevant for any kind of automated surveillance.

In the subjunctive world there is little coercion, yet human dignity, which makes its own contributions to the ideology of pre-modernity and modernity, has yet to find its role in digital modernity. In digital modernity, the individual is judged by the data generated by and about him or her, and policy takes a lead from the routes to perfectibility of the avatar. Yet the individual is strangely absent from the calculation, because of the asymmetry between him- or herself and the data system, both in terms of power and knowledge about the individual.

The individual under digital modernity is newly-positioned relative to major social and governmental institutions, still far less powerful, but potentially with less space in which to determine his or her own future. In the pre-modern world, this space was arbitrarily distributed, and often contingent on the relative lack of efficiency of the state. Under modernity, there was a principled private space of decision-making that was created (and often defended) by the state. Under digital modernity, the state threatens to invade that space with new efficiency, albeit with the well-being of the individual in mind, at least in the democracies. Yet the role of the individual in the new set-up has yet to be made clear.

Conclusions

At its most ambitious, the use of behavioural psychology is trying to square a circle of pushing people into a certain type of behaviour without coercing them. This can be done more or less transparently, and accountability must be maintained for the choice architects. However, even the fact of oversight may not be sufficient to define and defend the dignity of the data subject. Transparency may be necessary but not sufficient to even up the power asymmetry between the nudgers and the individual who is being moulded by the choice architectures with which they present him or her.

Whether this circle can be squared will depend on how data is used by governments, how data subjects push back, and how this public sector debate progresses alongside the similar debate with respect to private sector actors. Even the behavioural psychologists remind us that human well-being is strongly affected by the feeling of being in control (Halpern 2015: 239), which is a hallmark of modernity, but not the subjunctive world of digital modernity. There is therefore a question of their relationship with the expert services they receive.

Behavioural psychology can contribute in more than one direction. It could be used to derive feedback from clients to improve the responsiveness of the experts, or it could be used to make the clients *feel* more in control even when they are not (Halpern 2015: 259–61). Done well, feedback on service delivery and quality that is properly analysed and acted upon certainly focuses the attention of providers on how to treat their clients with respect and dignity (Halpern 2015: 261–2). This is an excellent idea, but it is not the only possibility. The task for lawyers, philosophers and data scientists is to magnify the human element in the system sufficiently to preserve dignity, while simultaneously realising the potential of the technology.

References

Barrat, J., *Our Final Invention: Artificial Intelligence and the End of the Human Era* (New York: Thomas Dunne, 2015).

Batty, M., K. W. Axhausen, F. Giannotti, A. Pozdnoukhov, A. Bazzani, M. Wachowicz, G. Ouzounis and Y. Portugali, 'Smart Cities of the Future', *European Physical Journal Special Topics* 214(1) (2012): 481–518.

Brynjolfsson, E. and A. McAfee, *The Second Machine Age: Work, Progress and Prosperity in a Time of Brilliant Technologies* (New York: W. W. Norton, 2014).

Coles-Kemp, L., D. Ashenden and K. O'Hara, 'Why should I? Cybersecurity, the Security of the State and the Insecurity of the Citizen', *Politics and Governance* 6(2) (2018): 41–8.

Eggers, W. D., D. Schatsky and P. Viechnicki, *AI Augmented Government: Using Cognitive Technologies to Redesign Public Sector Work* (Deloitte University Press, 2017), available at: https://www2.deloitte.com/insights/us/en/focus/cognitive-technologies/artificial-intelligence-government.html, last accessed 23 May 2018.

Formica, Piero (ed.), *Entrepreneurial Renaissance: Cities Striving Towards an Era of Rebirth and Revival* (Basel: Springer, 2017).

Gibson, W., *Neuromancer* (New York: Ace Books, 1984).

Halpern, D., *Inside the Nudge Unit: How Small Changes Can Make a Big Difference* (London: W. H. Allen, 2015).

Harvey, D., *The Condition of Postmodernity: an Enquiry into the Origins of Social Change* (Oxford: Blackwell, 1990).

Kitchin, R., *The Data Revolution: Big Data, Open Data, Data Infrastructures and Their Consequences* (London: Sage, 2014).

Kurzweil, R., *The Singularity is Near* (New York: Viking Penguin 2005).

Oakeshott, M., *On Human Conduct* (Oxford: Clarendon Press, 1975).

Oborne, P., *The Triumph of the Political Class* (London: Simon & Schuster, 2007).

O'Hara, K., 'Conflicts of Digital Modernity', *AI and Society*, 2018, doi:10.1007/s00146-018-0843-7.

Parkinson, B., D. E. Millard, K. O'Hara and R. Giordano, 'The Digitally Extended Self: a Lexicological Analysis of Personal Data', *Journal of Information Science*, 2017, doi:10.1177/0165551517706233.

Richards, S., *The Rise of the Outsiders: How Mainstream Politics Lost its Way* (London: Atlantic, 2017).

Ronson, J., *So You've Been Publicly Shamed* (London: Pan Macmillan, 2015).

Schmidt, E. and J. Cohen, *The New Digital Age: Reshaping the Future of People, Nations and Business* (New York: Random House, 2013).

Schwab, K., *The Fourth Industrial Revolution* (Geneva: World Economic Forum, 2016).

Shapiro, J. M., 'Smart Cities: Quality of Life, Productivity and the Growth Effects of Human Capital', *Review of Economics and Statistics* 88(2) (2006): 324–35.

Shils, E., *Center and Perphery: Essays in Macrosociology* (Chicago: University of Chicago Press, 1975).

Stephens-Davidowitz, S., *Everybody Lies: Big Data, New Data, and What the Internet Can Tell Us about Who We Really Are* (New York: HarperCollins, 2017).

Stevens, D., 'In Defence of Toma: Algorithmic Enhancement and Cultivating a Sense of Justice', in M Hildebrandt and K O'Hara (eds), *Law and Life in the Era of Data-Driven Agency* (Cheltenham: Edward Elgar, forthcoming).

Thaler, R. H. and C. R. Sunstein, *Nudge: Improving Decisions about Health, Wealth and Happiness* (New Haven, CT: Yale University Press, 2008).

Williams, B., 'Modernity and the Substance of Ethical Life', in *In the Beginning Was the Deed: Realism and Moralism in Political Argument*, ed. G. Hawthorne (Princeton: Princeton University Press, 2005), pp. 40–51.

Yeung, K., '"Hypernudge": Big Data as a Mode of Regulation by Design', *Information, Communication and Society* 20(1) (2017): 118–36.

TWO

Politics, Big Data and Opacity Respect

Carl Fox

Introduction

The future is here, and it is not hoverboards, space travel or simian rule. It is data analytics. The combination of masses of information and computer processing power is set to revolutionise our approach to just about everything. Algorithms will allow us to harness all this raw data to better understand human behaviour so that we can devise ingenious solutions to problems as diverse as falling voter turnout[1] and climate change.[2] 'Big data' thus promises enormous benefits. However, in this chapter I want to raise a serious problem that should give us pause. I shall argue that governments and other political actors have special reason to avoid using algorithms to 'look inside' us. This stems from an influential answer offered to the question: what is the basis of equality?

It is readily apparent that some people are physically stronger than others, or cleverer, or nicer, or prettier, and so on. Even when it comes to more abstract abilities, such as judging what is in our self-interest or how best to pursue one's particular conception of the good, some are better than others. It seems that in any dimension of human ability we can locate people at different points along a spectrum. But if we differ so markedly in our natural capacities, then what are we to make of the idea that there remains some important sense in which we are all equal, and so entitled to equal treatment? Ian Carter (2011) has argued that there is one crucial respect in which we are all the same, and that this explains why, and how, we are to be respected as equals. His thought is that we all have an interest in being able to conceal or cover up aspects of ourselves in order to maintain a level of outward dignity. Carter argues that our default position towards one another should thus be one of 'evaluative abstinence', in which we refrain from making judgements about how good or bad our fellows are at being agents. This is what it means to show each other what he calls 'opacity respect'. In this chapter I argue that the importance of opacity respect gives us reason to be concerned about public officials and candidates for public office using the combination of large datasets and powerful algorithms to crack us open and work us out.

The problem stems from the observation that our standing in the eyes of others is fragile. If an observer was able to listen to my thoughts then they would be privy to all my anxieties and eccentricities, my foolish notions and silly mistakes. Focusing on my weaknesses and idiosyncrasies will alter their perception of me and, over time, they may view me as something less than an independent, autonomous agent. In short, they may lose respect for me. It is especially stigmatising if it is the state that deems me to be less capable or less worthy since this undermines my standing as a full citizen. It is also dangerous. The awesome power the state wields provides a constant temptation to interfere in the lives of citizens for their own good. If my own state comes to view me, people like me or the citizenry as a whole as malfunctioning or compromised, then the temptation may become too great to resist. So, it is on these grounds that I will argue that the state and the people who do, or might, hold office within it ought to maintain an attitude consistent with the value of opacity respect.

I begin by examining the development and potential of big data with specific reference to the political sphere. I then raise and set aside some important concerns about the use of big data in politics to better focus on the significance of opacity respect. The fourth section outlines Carter's theory, expanding on the significance of opacity respect for the relationship between the citizenry and the state, before I move on, in the next section, to argue that big data presents a challenge to that relationship by tempting the state to abandon what Philip Pettit and Michael Smith (1996) call the 'conversational stance'. Finally, I consider the objection that this view is naive and fetishises opacity respect at too high a cost to well-being and knowledge.

Politicising Data

The Cambridge Analytica scandal sparked a period of fevered speculation about what data analysis firms might be able to do with only your star sign, mother's maiden name and top-five desert island discs. Whether or not such companies have the ability to deliver on their boasts, what they are claiming to be able do is certainly unsettling. One of the (many) striking claims is that by using algorithms they can effectively come to know a person better than they know themselves.[3] I contend that there are important reasons to refrain from trying to learn too much about each other and that these reasons should be applied especially stringently to elected officials and to candidates for public office. This section lays out the general strategy behind this branch of data analytics.

In the broadest terms, the idea is to sift through large datasets in search of correlations between apparently unrelated pieces of personal information. If people who like romantic comedies and long walks on the beach also tend to favour higher taxes on the wealthy, say, then access to someone's streaming preferences and their phone's GPS information could tell you their political orientation. These kinds of correlation can be extrapolated to individuals or groups about whom only partial data is available. They can thus be used to make all sorts of predictions about us: what our tastes and preferences are likely to be; what causes or ideals we might support; and perhaps even how our likely behaviour in some set of circumstances might be affected by various kinds of intervention. The insights gleaned allow companies and campaigns to tailor their communications to small groups or particular individuals in a process known as 'micro-targeting'.

Attempting to use data to get an edge is nothing new. The most dramatic example is the now infamous case in which an initially outraged father was forced to apologise to the American supermarket chain Target, whose algorithms had correctly deduced from his teenaged daughter's purchases that she was pregnant.[4] It is not even a new strategy in politics. John F. Kennedy's 1960 campaign for the presidency was rumoured to rely on a mysterious computer nicknamed the 'people machine', and did indeed commission analysis from a company called Simulmatics Corporation that segmented the American population into 480 distinct groups to better understand their concerns and probable responses to a range of potential strategies (Issenberg 2013: 116–23). The ending of Sidney Lumet's 1986 film *Power* is simply an entire floor of unattended machines tirelessly processing voter information.

Sasha Issenberg (2013: 325) notes that Barack Obama's re-election campaign used 'targeted sharing' protocols that 'mined Obama backers' Facebook networks in search of friends the campaign wanted to register, mobilize, or persuade'. In fact, Issenberg (2013: 328) reports that so much data was collected and collated the first time around that the campaign felt confident that they knew the names of every single one of the 69,456,897 voters who had elected him in 2008. The lesson to be learned here is a thoroughly unsurprising one: political campaigns have always sought to use the information at their disposal to deliver as many votes as possible.

If there is something new in the current wave of data-driven strategies, it is the drive to link them up with psychological profiles of potential voters and customers. This involves situating people in relation to the so-called 'Big Five' psychological traits.[5] The thought is that a person's psychological makeup can then be used to tailor messages to which they will be receptive, even if their conscious desires or commitments are in conflict with whatever suggestion is being pushed. Issenberg points out that for a long time it was more straightforward – and cost effective – to spend your money on getting potential voters who were already inclined to vote for your candidate to turn out on polling day. Persuasion is generally harder and more expensive than mobilisation. The promise of micro-targeting is that it may allow operatives to engage in a limited, but highly effective, form of short-term persuasion, pressing particular psychological buttons to motivate us to behave in very specific ways.

Initial Concerns

If this is just the latest variation on a well-established theme, then why should there be so much hype about it? In this section I briefly discuss some of the likely objections that might be raised to the application of big data to the practice of politics so that we can distinguish the concern about opacity respect.

There are two key reasons why one might think that democracy is justified as a system of government. The first is that pooling our decision-making capacities tends to produce good decisions. It is on this basis that David Estlund (2008) argues that democracies have epistemic authority and that their possession and use of the means of coercion is legitimate. The other reason for thinking that democracy is a good system of government is that it has the right sort of procedures such that it respects and secures the value of political equality, the idea that since we are all moral equals we should all have the same amount of control over the laws and policies that affect us.

The use of big data by political campaigns poses several fundamental questions for democratic theorists. If strategies such as micro-targeting really do allow campaigns to skew the results of our decision-making procedures then we have a problem. The assumptions behind it suggest that human beings are, on the one hand, less rational in their decision-making than we thought, and, on the other, more susceptible to external influences and manipulation than we suspected. If that is right, why should we be so optimistic either that citizens are generally good at making decisions or that increasing the numbers involved in a decision will tend to produce better results? If people are easily persuaded to vote against their own values and interests, then it seems to follow that the more people who are included in the decision-making process, the greater the chances of getting it wrong.

A related problem arises from the perspective of political equality. Cutting-edge data analytics cost money. Those candidates and causes that have access to greater resources will thus be able to wield a potent political weapon that is not available to everyone. The ability to convert wealth into political advantage clearly contravenes the principle of political equality by enabling some citizens to exercise greater influence over the political process than others.

These are genuine concerns and merit proper consideration.[6] However, they are not what interest me in this chapter. I think that they point us towards another issue. Big data research may fundamentally alter the relationship between citizens and the people they elect to exercise power in their name. In this category I include not only elected officials, but also civil servants and candidates for public office. The former carry out the policies of office-holders, while the latter hope to be in a position to give such orders. For the rest of this chapter I concentrate on the relationship between citizens and the elected members of government. However, with some tweaking, everything I say can be applied to civil servants and candidates for public office.

To set up my concern I would like to consider a fascinating piece of social science. Milkman et al. (2009) had a hunch that the kind of films that people say they want to watch differs markedly from the content they actually consume. And that is exactly what they found. When we add documentaries or foreign-language films to our 'to watch' lists on Netflix, for example, they tend to stay in televisual purgatory for a long time before we actually get around to pressing play. Brainless action films and insipid romantic comedies, on the other hand, we watch immediately. They highlight a tension between what they call (2009: 1048) 'should goods', or goods that we think we ought to desire, and 'want goods', or goods offering less long-term or overall satisfaction but which we nonetheless prioritise. In doing so, they expose an irrational behaviour pattern to which all of us are subject to some degree. If it is possible to use big data to discover facts like this about people of which even they are not aware, or only dimly aware, then this cuts against the Millian belief that people are usually the best judges of what is in their interests. With a dataset large enough and processing power strong enough, a data analyst could become a better judge of our interests than we are. But is this something that we want our governments to do? Should our politicians be in the business of making judgements about how good or bad we are at making decision for ourselves?

Opacity Respect

The broad answer that I give to these questions is no. Although I shall qualify this somewhat, we should generally oppose the idea of governments commissioning or using research that 'looks inside' people to determine how well they can exercise core abilities that underpin agency. I support this conclusion by appealing to Carter's (2011) notion of 'opacity respect'.

So, what is opacity respect and why is it so important? Carter's project is to uncover the basis of equality, to discover the feature, or features, of human beings that explain why they are entitled as a matter of justice to be treated in the same way when it comes to such things as standing before the law and accessing basic services.[7] No matter what property of persons we hold up to the light, it turns out to be one that we do not all possess in equal measure. Those of us committed to the notion of fundamental moral equality will want to avoid establishing a 'hierarchy of human entitlements' (2011: 542), but how can we do so in a non-arbitrary way? We could stipulate that we must treat all human beings equally regardless, but as Carter points out: '[i]f unequals ought nevertheless to be accorded equal entitlements, why not accord equal entitlements indiscriminately to humans and cats and oysters?' (2011: 541).

Carter finds the germ of a solution in John Rawls' idea that equality might be grounded in a special kind of property called a 'range property'. 'To possess a range property is to possess some other, scalar property, within a specified range' (Carter 2011: 548). Being over 180 cm tall is a range property as it encompasses being 181 cm, 182 cm, 183 cm, and so on, but rules out being 179 cm, 178 cm, 177 cm, etc. Since the presence or absence of the relevant scalar property, or properties, above a certain threshold establishes that one either does or does not have the range property, it looks like it might allow us to draw a circle around those entities we care about, while excluding all those cats and oysters less fortunate than ourselves. However, Carter flags up two further worries that must be addressed, namely, why should we think that any particular range property is morally relevant in the first place, rather than the basic property on which it supervenes, and why draw only on the range property and ignore the more fundamental characteristic? His solution is to look for a range property that matters for reasons that are independent of the importance of the properties on which it supervenes. Possessing the relevant properties to the requisite degree will thus be what qualifies one for consideration as an equal, but the justification for the equality of treatment itself will have to come from a different source.

What is the property or properties upon which the range property is going to supervene? Carter is relatively unspecific here, pointing to such capacities as the ability to reflect on one's desires, set and revise ends, and to make plans to achieve those ends (2011: 552). We do not need to get into the weeds here, as it is clear enough that Carter is interested in those features that distinguish thinking, feeling, self-directed entities from other forms of life. They are the core capacities that constitute agency and are sufficient to allow us to explain what is so special about possession of the accompanying range property. The next move is the crucial one for our purposes. Carter argues that autonomous rational agents have an interest in being respected just as such and that being respected as an agent precisely involves not having one's core capacities scrutinised too closely. If true, this gives us the reason we need to guide our behaviour only by the range property and not by the properties on which it supervenes, because it gives us cause to avoid trying to determine how capable anyone is above the threshold.

Why should agents be so loath to have their capacities evaluated in this way? The answer is that such evaluation is incompatible with having and maintaining human dignity. On one conception of dignity, it is a special status that a person has as long as they retain the capacities necessary for agency. It shines through in even the most degrading circumstances of poverty, incarceration or oppression. Only the obliteration of the capacities themselves, as in death or severe mental deterioration, can tear it from our grasp. Carter sets this highly idealised conception aside, though, for a more mundane sense of dignity which he describes as 'a feature of a person's character, behaviour, or situation' (Carter 2011: 555). This idea of 'outward dignity' (ibid.: 555) has more to do with how we are able to present ourselves, and depends upon our ability to hold something back from the gaze of others.[8]

To be sure, dignity in the first sense is necessary for outward dignity, but it is not sufficient. Carter (2011: 556) points out that precisely how outward dignity is realised in practice will depend on social norms, but follows Thomas Nagel (1998) in holding that it will always involve the ability to conceal elements of oneself or one's activities. The importance of concealment can be seen in everyday examples such as the store we set in having clothes to cover our literal nakedness, or privacy on the toilet. We have an interest in being able to exercise some control over how we present ourselves to others since everyone starts to come apart when put under a microscope.[9] We are not always consistent, or sensible, or even coherent in all of our thoughts and actions. However, because of the many ways in which we fall short of the ideal of rational agency, once we clear the bar for consideration as that kind of entity it is better that our fellows do not ask the further question of how good we are at being an agent and instead mind their own business. If they peer too closely then they will start to think of us in terms of our limitations and malfunctions. Drawing on the work of Peter Strawson (1962), Carter (2011: 559) warns of this 'objective' perspective and argues that it reduces its target to nothing more than the sum of their parts.

Showing respect to one another as agents therefore means treating their core capacities as opaque, hence 'opacity respect'. Opacity respect is due when our reasons for respecting an individual are also reasons to avoid making determinations about the degree to which they possess certain core capacities. Carter argues that once a person clears the threshold for moral agency, we ought not to make further judgements about how good they are at being a moral agent. He calls this 'evaluative abstinence', and describes it as 'a refusal to evaluate persons' varying capacities' (2011: 550). Treating someone as a moral agent, for Carter, is to hold them responsible for their actions in the same way we do all other moral agents, even though there are abilities relevant to being a good moral agent that clearly come in degrees. 'Respect, on this alternative interpretation, is a substantive moral attitude that involves abstaining from looking behind the exteriors people present to us as moral agents' (Carter 2011: 551). If in the course of our everyday interactions we happen to witness variances in the capacities of different people, we are required to wall off those perceptions and continue to, as Carter says, 'take the subject as given' (2011: 552).

There will be some contexts in which this is not possible, and others in which it is not desirable. Doctors must determine the capacity of their patients and teachers need to measure the progress of their students. This means making judgements about individuals' capacities. We also choose to share more of ourselves with friends and partners. Finally, we must determine that someone passes the threshold for moral agency in the first place if they are to be entitled to opacity respect. However, these are all exceptions that serve to emphasise the ordinary operation of the rule.

There is a final piece to this puzzle, and it is to establish not just that we have an interest in being respected in this way, but that there are relationships in which it is actually owed to us. Carter (2011: 556) posits that one such relationship is that between citizens and their political institutions, and that is what we shall discuss next.

Citizens and their States

To understand the full significance of being able to present an opaque exterior, it is worth considering a mundane and yet remarkable fact highlighted by Philip Pettit and Michael Smith (1996: 430), which is that people 'listen to one another in the course of belief formation and they invest one another's responses with potential importance'. They do this because they 'assume that they are each authorities worth listening to, even if the likelihood of error varies from individual to individual' (Pettit and Smith 1996: 430–1). In fleshing out their notion of the 'conversational stance' (ibid.: 429), Pettit and Smith argue that we each assume that when our interlocutors make mistakes it is down to absent or inconclusive evidence, or else something like laziness or inattention. 'By taking one or another of these views, people are saved from having to conclude that those who dissent are out of their minds and not worthy of attention: that they are not even presumptive authorities. They may be driven to the out-of-their-minds conclusion as a last resort but the default position is more optimistic' (ibid.: 431). They note that not only do people believe in these claims, but they believe that everyone else believes them too. We rely on other people to treat us as presumptive authorities and they rely on us to treat them in this way too. It is this optimism about each other's core capacities that we have an interest in protecting by being able to screen at least some of our internal life from view.

Presumptive authority is also what is at stake in the relationship between citizens and the state, and so this template for interpersonal relationships can be extended to cover that case. My claim is that states' default position must be that their citizens are authorities when it comes to their own lives. This will include such things as deciding what is in their interests, how they wish to live their lives, what their political views are, and so on. Therefore, states ought to refrain from scrutinising citizens, since to do so would be to show a distrust which is incompatible with treating them as authorities. Let us take a step back and ask first, what it is to treat someone as an authority, and, secondly, why states should treat their citizens in this way.

The key to understanding authority is the notion of content independent reasons. Content independent reasons operate at one remove from the familiar first-order considerations that we ordinarily count and weigh when deciding whether we should perform some action. To have authority in some domain is to have the ability to create reasons for other people that supersede and replace those first-order considerations, so that they ought to act on the basis of the authority's recommendation or directive and not their judgement of where the balance of reasons lies. We treat people as authorities when we take their word for something rather than attempt to decide for ourselves if we should agree with them.[10] This is not to say that we must defer to a genuine authority on every point, but if we do not defer on the subject over which they have mastery, then we do not treat them as an authority. For instance, if Michael is talking to an economist about the overall desirability of Brexit he does not have to agree with her conclusion. If, however, he refuses to trust her when she says that the value of the pound will fall because investors abhor instability, then he is not treating her as an expert.

Why should governments treat their citizens in this way? One obvious answer is that opacity respect protects against unjustified paternalistic interference. History seems to show that it is especially hard for the state to maintain an appropriate distance once it identifies what it views as a problem with its citizens. Carter (2011: 559) plugs into a long liberal tradition in political philosophy when he warns against taking legitimate reasons for supporting positive liberty too far. The more the state focuses on the things that limit human agency, the more natural it becomes to view particular human beings as objects in need of repair. From there it is a short step to dismissing what they say and do as symptoms of an underlying disorder, and that is a recipe for disaster.

Another answer has to do with the notion of separateness of persons and the requirement that each citizen be treated as an individual. Why should big data not make the idea of consulting individual citizens to find out their preferences redundant? After all, conducting large-scale interactions such as elections is costly and cumbersome. Why bother with it if you can collapse distinct individuals into statistical probabilities to get the same result faster, cheaper and perhaps even more accurately? Evaluative abstinence, on the other hand, means continuing to treat each person as someone whose actions and desires cannot be perfectly predicted. Governments work for us. Their authority is justified because they serve our interests, and we have an interest in opacity respect. What, if anything, does this mean in practice for political actors? I think it means that they should neither commission nor use algorithms for the purpose of 'looking inside' citizens to see how good or bad they are at exercising the core capacities that constitute agency. They should treat citizens as authorities when it comes to the running of their own lives. It is worth stressing that this injunction should be understood to include the pursuit of such knowledge as a stepping stone to some other ultimate end, such as votes, economic growth or welfare, since too much familiarity of this kind might breed contempt.

This is still unhappily vague. Fleshing out this conclusion and assembling specific guidelines will require greater expertise in data analytics than

I possess. However, we can become a bit clearer about what it will involve by considering an important objection.

Opacity Respect and Bounded Rationality

I have argued that elected officials, civil servants and candidates for political office should eschew algorithms that allow them to look inside citizens. I noted some pragmatic reasons for concern since it might encourage paternalistic impulses and thus give rise to unjustified interference in citizens' lives, but the deeper problem is simply that we are entitled to a degree of distance as part of the respect we are owed by our politicians. They should not attempt to peer too deeply into our capabilities, and get on with the work they do for us on the basis that anyone who qualifies for full citizenship is a rational agent. The objection that I consider in this section is that this position, while perhaps attractive in a rigid, principled sort of way, is fatally naive. When it comes to constraints on our agency, the cat is already out of the bag. Politicians would be remiss if they failed to tailor their policies to account for the facts, and in order to do this they must be allowed to get a proper handle on them. Further, we may be rewarded for some flexibility here since big data has the potential to deliver enormous social benefits. Does my argument fetishise opacity respect?

One point on which there is now widespread agreement is that it is long past time that we surrender the Enlightenment ideal of the perfectly rational person. The work of psychologists Daniel Kahneman and Amos Tversky has become hugely influential for showing the many ways in which human beings err because of our reliance on biases and heuristics even when they deliver very poor results.[11] The first step to resolving a problem is to admit that you have one. Philosophical, political and economic theories predicated on the ideal of perfect rationality have a problem: human rationality is bounded.

Recognition of our limitations presents new avenues for dealing with old problems. For instance, let us say that the Department of Health decides that it is going to tackle obesity by developing a policy about the location of salads in food buffets based on Richard Thaler and Cass Sunstein's (2009) 'nudge' strategy. To get it right, they will need to use data analytics to discover how people will react to different circumstances. They will also need to determine just how malleable people's preferences are if they are to guide the formation of healthier ones. Does this not entail looking inside us? And isn't it worth it to deliver sensible policies such as healthier eating, automatic enrolment in pensions and opt-out organ donation schemes?

This is a forceful objection, but it is overstated. When placed in perspective we can see that the pursuit of neither self-understanding nor general welfare demands that we sacrifice opacity respect.[12] Division of labour comes to the rescue. Government can keep its nose out of academic study and leave researchers to get on with their work. The insights they glean can then be allowed to work their way through the normal process of critique and refinement in academic circles, before entering the fringes of the public sphere where they can be debated on a more general level. The policy options produced by this process will gradually bubble up into the mainstream political discourse and then stand a chance of being adopted by a candidate or party and subjected to the formal democratic process. It will then be up to the people to decide whether or not to endorse them at the ballot box.[13] Research showing that agency is compromised in various ways is thus filtered through procedures that assume and enshrine opacity respect.

This space between politics and research is vital since research must always be tested, confirmed and interpreted before it is applied to political problems. Public funding is indispensable to a thriving academic community and so there will always be pressure on government to show that it is distributing scarce resources wisely by demanding ever greater 'impact' and 'engagement' from researchers. This pressure must be resisted, especially when it comes to research that suspends a value as fundamental as opacity respect. Putting policies inspired by academic research to the people might slow down state efforts to use them to increase well-being, but this seems a good idea in any case.

And let us not forget that states always retain the option to engage with citizens as rational agents and offer us reasons to alter behaviours that might be ill-advised. Indeed, we might wish to go further and argue that it can be permissible for states to engage in so-called 'soft paternalism', where someone is temporarily prevented from completing an apparently self-harmful action in order to ensure that they are freely choosing to perform that action and understand the consequences.[14]

Conclusion

I have argued that elected officials, civil servants and candidates for public office should neither commission nor use existing algorithms for the purpose of 'looking inside' citizens to see how good they are at exercising the core capacities that constitute agency. Anyone who qualifies as a full moral agent has an interest in being able to control and maintain their outward dignity, and to demand that others respect that dignity by refraining from evaluating their capacities any further. In the relationship between citizens and the politicians who run their state, this means treating citizens as presumptive authorities when it comes to their own lives.

This conclusion also provides a basis on which to respond to the corrosive impact of the various data-harvesting and dark propaganda scandals swirling around the twin electoral shocks of Trump and Brexit. The fear that shadowy political operatives can decide national elections and referendums, and the ensuing scramble to portray human beings as helpless victims of this malign influence, undermines the basic democratic idea that the public can be trusted to make decisions. This is a big deal. Perhaps there will come a day when we are forced to conclude that the notion of self-government is outdated and we would all do better to be ruled by experts, artificial intelligence or the I-Ching, but I doubt it. As imperfect as we are, we are surely agents. Replenishing faith in democracy will mean restoring outward dignity, and that in turn requires a firm and enduring commitment to securing opacity respect.

Notes

1. See, for instance, Green and Gerber (2015).
2. See, for instance, the 'Data for Climate Action' challenge set by the United Nations Global Pulse project, available at: https://www.unglobalpulse.org/data-for-climate-action, last accessed 22 May 2018.
3. Available at: https://www.bloomberg.com/news/features/2015-11-12/is-the-republican-party-s-killer-data-app-for-real-, last accessed 24 September 2019.
4. Available at: https://www.forbes.com/sites/kashmirhill/2012/02/16/how-target-figured-out-a-teen-girl-was-pregnant-before-her-father-did/#2d1838ab6668, last accessed 24 September 2019.
5. That is, openness, conscientiousness, extraversion, agreeableness and neuroticism. For a helpful discussion of the relationship between this approach to psychology and politics, see Gerber et al. (2011).
6. For instance, see Joe Saunders' chapter in this volume, below.
7. See also Williams' (2009) hugely influential remarks in 'The Idea of Equality'.
8. Degrading treatment is so dangerous for dignity because it is designed to undermine the idea that some individual is a competent and independent agent. It works by emphasising or focusing attention on weakness, and when it succeeds, it does so by evoking the 'appropriate' response of pity for the pathetic spectacle on display.
9. This fixation with concealment may seem strange since at least some crude form of evaluation must take place in order to determine that the threshold for agency has been passed in the first place. Carter grants this, allowing that we 'perceive individuals as moral agents because we perceive them as having at least a certain

minimum of agential capacities' (2011: 552). However, he asserts that once this minimum is acknowledged that is when opacity respect kicks in.

10. Now, we might wish to distinguish here between theoretical and practical authority, or the authority of experts and the authority of leaders. The former give advice while the latter give orders. So far as it goes, this is true. However, Joseph Raz (1986) suggests that there is no deep difference here. The directives of practical authorities simply sum up and replace more of the reasons that apply to us – including the autonomy-based reasons we have for being allowed to make up our own minds. The key point is that authority has to do with the structure imposed on the reasons that apply to us. If it were sufficiently important to get something right then a theoretical authority could become a fully-fledged practical authority. For further discussion of this point, see Fox (2015: 175–6).

11. See, for instance, Kahneman (2011).

12. How worried should we be that scientists studying human frailty will come to adopt the objective viewpoint permanently? In fact, although I will not pursue it any further here, it is worth noting that 'maintaining their humanity' at the same time as professional detachment has always been seen as a challenge for scientists and doctors.

13. This is, of course, an idealised story about the public sphere, but as I am trying to outline an alternative to governments directly becoming party to research that objectifies it will suffice.

14. For a discussion of soft paternalism see Begon (2016: 357–60).

References

Begon, J., 'Paternalism', *Analysis* 76(3) (2016): 355–73.

Carter, I., 'Respect and the Basis of Equality', *Ethics* 121 (2011): 538–71.

Estlund, D. M., *Democratic Authority: a Philosophical Framework* (Princeton, NJ: Princeton University Press, 2008).

Fox, C., 'Political Authority, Practical Identity, and Binding Citizens', *International Journal of Philosophical Studies* 23(2) (2015): 168–86.

Green, D. P. and A. S. Gerber, *Get Out the Vote: How to Increase Voter Turnout* (Washington DC: Brookings Institution Press, 2015).

Gerber, A. S., G. A. Huber, D. Doherty and C. M. Dowling, 'The Big Five Personality Traits in the Political Arena', *Annual Review of Political Science* 14 (2011): 265–87.

Issenberg, S., *The Victory Lab: The Secret Science of Winning Campaigns* (New York: Broadway Books, 2013).

Kahneman, D., *Thinking, Fast and Slow* (London: Penguin, 2011).

Milkman, K. L., T. Rogers and M. H. Bazerman, 'Highbrow Films Gather Dust: Time-Inconsistent Preferences and Online DVD Rentals', *Management Science* 55(6) (2009): 1047–59.

Nagel, T., 'Concealment and Exposure', *Philosophy & Public Affairs* 27(1) (1998): 1–30.

Pettit, P. and M. Smith, 'Freedom in Belief and Desire', *Journal of Philosophy*, 93(9) (1996): 429–49.

Raz, J., *The Morality of Freedom* (Oxford: Clarendon Press, 1986).

Strawson, P. F., 'Freedom and Resentment', *Proceedings of the British Academy* 48 (1962): 1–25.

Thaler, R. and C. R. Sunstein, C. R. (2009), *Nudge: Improving Decisions about Health, Wealth, and Happiness*. London: Penguin.

Williams, B., *Problems of the Self: Philosophical Papers 1956–1972*. Cambridge: Cambridge University Press, 2009, available at: https://www.bloomberg.com/news/features/2015-11-12/is-the-republican-party-s-killer-data-app-for-real-, last accessed 22 May 2018.

United Nations Global Pulse, 2018, available at: https://www.unglobalpulse.org/data-for-climate-action, last accessed 22 May 2018.

THREE

A Pre-Occupation with Possession: the (Non-) Ownership of Personal Data

Kevin Macnish and Stephanie Gauttier

Introduction

Data which relate to and may be used to identify living people ('personal data') have become commodified in a manner unimaginable to most just fifteen years ago. Companies prolifically collect data on people's health, shopping habits, driving behaviour, likes and dislikes with the goal of making money from an abundant, cheap and never-ending supply. In return, those people to whom the data relate (because the data reveal *their* shopping patterns or *their* driving behaviour) may be offered coupons, lower insurance premiums or access to services, which they frequently take.

The realisation that data relating to people may be worth something financially is dawning. There is an awareness that if the data I hand over to a company is worth something to those running the company, then they should give me something in return. Seizing on this growing realisation, a number of companies have been formed in recent years aimed at enabling people to profit from the sale of this data, such as CitizenMe (CitizenMe 2018; Finley 2014) and Data Wallet (Datawallet 2018). However, in order to sell something you must first own it, or have permission to sell it on behalf of another, and so there is an implicit assumption that people own data that relate to them such that they are justified in profiting from the sale of these data.

It is not all about money, though. Irrespective of the financial value of data, there is a deeper moral concern that I should have a (arguably controlling) say in what happens to 'my' data. This is captured in a quote by President Obama in 2016 concerning how to approach issues of harm and control in personal data: 'It requires, first of all, us understanding who owns the data . . . And I would like to think that if somebody does a test on me or my genes, that that's mine' (Obama 2016). Further, while other political bodies have argued that ownership should not be private but rather public or joint, they do not question that data are owned (Mascarenhas, Kesavan and Bernacchi 2003; Rodwin 2009).

In academia it is often simply assumed that personal data are owned by the person to whom the data relate (Al-Khouri 2007; Chen and Zhao 2012). In academic legal debate there is similar recognition that, in European law at least, personal data are owned by the person to whom they relate (Rees 2014; Berlioz 2015; Beyneix 2015; Bensoussan 2010). Finally, social science research has demonstrated that, at least in some instances, people view personal data relating to them as simultaneously owned by them (Spiekermann, Korunovska and Bauer 2012).

Perhaps most significantly for this book, though, is the problem as to who can do what with data that relate to people when those data may have political significance. This came to light most clearly in the Cambridge Analytica scandal of 2016–18 in which a private company gained data freely submitted to an app on Facebook in 2013 (Cadwalladr and Graham-Harrison 2018). The app had no obvious political significance, but the contributions of people to the app created a large store of data. In gaining access to these data, Cambridge Analytica used them to shape the direction of political campaigns and, it is at least alleged, engage in political manipulation. This therefore presents a strong democratic concern as to the control of personal data.

In this chapter, we argue that the existing models of ownership do not account for our relationship to personal data in a satisfactory manner. Based on the idea that one wants to minimise the harmful consequences that the use of the data might have for themselves, and acknowledging that the data is a product of mixed labour between the individual and the platform collecting the data, we argue that both individuals and platforms are responsible for the way the data are used and must be able to control them. Furthermore, whenever the data are shared with others, those others adopt a share in that responsibility.

What are Personal Data?

We have defined personal data as data which relate to, or can be used to identify, a living person. This is drawn from the definition of personal data offered by the General Data Protection Regulation (GDPR) (EU Parliament 2016). This definition has some obvious drawbacks, such as whether the contents of my diary (relating only to my thoughts about myself) cease to be personal data when I die, whether data that are about me but cannot be used to identify me are not personal, and the obvious context-dependent nature of identification (such as one being male could be used to identify a man in an otherwise all-female line-up). However, these are not our concern in this chapter. Rather, we adopt this approach as a workable definition of personal data in order to better understand theories of ownership in relation to those data.

Why Ownership?

The concept of ownership is both intuitive to many and a seemingly popular approach to managing the benefits and harms that can arise from the use of personal data. A classic contemporary definition of ownership is that expressed by C. B. Macpherson as 'a right to dispose of, or alienate, as well as to use . . . which is not conditional on the owner's performance of any social function' (Macpherson 2014: 126). More recently, Jeremy Waldron has ownership as determining 'how, by whom, and on what terms the resource [is] to be used. An object is mine if it is for me rather than for anyone else to say what is to be done with it' (Waldron 1991: 158).

Taking these definitions as relatively uncontroversial, ownership can be seen to confer control over property. This control allows a person to exercise influence over harm threatened to themselves and others. If I own a large stick then you cannot use that stick to harm me, and I could use it to defend myself should you attempt to harm me with your large stick. As such, ownership gives one a sense of control (albeit possibly misguided) and, through that, a sense of security. Furthermore, in many cases I am best placed to know what will hurt me. Public knowledge that I am homosexual may be so embarrassing that I would consider suicide, or it may be something I wear as a badge of pride. Either way, I am best placed to know whether that information would harm or help me. As such, it is clear why a person would want to exercise control over their personal data, and particularly data which could be used to harm them or the state in which they live. Using an ownership approach appears to offer the owner of the data that control.

The implications of ownership are significant. As noted, other people and companies are interested in accessing personal data: the use of personal data is the business model of social media platforms such as Facebook. It is in Facebook's interest to lay claim to own the data which are uploaded to its platform. At the same time, were they my data I had uploaded, I might reasonably lay claim to owning those data myself. In each of these cases, ownership of the data provides intuitively strong grounds for controlling what happens to them. If I own the data, then I have strong grounds to resist Facebook using those data as it pleases. If Facebook owns the data, then my resistance is weakened.

In the latter case I may fear that if a social media company controls data that are about me, it is likely to be risk-prone in its use of those data, as any harm will most likely accrue to me rather than to the company, while the party to benefit will be the company or, in some cases, society at large (Wolff 2010). Hence, it is important to this line of thinking not only that personal data can be owned, but that I own the data which relate to, and can be used to identify, me. We take this to be a central thesis which we will challenge in this chapter:

> ownership of personal data sits (or can be assumed to sit) by default with the person to whom the data relate.

Our argument in what follows is not that *theories* of ownership do not apply to personal data. We believe that they do, or can be made to do so. Our challenge is rather that these theories do not support the thesis outlined above. As such, our argument is that we must either accept that the thesis is false, or reject the ownership model when it comes to personal data.

Models of Ownership

There are two means by which a person may come to own something ('property'). The first, intrinsic, applies in the case of things which are owned by a person as a matter of natural right. The second, acquired, describes how things are properly acquired by a person, thus becoming that person's property. We shall treat each of these in turn as regards personal data in this section.

Intrinsic

The classic starting point for intrinsic (or self-)ownership is frequently given as the eye, following an article by Gerry Cohen in which he argues that it would be wrong to force me to have an eye transplant with you, even if I have two working eyes and you have none (Cohen 2010: 69–71). Despite the aggregate benefit (the eye transplant would mean that two people, rather than just one person, could see), I am under no obligation to surrender my eye to you. My eye is owned by me and as such I have the right of use and disposal of my eye, along with a right of non-interference, described by Macpherson and Waldron above.

Stephen Munzer challenges this position, arguing that I do not have the right of destruction of my body. Hence, I do not have ownership of it, but

I do have some property rights over it (Munzer 1990). In a similar way, I may not have ownership over data relating to me, but have (some) property rights over those data. Leaving aside the contention that I may have a right of destruction of my own body, there are other things that we might properly be said to own and yet lack the right of destruction. Were one of us the owner of a van Gogh painting, we do not think that we would have the right to destroy that painting. We may own it, but the work retains social value that cannot be ignored. However, it would be strange to say that, having just parted with €30 million to have it in our private collection, we do not own the painting. Hence, ownership does not always confer an absolute right of disposal.

That some people do hold an intrinsic view of ownership of personal data is evident in the following quote by Luciano Floridi: '"My" in "my information" is not the same "my" as in "my car" but rather the same "my" as in "my body" or "my feelings": it expresses a sense of constitutive belonging, not of external ownership, a sense in which my body, my feelings and my information are part of me but are not my (legal) possession' (Floridi 2005: 195). Hence, to Floridi at least, there is a sense that the ownership of personal data is intrinsic rather than acquired, more akin to Cohen's eye than to his car.

While there may be intuitive strength to Floridi's position, there are a number of challenges that can be levelled here. In the first place, personal data are significantly different from a body or an eye and seem closer in nature to knowledge: as I share data that relate to me, I do not lose those data (they do not cease to be 'my' data because Facebook now has a record of them). By contrast, the strength of Cohen's claim lies in the fact that were I to have an eye transplant I would lose that eye. Were Cohen's eye example to be continued in a manner such that I could offer you sight with no significant loss to myself, then I should do so. In this new situation it is harder to argue that I should not share my data with Facebook if in so doing I would significantly help another's need and I would not risk significant and obvious harm to myself.

If personal data are closer in nature to knowledge than to tangible things, then an analogy could be drawn with intellectual property (IP). IP can be shared with no immediate loss to the originator. Loss occurs only when a person uses IP without correct attribution or payment. However, IP is rarely, if ever, justified as being intrinsically owned by the property-holder, even if that property-holder is the author. Rather, typical justifications rest on Lockean, Hegelian or other interpretations of property acquisition (Fisher 2001). As such, we shall return to considering this analogy when looking at property as acquired.

Secondly, if you take a part of my body without my permission, I would probably describe that as some manner of theft. By contrast, Cambridge Analytica encountered data uploaded to Facebook without gaining the data in such a way that we would refer to as theft. Once again, then, it does not seem as if I can rightly be said to own my personal data intrinsically.

A final point is that at a later stage in his life Cohen questioned the notion of self-ownership described above. He was considerably less sure of the intrinsic right of the person whose eye it was to deny the use of that eye to another. This is not to say that Cohen was right, but merely to remark that the *locus classicus* of intrinsic self-ownership was perhaps not as obvious as its author once thought (Cohen 2010: 243–4).

Acquired

If personal data are owned, but are not owned intrinsically, then they must be acquired. The acquisition of property has been described by Vinding Kruse as 'taking into possession of an ownerless thing or other valuable good belonging to no one, or any other act by which a person unilaterally determines such an object of value as belonging to him in future' (Kruse 1939: 277). While this captures the approach taken by the theorists we shall consider below, it does not account for the most common means of acquisition through purchase and gifting. Indeed, the original Latin word *datum* refers to the giving of a gift.

Of the principal theories of acquisition, the best known is probably Locke's theory of mixing labour with a thing previously unowned, through which the labourer comes to own the product of that labour (Locke 1988, ss. 2:27–51). However, it is not obvious how this could be applied to personal data. One might say that my effort in thinking through and uploading data to a social media platform is labour of a sort. However, it is more plausible to claim that the company that analyses those data and provides me with a personality profile based upon them, has mixed more of its labour with those data than I have. If so, then the Lockean account would tend towards the company owning the data rather than me.

Robert Nozick's alternative account calls for a just principle of acquisition and a just principle of transfer (Nozick 2001). Provided both principles have been met, Nozick argues, all property is held justly. Whether Nozick is correct in the transitivity of justice in this way is not at issue here, but rather his principle of just acquisition, on the precise nature of which he is quiet. He famously challenges Locke's account by suggesting that mixing a teaspoon of tomato juice with the ocean does not entitle me to ownership of the ocean, but fails to suggest an alternative.

Georg Hegel did provide an alternative account of acquisition, and arguably one much simpler than Locke's, in suggesting that it was a matter of first occupancy (Hegel 2016: 73). This was not simply a matter of 'first come, first served', but part of a richer theory that ownership of property was fundamentally good for a person's character and promoted notions of responsibility. As such, the desire to own was also a good and so a person should be permitted to own that which was otherwise unclaimed to develop their character.

Hegel's account lacks persuasive force in the early twenty-first century when so much of the world's resources are owned by so few and at the expense of so many. Despite this concentration of ownership, there has been little evidence of the benign effects of property ownership on character development in the neo-liberal globalised economy. Even if we were to accept this theory, though, it would not take us to a place of ownership of personal data. Rather it would suggest that any data previously unclaimed are 'up for grabs', including personal data. Hence, if I have not staked a claim on my data then it is fair game for others to do so. Furthermore, Waldron argues that Hegel also allowed for the redistribution of property by the state to account for those without property. Property rights, according to Hegel, were not absolute in the face of competing demands from 'higher stages of ethical development' (Waldron 1991: 387). Hence, even if I were to argue first occupancy of my data on grounds of character development, the Hegelian approach would allow the state to forcibly redistribute my data if in so doing it would benefit others in society.

Adam Henschke has recently argued in favour of Hegel's account, noting that his theory of property makes the claim that 'all people have a property claim in things that are necessary for individuation, those things central to self-development' (2017: 73–4). This, as Henschke points out, does give the Hegelian account stronger grounds for arguing in favour of the individual's ownership of personal data than Locke's. In combination with the principle of first occupancy, Hegel's account allows for general private ownership as long as people are able to access that which is necessary for survival and the exercise of free will. In this regard, it is similar to Locke's proviso that ownership is acceptable as long as it does not entail property going to spoil while others die in want of that property. However, there are at least two arguments which give reason to think that Henschke is mistaken in his account.

One crucial distinction is whether personal data, or control of those data, are indeed 'necessary for individuation'. It is not immediately clear that this is the case, at least of necessity. Certainly, a case can be constructed, as Henschke demonstrates, whereby information relating to a person's skin colour, for example, can have an impact on their individuation and exercise of free will. However, there are also cases where this need not be the case. In what way is ownership of the personal data that I bought a chocolate bar yesterday a matter of individuation? So it does not follow on the Hegelian account that we should have ownership of all personal data, but only of those data which impact those things central to our self-development.

Even if we agree that personal data are always necessary for individuation, there is also an argument about scope, which asks what constitutes a thing as necessary for my individuation or self-development. In contemporary society it might be that my individuation and self-development require that I have a computer. Does this mean that therefore I now own a computer? Of course not. At best it can mean that you have no right to stop me from owning a computer. Hence, this Hegelian position cannot be that the need for individuation grants ownership of that which is needed, but rather that the need for individuation means that I cannot be denied ownership of that which is needed. But that is entirely different from the case in hand. Our argument is *not* that you cannot own data which are about you; you can. Our point is rather that you do not own those data as a matter of default. Hence, Hegel's theory, despite Henschke's attempts to salvage it, does not work either.

Hume's conventionalist theory of property was more laissez-faire than Hegel's, and arguably even less applicable in a contemporary environment (Hume 2015: 489). His position was that the system of property that we have today may have originated by force, but that it has been 'transformed into a system of private property by consent' (Waldron 1991: 339). This is an intriguing position given Hume's well-known refutation of the social contract theory, and one wonders how consent was to be understood in this context. Even if we accept Hume's theory, though, it likewise has no obvious application to personal data as there are no conventions in this case. With the possible exception of IP, we have not hitherto been in a position of discussing ownership of something as different from physical property as data. Furthermore, if we are to accept with Hume that we can legitimise the forcible seizure of property over the course of time and general acceptance, then this would seem to argue in favour of people taking what data they can get and keeping them for as long as is necessary to gain public acceptance.

That ends a cursory overview of the leading historical theories of property acquisition. There are of course others (not least Marx, although it will not take much reflection to see that a Marxist interpretation will similarly fail to give ownership to the individual but rather to the state), but the forgoing is sufficient to make our point.

In response to this overview, it may be argued that these theories were all developed prior to the realisation of the value of personal data, so the fact that they cannot account for the ownership of personal data merely suggests that new theories (or significant modifications) are needed. In response to this, we would note, first, that the challenge is not that the *theories* do not apply to personal data; they do. It is quite plausible to apply a Lockean, Hegelian, Marxist or other theory to personal data. The challenge is that such applications do not result in the ownership of personal data being allocated to the person to whom those data relate, which we take to be the desired position. Rather, they suggest that ownership should rest with the company analysing the data, the state or some other entity. This raises issues pertaining to how the individual can control the use of the data that can harm him or her, if the data are owned by someone else. Secondly, if none of the accounts of ownership apply in such a way as to arrive at the desired outcome, then it is more obvious to conclude that the desired outcome is unattainable by appealing to ownership than to conclude that new theories are needed.

We have claimed that there is a desire for people to be able to control (at least some of) the data which describe them. We have also argued that no existing theory of ownership can satisfactorily account for that relationship, such that ownership of personal data would confer control to the person described by those data. This undertaking has been, in part at least, motivated by consequentialist concerns: which theory will arrive at the consequences we desire, rather than which theory is right. Once started on this road, why not go the rest of the way and look at a consequentialist justification for ownership of personal data?

The Consequences of Ownership

Adopting a model of ownership in thinking about personal data, irrespective of any deontic justifications, would not take us any closer to the desired goal of my having control over the personal data which relate to me. The immediate consequences of owning personal data would certainly be that I would get property rights over data which relate to me: I would have the right to use and dispose of my data as I chose. This appears to take us where we want to go. However, it is important to remember that the right to dispose of data, or indeed any property, includes the right not just to destroy those data, but also to trade them. Furthermore, it is apparent that there are people willing to pay for my data, such that even if I did not want to part with those data, the money offered would make their sale very attractive.

Being able to trade personal data is not obviously a bad thing: individuals freely choose to trade their data for coupons, suggesting they find benefits in this trade. The challenge that is presented in trading personal data is that, through the trade, a person loses control of the data which relate to him or her. Hence, the control of personal data that is promised by the ownership model would be short-lived. If I own the data relating to me and can therefore sell you those data, and I do, then I find myself in a post-sale situation where you have the right to use and dispose of the data which relate to me and the right of my non-interference in so doing. Once more, this seems to take us to a position that is orthogonal to the outcome originally desired regarding control and minimising harm.

In that case, it is plausible that it is not the trade itself that is the problem but the unconstrained trade. It might be that trading, or donating, personal data would be acceptable if it were sufficiently regulated, so that individuals are less open to exploitation. However, the fact remains that the person to whom the data relate no longer has control over those data. Control now rests with the company that possesses the data and possibly a regulator. Furthermore, if it is the case that I own personal data relating to me, and the sale or donation of those data would not harm anybody other than me, then it is very paternalistic for the state to say what I can and cannot do with it.

Finally, as is often the case with consequential considerations which are not time-bounded, it is difficult to know what the consequences will be in the future of having parted with control of my information in the present. Given that those uploading their data to an app on Facebook did not know at the time what use would be made of it by Cambridge Analytica three years later, and the current expansion of technical capabilities, it is virtually impossible to say what uses of personal data will become possible within a lifetime.

Hence, in coming to a consequentialist consideration of the question of ownership, the benefits are that the person to whom the data relate does indeed gain short-term control of those data and that person could gain some money by selling 'their" data. However, this is more than counterbalanced by the loss of control of those data which occurs because of the sale.

An Alternative Approach

One way around the problem of ownership would be to refocus attention from the rights of the person affected to the responsibilities of the parties controlling the data, that is, those who hold the data. These individuals or entities with access to data are responsible for using the data in a way that does not harm others, including those to whom the data relate. Their function is not that of a data controller or processor as defined in the GDPR as they are not meant to control legal compliance. Rather, those with access to data become, by virtue of that access, custodians of the data: they have the ability, and with it a moral responsibility, to determine what happens to the data and, hence, to ensure for their part that the use of the data does not lead to harm.

As anyone with access to personal data is a custodian of this data, the person to whom the data relate may also be a custodian and, hence, have responsibility to ensure that the data are not used in such a way as can harm them. This means that there is a responsibility on the part of the person to whom the data relate in disposing of those data. Individuals should discern between those entities which might use the data in ways that could foreseeably harm individuals, and those others which would use the data without harm. Any entity which accesses the data must apply the same discernment in deciding whether and with whom to share the data as well as in deciding how to use the data.

There is therefore a co-responsibility between all custodians of data to make sure that data is not shared or used in ways that may be harmful. Current approaches focusing on ownership do not consider this as they imply that the person owning the data can dispose of the data as they see fit. The responsibility of the person to whom the data relate to make sure that their data is not used in harmful ways is not considered. The responsibility of any entity towards the person to whom the data relate is also absent from this approach. In this way, our approach refocuses attention from the rights of the putative data owner to the responsibilities of the custodians of those data.

Applying this approach to the case of the Cambridge Analytica, the company had a responsibility not to use the data in a way that could harm others. Likewise, Facebook had a responsibility to make sure that entities accessing data were trustworthy. Facebook should have applied their responsibility by enquiring about the purpose of the data acquisition. Cambridge Analytica might have lied in response, in which case Facebook's responsibility would be waived in this instance, provided they had engaged with due diligence. When Cambridge Analytica placed advertisements on Facebook, the social media platform could have audited the purpose of these advertisements. This is especially true knowing that the advertisements might be related to the analysis of a set of data which was initially under their responsibility and used to accomplish something on their platform. In the event, both Facebook and Cambridge Analytica appear to have failed to engage with their responsibility for the data of which they were custodians. Individuals who generated the data, on the other hand, could not see the end use, which developed after the data were uploaded, and then could only deal with their personal data, while the problem arose from using a large pool of data. Individual user responsibility lay in choosing to upload their data to Facebook while knowing that the business model of Facebook is based on the utilisation and selling of personal data.

A second example is of employees voluntarily giving their physiological data to their employers to allow them to understand individual stress levels at work to improve that employee's work conditions. This data could reasonably be foreseen to produce potential harm were it to become identifiable and known by line management. In this case, both the employee and the employer are custodians of the generated data.

There needs to be shared control of the data between the custodians of the data. In accepting the data, the employer assumes shared responsibility (with the employee) of the data and should ensure to the best of their ability that the data do not lead to harm. Were the data leaked from my employer to my line manager, then my employer would be responsible for any harm that may arise. If the data were leaked from me, then my employer would not be responsible for any harm that may arise, but rather I and the new custodian of my data (the recipient of the leak) are. If my employer shares my data with my line manager, then that manager becomes a custodian and adopts shared responsibility for those data. If reasonably foreseeable harm arises from my line manager's use of the data then she or he bears responsibility for that harm, coupled with the employer if it was reasonably foreseeable that harm would result from sharing the data.

Employees in this situation who have not generated data yet work in the same location can be affected by the consequences of the use of this data, such as through any changes that are made to manage stress differently. These new dispositions might not suit the non-participants and could even harm them. A difference here with the Cambridge Analytica case is that in the latter everyone was affected by the consequences of the use of the data, but no one knew what data were collected or for what purposes. No individual outside Cambridge Analytica or Facebook would bear responsibility. In the case of the workplace, by contrast, it is reasonable to assume that the individuals who are affected by the sharing of data are easy to identify: they are the co-workers of those who share the data. They would not have any say in the matter if we were to adopt an ownership approach to the data. However, if we adopt the proposed approach based on custody and responsibility for harm, then their interests should at the least be considered by those using the data. Ideally, those at risk of harm should have the right to observe what happens with the data and be given means of redress if they are wrongly affected by these data and the ways they are shared.

Conclusion

In this chapter, we have argued that the ownership of personal data is flawed. While this approach appears to provide control and a means of minimising harm, we have demonstrated that it fails to do either. Furthermore, there are no grounds for a concept of ownership to be applied to personal data through employing existing theories. While this may not be fatal for the approach, it robs it of a significant intuitive strength if, in holding that we own 'our' data, we must also re-define how it is that we come to own them.

There are three areas which arise from this chapter crying out for further research. The first is the intuitive attraction of owning personal data. This may relate to the use of the possessive pronoun 'my' and equivocating on different meanings of this word. The second is the concept of self-ownership. Given that Cohen is both the common point of reference for justifying this intuition and yet has also questioned it, further work could usefully be carried out in exploring whether self-ownership is a meaningful or useful concept. The third is the development of a suitable alternative approach to ownership in accounting for the relationship between a person and the data that describe them. We have considered focusing on custody of data and responsibility for the reasonably foreseeable harm arising from those data. Unlike ownership, this responsibility is not exclusive but is based on the potential for harm. This therefore presents an intuitively powerful and theoretically grounded alternative to the ownership model.

References

Al-Khouri, A. M., 'Data Ownership: Who Owns "My Data"?' *International Journal of Management & Information Technology* 2(1) (2007): 1–8.

Bensoussan, A., 'Propriété des Données et Protection des Fichiers', *Gazette du Palais*, No. 2 (2010).

Berlioz, P., 'Consécration du Vol de Données Informatiques. Peut-on Encore Douter de La Propriété de l'information?' *Revue des Contrats*, No. 951 (2015).

Beyneix, I., 'Le Traitement des Données Personnelles par les Entreprises: Big Data et Vie Privée, État des Lieux', *Semaine Juridique*, No. 2113 (2015): 46–7.

Cadwalladr, C. and E. Graham-Harrison, 'Revealed: 50 Million Facebook Profiles Harvested for Cambridge Analytica in Major Data Breach', *The Guardian*, 17 March 2018, available at: https://www.theguardian.com/news/2018/mar/17/cambridge-analytica-facebook-influence-us-election, last accessed 22 May 2019.

Chen, D. and H. Zhao, 'Data Security and Privacy Protection Issues in Cloud Computing', 2012 *International Conference on Computer Science and Electronics Engineering* 1 (2012): 647–51, available at: https://doi.org/10.1109/ICCSEE.2012.193.

CitizenMe, available at: https://www.citizenme.com/public/wp, last accessed 22 May 2018.

Cohen, G. A., *Self-Ownership, Freedom, and Equality* (Cambridge: Cambridge University Press, 2010).

Datawallet, available at: https://datawallet.com/#get-the-app, last accessed 22 May 2018.

EU Parliament, *Regulation (EU) 2016/679 of the European Parliament and of the Council of 27 April 2016 on the Protection of Natural Persons with Regard to the Processing of Personal Data and on the Free Movement of Such Data, and Repealing Directive 95/46/EC (General Data Protection Regulation) (Text with EEA Relevance)*, OJ Law 119 (2016), available at: http://data.europa.eu/eli/reg/2016/679/oj/eng, last accessed 22 May 2018.

Finley, K., 'The App that Lets You Spy on Yourself and Sell Your Own Data', *Wired*, 7 September 2014, available at: https://www.wired.com/2014/07/citizenme, last accessed 27 September 2019.

Fisher, W., 'Theories of Intellectual Property', in S. Munzer (ed.), *New Essays in the Legal and Political Theory of Property* (Cambridge: Cambridge University Press, 2001), pp. 168–99.

Floridi, L., 'The Ontological Interpretation of Informational Privacy', *Ethics and Information Technology* 7(4) (2005): 185–200.

Hegel, G. F. W., *Hegel's Philosophy of Right*, trans. S. W. Dyde (Charleston, SC: CreateSpace Independent Publishing Platform, 2016).

Henschke, A., *Ethics in an Age of Surveillance: Personal Information and Virtual Identities* (New York: Cambridge University Press, 2017).

Hume, D., *A Treatise of Human Nature: Being an Attempt to Introduce the Experimental Method of Reasoning into Moral Subjects* (Charleston, SC: CreateSpace Independent Publishing Platform, 2015).

Kruse, V., *The Right of Property* (London: Oxford University Press, 1939).

Locke, J., *Two Treatises of Government*, ed. P. Laslett (Cambridge: Cambridge University Press, 1988).

Macpherson, C. B., *Democratic Theory: Essays in Retrieval*, rev. edn (Don Mills, Ontario: Oxford University Press, 2014).

Mascarenhas, O. A. J., R. Kesavan and M. D. Bernacchi, 'Co-managing Online Privacy: a Call for Joint Ownership', *Journal of Consumer Marketing* 20(7) (2003): 686–702.

Munzer, S., *A Theory of Property* (New York: Cambridge University Press, 1990.

Nozick, R., *Anarchy, State and Utopia*, new edn (Oxford:Wiley-Blackwell, 2001).

Obama, B., 'Remarks by the President in Precision Medicine Panel Discussion', *Whitehouse.Gov.*, 25 February 2016, available at: https://obamawhitehouse.archives.gov/the-press-office/2016/02/25/remarks-president-precision-medicine-panel-discussion, last accessed 22 May 2018.

Rees, C., 'Who Owns Our Data?' *Computer Law & Security Review* 30(1) (2014): 75–9.

Rodwin, M. A., 'The Case for Public Ownership of Patient Data', JAMA 302(1) (2009): 86–8.

Spiekermann, S., J. Korunovska and C. Bauer, 'Psychology of Ownership and Asset Defense: Why People Value Their Personal Information Beyond Privacy', SSRN Scholarly Paper ID 2148886. Rochester, NY: Social Science Research Network, 2012, available at: https://papers.ssrn.com/abstract=2148886, last accessed 22 May 2018.

Waldron, J., *The Right to Private Property*, new edn (Oxford: Oxford University Press, 1991).

Wolff, J., 'Five Types of Risky Situation', *Law, Innovation and Technology*, 2(2) (2010): 151–63.

FOUR

Policing with Big Data: DNA Matching vs Crime Prediction

Tom Sorell

Many large data sets are relevant to the detection and prosecution of crime. For example, DNA profiles can be extracted from databases and matched with samples collected at crime scenes to aid in the identification of suspects. There is evidence that storage and matching of DNA profiles not only solves particular crimes but reduces crime rates.[1] More controversially, patterns in the intensity and spread of burglaries in a city can inform opinions about where burglaries will occur locally in the future. Since liberal democracies promise the law-abiding that they will protect them from crime, do those jurisdictions not have an obligation to use relevant data sets to prosecute, and, where possible, prevent, crime? Even if the answer is 'Yes', those obligations may be limited significantly by liberal rights. Ordinary citizens have rights to pursue law-abiding activities unmolested, and the surveillance underlying some of the relevant data collection and matching may amount to a sort of molestation or at least an invasion of privacy. Besides, pattern recognition in crime data may be affected by bias in choices of characteristics that matter to crime, and data sets are subject to theft, deletion and contamination of various kinds.

In previous work, I have defended large-scale data collection and analysis of data in the prosecution and prevention of the most serious crime, including terrorism (Sorell 2011, 2016, 2018a, 2018b). In particular, I have tended to be sceptical of objections based on privacy to large-scale collection and analysis for those purposes. But, clearly, the propriety of using big data in policing decreases the less serious the relevant crimes are, the more speculative the algorithms generating the predictions and the less well governed the databases. The use of big data is also called into question in jurisdictions that suffer from over-criminalisation, disproportionately severe punishment and very expensive legal representation. Differently, secrecy and the relative accountability of the collectors and users of the data matter to the democratic legitimacy of uses of big data. Police forces are not meant to operate out of sight of at least a subset of democratically elected legislators and the judicial system. Nor are they supposed to operate ad lib. They are subject to protocols intended to maximise the harmless liberty of those who are policed.

In this chapter I defend the construction of inclusive, tightly governed DNA databases, as long as police can access them only for the prosecution of the most serious crimes or less serious but very high-volume offences. I deny that that the ethics of collecting and using these data sets the pattern for other kinds of policing by big data, notably predictive policing. DNA databases are primarily used for *matching* newly gathered biometric data with stored data. After considering and disputing a number of objections to this practice, I conclude that DNA databases used in this way are ethically acceptable, if not valuable, contributions to legitimate policing.

DNA Databases

In developed liberal democracies DNA databases are composed of profiles rather than samples. A DNA sample is biological material that, under the right conditions and with the right techniques, can be used to identify a unique individual. A sample is also a basis for very probable inferences about an offender's gender, certain medical conditions and physical characteristics, such as eye colour. In both the US and UK, there are severe restrictions on the retention by the authorities, including the police, of DNA samples. DNA *profiles* are different. Each profile is a set of markers of gender and Standard Tandem Repeat (STR) DNA sequences – sequences that do not code for genes (and therefore do *not* sustain the inferences just mentioned). These profiles are virtually unique to a single human being – identical twins apart – and are excellent evidence of identity if derived from uncontaminated, undegraded DNA samples.

In the UK until 2008, DNA samples could be collected without consent from anyone arrested for virtually any crime. They could be kept permanently, whether or not people whose samples were taken were subsequently convicted. A European Court of Justice ruling in 2008 prohibited the retention of DNA profiles of people with no convictions. Rules introduced relatively recently in the UK limit the periods of time profiles can be retained for non-convicts. In general, the more serious the crime for which someone with no convictions is arrested, the longer a profile taken at the point of arrest can be retained. Retention beyond three years sometimes requires a special application to an official, and five years tends to be the limit. However, it is still customary near the time of arrest for a profile to be checked for matches with samples independently collected from scenes of crime, and with profiles of convicted offenders, lest arrestees who have convictions but who are operating under an assumed name escape detection.

Although thousands of DNA profiles in the UK are now deleted annually in order to meet the provisions of the Protection of Freedoms Act (POFA) (UK Government 2012), the DNA database in the UK remains the largest in the world, with profiles of over 5 million people (out of a UK population of around 65 million). The deletion rules under POFA defer from the 2008 European Court of Justice ruling in *S and Marper* v. *UK* (Council of Europe 2008) – according to which keeping indefinitely the DNA profiles and fingerprints of people who were once suspected of a particular crime but who have been acquitted, infringes their right to private and family life. The Court particularly objected to a police practice in England and Wales that made collection and retention of biometric data routine for adults and minors alike, regardless of the severity of the crime. (S had been a child suspect in a burglary case, and Marper was charged with harassment in a case brought by a partner who subsequently resumed a relationship with him.) The Court did not object to the general purpose of the collection and retention of biometric data, namely, the detection and prosecution of crime. Its focus was on the disproportionate effects of pursuing that policy on Marper (against whom harassment proceedings were dropped) and S, a child when arrested, who was acquitted).

The Privacy Objection

Without denying that the former collection and retention policy in the UK was heavy-handed in the case of *S and Marper*, must we say that there are objections on the basis of the value of privacy or other values to any DNA database that covers 8 per cent of the population? It is not obvious to me that we must.

Violations of privacy, as I have tried to argue in the past (Sorell 2011, 2018b; Guelke and Sorell 2017), are penetrations of zones conventionally protected from observation or reporting. The zones in question are those of the body, the home and the mind.[2] By 'the body' is meant primarily the exposed or naked human body. The conventions of covering the body or, differently, of not uncovering the body, support a convention of refraining from surveillance of the body. Looking at close quarters is intrusive unless it is invited, and so is camera surveillance, which produces pictures simulating direct visual experience of the body. Privacy conventions put the control of exposure of the body in the hands of the self, and limit the unwanted social effects of observation or reporting about the body by others.

The home, for the purposes of this chapter, is the default location occupied daily by a person when not otherwise active. It is the zone where people rest and sleep and expect to be safe when engaged in either. There can be temporary default locations, like hotel rooms, or passenger aircraft or cars that also count as home spaces, and the conventions for not entering or inspecting the home uninvited can apply to the hotel room or one's airline seat. These, too, are normally not to be observed or reported on without the permission of the person whose space it is.

The third and most important zone of privacy is the mind, understood as the set of capacities for arriving at what to believe and what to do. The mind is not, for our purposes, private in the sense – famously called into question by Wittgenstein – of being accessible only to the subject, or being the place where 'what it is like' to experience something registers. It is *normatively* private, meaning that it is wrong to force people to disclose their thoughts or convictions or to think aloud in some substantial sense (Nagel 1998). Especially in contexts where there is some strongly enforced political or religious orthodoxy, and expectations that each person will publicly proclaim adherence, the freedom to make one's own mind up privately – *without* thinking aloud and without declaring one's possibly unorthodox conclusions – comes into its own.

More generally, the mind is the arena where, by arriving at reasons for beliefs, or beliefs on the basis of reasoning, one *makes* those beliefs one's own. In the absence of the normative privacy of the mind people are likely to be mouthpieces for the views of their parents, religious or political leaders, or their class. The normatively private mind is also in some sense the *pre-eminent* zone of privacy, because it is by using its capacities that an adult in a liberal democratic society can determine the limits of exposure of the body and public access to the home. Normative mental privacy, then, is typically a condition of an individual's governance of other normatively private zones, but not the other way round.

If privacy is what one enjoys when experiential and informational access by others to one's body, home, beliefs and choices is significantly limited, then it is easy to see that privacy facilitates the exercise of autonomy. The normative privacy of the mind helps one to think and choose for oneself, but the public conventions licensing limited access to the home also facilitate the exercise of the capacity to choose and to believe for reasons. It is at home that one can be oneself and expose oneself most easily, and the home space therefore provides opportunities for trying on different views with one's friends and family before expressing them publicly.

Privacy is often, but disputably, connected with being in control of information about oneself. I say this is disputable, because loss of control, or absence of control, does not necessarily amount to a violation of privacy. When a powerful politician tries to prevent publication of damaging but accurate information about him- or herself – for example, the fact that he or she has taken a bribe – that is not necessarily a case of preserving the privacy of properly private information, and when, despite the politician's efforts, the information becomes generally known, that is not necessarily a violation of privacy. It could instead be a case of people finding out what a public figure is really like, which might properly affect their votes in a future election. This is because there is a legitimate public interest in news of the bribe: electors are entitled to know whether their representative's votes can be bought with money, especially where the use of paid-for influence could go against the interest of constituents.

On the other hand, publishing photographs of the interior of the politician's home to satisfy newspaper readers' curiosity about what it looks like is a violation of privacy quite apart from the politician losing control of the information in the photos. This is because of conventions that define the privacy zone of the home are so well entrenched in everyone's thinking about privacy.

How do DNA samples and DNA profiles fit into this picture of the protected zones? DNA *samples* certainly give a scientifically trained third-party insight into a person's body and even the bodies of members of that person's biological family, their parents in particular. Publicising some of this information could disadvantage those with identifiable genetic predispositions to expensive and hard to insure, or stigmatised, medical conditions. Even if the information were not public but were disclosed only to the person whose DNA it is, knowledge of the condition could drastically reduce quality of life. These adverse consequences of the availability of DNA samples do not show that DNA samples should never be taken or be the subject of published research. At most they call attention to the importance of insurance safety nets and the difficulty of adjusting to news that indicates one's days are numbered.

What about the fact that information derived from a DNA sample is for all intents and purposes *uniquely* identifying? What does this have to do with privacy? Claims that DNA is essential to a person's *identity* do not mean that sequencing or collecting DNA is more intimate than collecting, say, information about a person's preferred sexual practices or their sexually transmitted diseases, which are often *not* uniquely identifying.

It is true, as already acknowledged, that genetic information may need protection or rationing for communicative purposes, for example, because it will trigger prejudices and disadvantage someone. But this is not to say that just any disadvantageous information about a person is therefore private and incommunicable. The fact that someone has been convicted of murder is normatively public (because the result of a normatively public trial), *not* private.

The collection of uniquely identifying information, including genetic information, is not necessarily more of an intrusion than the confiscation of a diary. On the contrary, it can be entirely non-intrusive, because the information in question is not personally revealing. For example, the fact of being female and winning two Nobel prizes uniquely identifies Marie Curie (so far), but a contemporary of Marie Curie who knew only this fact did not come close to knowing Marie Curie 'personally', and fell even further short of being aware of private information about her. The same, I think, is true of knowing the results of the sequencing of one's own DNA. To know this sequence is to have impersonal knowledge, albeit biologically revealing knowledge, of someone. This is not necessarily private in the sense of penetrating a protected zone.

The fact that DNA is uniquely identifying does not show that it is tied to no-one else. If it is private or private property, it is private property shared by someone with their genetic parents, siblings and children. So not only is the inference from

(1) X uniquely determines the identity of person P

to

(2) X is private to person P

disputable,[3] in view of the inheritance of half of one's genetic material from each of one's parents. So, too, is the inference from (1) to

(3) Third-party collection of X violates P's privacy, *ceteris paribus*.

But, in any case, most DNA databases are *not* collections of DNA samples but of DNA *profiles*, which are much less revealing than DNA samples even if, for all intents and purposes, uniquely identifying.

The Suspect Population Objection

A second objection to large-scale collection and storage of DNA profiles arises from the size of the DNA database when it contains, as it does in the

UK, profiles of around 8 per cent of a large population. This time the problem concerns the relation between police and citizens in a liberal democracy. A citizenry is supposed to control and authorise the actions of police through representatives who legislate in the interests of everyone or most people in the jurisdiction. When law enforcement holds potentially incriminating information on so many, is not the direction of the control reversed, so that police and not citizens have the whip hand?

A related question is asked about the use by the police of large-scale closed circuit television systems whose cameras are openly trained on large public spaces. Does not this kind of surveillance either make a population suspect or help to keep them under the thumb of the authorities? Granted that the police are not *actively* targeting each person in those large spaces for attention, is not the indiscriminate retention of the images of so many, and in places where levels of crime may not be high, an expression of distrust or suspicion of the population? It is no more an expression of distrust or suspicion than the fact that everyone is now checked at airports before boarding. The authorities know that very few people come to the airport with concealed explosives or weapons. Still, the consequences, if just a few people are successful, are so great in lives lost, injury suffered and fear created, that sweeping searches are arguably not disproportionate. Nor are they discriminatory, since the premise of the argument that they *are* disproportionate is that *everyone* is treated the same way.

In the case of the national DNA database in the UK, there is no question of the collection of data turning people *into* suspects, as allegedly happens with mass surveillance. If anything, it is the other way round: only if someone is already officially suspected for some crime inasmuch as they have been *arrested*, does their profile get added to the database. Against this background, the collection of DNA samples is far less indiscriminate than the collection of CCTV images, and might for that reason be more proportionate as well.

Not only must subjects of DNA profiles reach a non-trivial threshold – arrest – to be included at all in the UK national DNA database, further non-trivial conditions need to be met if those profiles are to be retained for more than three years. There are three kinds of relevant suspects: (a) convicted; (b) unconvicted but charged with a relatively serious or 'qualifying' offence under the Protection of Freedoms Act; and (c) those charged with or arrested for a relatively minor offence. There is no retention in type (c) cases except by permission of the UK Biometrics Commissioner. Type (b) cases involve the retention of profiles for three years with the possibility of applying to the Biometrics Commissioner for a two-year extension. Type (a) cases call for indefinite retention of profiles. There is more lenient treatment for offenders under 18 with a single conviction, and guidelines for early deletion of profiles in a range of special cases (UK Government 2016: 30–1, table 6a).

The large size of the UK DNA base notwithstanding, the current restrictions on inclusion and retention of profiles seem sufficient to rebut the charge that it is an instrument for making a whole population suspect. Indeed, the restrictions rebut the charge that the DNA regime is disproportionately unforgiving of the population of arrested people or the population of previously charged people.

Whole Population DNA Profiling

I have argued that collecting DNA profiles of arrestees falls well short of making a whole population suspect. Would collecting DNA profiles not involve injustice, however, if arrestees, and therefore profiles, were overwhelmingly from a section of the population who was despised, or subject to some kind of prejudice? Here the answer is 'Yes'. In the UK, as it happens, profiles are currently in proportion to the ethnic mix of the country, with, in particular, the majority white population being reflected in the proportion of white people's profiles in the DNA database (UK Government 2016: 11, fig. 3b). It has not always been this way (*Independent* 2007). Indeed, it is conceivable that in another jurisdiction, or even in a possibly illiberal future UK, arrests and convictions would start conspicuously to disadvantage minority or ethnic populations. In jurisdictions of that kind, there would be an argument for reforming conditions under which someone could be arrested.

But would there not also be an argument for treating majority and minority populations alike by collecting DNA profiles of *everyone*? This would counteract some effects of prejudice in arrests, and would obviate the singling out of arrestees for DNA profiles. But would not *that* have the effect precisely of making a whole population suspect, if what the profiling was for was to find those guilty of any crime? And what if the jurisdiction in question were characterised by over-criminalisation and unduly severe sentences?[4] Would not universal collection of DNA profiles make it easier for unjust governments to convict anyone of offences that should not exist in the first place?

Let us for now leave aside special issues arising from over-criminalisation and unduly severe sentences: is there anything wrong with collecting profiles of everyone in a jurisdiction in which criminalisation and sentencing do seem proportionate, and arrests are not discriminatory? For example, if we hold constant the current range of criminal offences, sentences and investigatory techniques in the UK, what would be wrong with trying to match crime scene profiles with the profiles of 65 million people rather than 5 million profiles? (Smith 2006; Seringhaus 2009).[5] Unless one thinks (incorrectly, in my view) that knowledge of a DNA profile gives whomever has it dangerously direct access to the profile-owner's identity, allegedly the most private information of all, I do not see what is morally wrong with this idea on its face. Universal DNA profiling would support both law enforcement and the rule of law. It would treat everyone the same. If the current UK rules for accessing the database were preserved, the number of officials able to get at it would be extremely small.

Would universal profiling make a whole population suspect? That depends on whether inclusion in a universal database is enough to make one a suspect. I have already expressed scepticism about the related idea that the policy of checking every airline passenger for dangerous implements makes every airline passenger a suspect: a person can be checked just because checking everyone is thought to be the best (fairest and most thorough) way of finding dangerous substances or devices. Such a regime is compatible with checks on people who are regarded by the checkers and everyone else as very improbable potential terrorists. Universal checks in the *absence* of universal suspicion is what we find in airports.

What about being included in a universal DNA database? In some ways this is much *less* likely to trigger suspicion than being a traveller at an airport: the threshold for being singled out for investigation is much higher than in an airport where everyone is put through a scanner individually and sometimes searched. Most profiles in a universal database would lie permanently inert and unexamined on the database. Only a small minority would get attention, and only when a profile derived from a crime scene was run through the system and got a match. Until that occurs, a universal DNA database with a capacity for matching makes *no one* a suspect.

Furthermore, and just as important, the matching procedure is able to establish conclusively, and without the intervention of interested parties, including police with strong hunches, that someone's DNA does *not* match crime scene DNA. In this way, it can counteract the unreasonable suspicions, or the reasonable but mistaken suspicions, of investigating officers. A burglary may look to a policeman to be the characteristic work of X, whom the policeman has arrested many times, but if the profile extracted from the DNA found at the scene fails to match X's profile, then the work of showing X is the culprit gets harder, not easier. In conjunction with the presumption of innocence, a failure to match is a strong basis for reasonable doubt in the absence of other compelling evidence.

I am claiming that universal searches of people's bags and clothing at airports are more likely to be heavy-handed and clouded by prejudice than inclusion in a DNA database capable of identifying matches. This is precisely because the threshold for becoming a suspect is a DNA match and *not* mere inclusion on a database. In the airport case, merely starting the process of moving to a boarding area is enough for being searched. But in the universal DNA collection case, according to me, there is no counterpart of this low threshold for attracting the individual interest of the authorities.

In American jurisprudence my claim would be challenged, because taking a DNA sample is itself construed as a search under judicial interpretation of the Fourth Amendment to the US Constitution. American jurisprudence calls for a search to be reasonable, and although taking DNA through a mouth swab might be reasonable in the context of a reasonable arrest (US Supreme Court 2013) – for the purpose of collecting uniquely identifying information about the arrestee – search under a policy of taking DNA from everyone – whether arrested or not – would *not* count as reasonable. DNA would be taken not for the legitimate purpose of investigating a particular crime, but for the allegedly questionable purpose of eliminating most people from enquiries into any crime for which DNA evidence existed.

Does a buccal swab for DNA amount to an unreasonable search when such swabs are taken from everyone? That depends on the acceptability of treating DNA sample-taking as a 'search' in any sense of that term. A 'search' in the primary sense is systematic examination of the contents of a place. Presumably, taking a DNA sample is, in some metaphorical sense, a 'search' of a person or a person's body or a person's genome. But is it literally a search of this kind? It is not.[6] Taking the DNA sample is not necessarily a step in sequencing a person's genome, and the profile used in matching does not code for genes connected to a person's physical characteristics. At most it is a search in someone's 'junk' DNA for standard tandem repeats.

Although distinctive for each person, making a profile from STR does not seem to involve intrusion in the sense of revealing something incriminating, secret, hidden, embarrassing, deeply felt, deeply considered or deeply valued. Again, submitting to a buccal swab for a DNA sample is not to undergo a search of one's body or person except on some false assumptions about the relation of a profile to a body or a person. So the usual moral connotations of 'unreasonable search' in the ordinary sense of 'search' are missing.

If all this is right, it is not clear that universal data-profiling does involve unreasonable searches on a large scale. It is also not obvious (at least to me) that there would be much wrong with permanent retention of DNA profiles, if that practice extended to everyone rather than arrested people and convicts only. It is true that it is difficult now to remove the associations with suspects and convicts of retained DNA profiles, so that extending profile collection and retention to everyone would probably be construed now by the public as treating a whole population as criminals. I do not deny that this is probable or that it counts against a universalisation of profile collection and retention starting now. What I do deny, for reasons already given, is that is universal profile collection and retention actually criminalises a population.

So there is nothing necessarily wrong, according to my account, with universal DNA profile collection. This is different from saying that things never do or would go wrong if everyone's profiles were collected. In developed liberal, criminal jurisdictions, profile-matching produces a few false positives, and it can give erroneous results when DNA samples are contaminated or minute. A high false positive rate can and ought to undermine the use of a forensic technique. The more common it is for erroneous results to be produced in a jurisdiction, the more formidable the problems with convicting on the basis of DNA evidence. It is also true that false inferences can be drawn from the actual presence of someone's DNA at a crime scene. Mere presence at a scene is a ground for further investigation of the person whose DNA it is, but not necessarily for charges or a conviction. In addition, I have already conceded that in jurisdictions which suffer from over-criminalisation and disproportionately severe penalties, convictions should not necessarily be made easier by resort to DNA collection for *every* crime. The moral necessity of reducing the crime rate varies with the degree to which criminalisation and sentencing are reasonable and liberal democratic protections for suspects are in force. These are risks, but unless there is a high probability of their being realised, they do not rule out universal DNA databases in jurisdictions with the usual due process protections.

Repurposing Data

DNA can be collected for one purpose and used for another. It can be collected from someone arrested on suspicion of a particular crime and yet be used in an investigation of that suspect's family when a crime scene sample throws up a partial match. Is repurposing a risk particularly associated with DNA databases? Elizabeth Joh (2014) has suggested as much. She thinks that this risk arises particularly in big data research, because, according to her, big data research departs from standard methods of collecting data for research purposes. She claims that, standardly, researchers form hypotheses and selectively collect data that would confirm or falsify them. With big data, it is the other way round. It starts with comprehensive collection, and then identifies patterns that it interrogates for commercial, forensic or other purposes. For example, a sudden increase in Google searches for cold and 'flu symptoms might give early warning of a 'flu epidemic. If search data were correlated with location data for those searching, it might be possible to map the spread of the epidemic.

As this example shows, not all repurposing of data is sinister or in the service of some narrow self-interest. So, why should repurposing in general be flagged up as a danger? Again, *is* it true that research outside big data research – standard research – takes account only of data collected by researchers for the confirmation and disconfirmation of hypotheses arrived at by those researchers? To take this last question first, the answer is a clear 'No'. Data sets are often comprehensive and made available as a national research resource to answer questions that did not originally generate the data sets. For example, the British Household Panel Survey (BHPS 2018) is a multi-purpose study stretching over nearly thirty years, and is both usable and used for spotting patterns in much the way that more quickly collected and analysed internet-derived data sets are.

There are many repurposings of data sets that seem to me to be unobjectionable, because a new purpose served is a legitimate purpose, including a criminal justice purpose. CCTV camera output is a case in point. It is collected from many different cameras, installed for different purposes. For example, in petrol stations, cameras collect number plate data and images of customers, in case drivers fill up and drive off without paying. But the same images can establish where and when a victim was last seen in a murder investigation. Relatedly, data collected from mobile telephone masts can establish locations of mobile telephones and their users in a murder investigation. Surely these repurposings are entirely in order? The seriousness of the crime and the urgency of identifying, arresting and prosecuting culprits trumps privacy interests related to telephone location data and images of people in public places.

The less serious the crime, the less might be the moral justification for using CCTV camera footage collected for one purpose and used for another purpose.[7] For example, burglary is a less serious crime than murder: it does less harm to its victims, other things being equal. But it is a very high-volume crime: there are many burglaries in many places doing considerable harm, though not usually fatal harm, to many victims. The volume of this kind of crime counts towards it being classified as relatively serious, and towards the repurposing of CCTV camera data or other data, for the solution of burglaries.

Although Joh approvingly quotes David Lazer and Viktor Mayer-Schonberger as saying that the DNA samples from which profiles are derived *invite* repurposing (Joh 2014: 53–4), in the UK at least they are mostly destroyed very soon after a profile is derived. Since repurposing requires the preservation of these samples, the 'invite' claim seems tendentious, at least in relation to Great Britain.

Conclusion

Big data in policing does not always constitute a risk to a policed population. The use of DNA databases seems to me to be both relatively non-intrusive and reliable in the identification of suspects for elimination from enquiries. Other big data applications are more questionable the more they have pretensions to predict and profile accurately. Overall, big data is not making whole populations suspect in democracies. Nor do certain kinds of big data reach right into the essence of an individual identity. The real risks are closer to the surface: high false positive rates for some methods of biometric identification, and questionable assumptions associated with certain algorithms that aspire to the prediction of crime.

Notes

1. See Doleac, Anker and Landerso (2017). The criteria used to judge a DNA database as 'effective' are themselves fairly crude. See Walsh, Curran and Buckleton (2010).
2. The next nine paragraphs are adapted from Sorell (2018a, b).
3. I disagree with the view that is attributed to Baroness Hale of Richmond in the judgement in *S and Marper v UK*: 'Baroness Hale of Richmond disagreed with the majority considering that the retention of both fingerprint and DNA data constituted an interference by the State in a person's right to respect for his private life and thus required justification under the Convention. In her opinion, this was an aspect of what had been called informational privacy and there could be little, if anything, more private to the individual than the knowledge of his genetic make-up' (Council of Europe 2008: 5).
4. As Douglas Husak has argued is the case in the US (Husak 2008).
5. In the UK Lord Justice Sedley was a proponent of a universal database in 2007, when certain racial groups were over-represented in the profiles. As he understood it, visitors as well as UK residents or nationals would have profiles on the database (Independent 2007).
6. For further criticisms of anachronistic understandings of informational technology in Fourth Amendment jurisprudence, see Kerr (2004) and Solove (2002).
7. For a criterion of serious crime, see Sorell (2016).

References

BHPS, *British Household Panel Survey* (Colchester: University of Essex), 2018, available at: https://www.iser.essex.ac.uk/bhps, last accessed 22 May 2018.

Council of Europe, Case of *S and Marper* v. *The United Kingdom*, 2008, available at: https://rm.coe.int/168067d216 p.5, last accessed 22 May 2018.

Doleac, J., A. S. T. Anker and R. Landerso, 'The Effects of DNA Databases on the Deterrence and Detection of Offenders', 2017, available at: http://jenniferdoleac.com/wp-content/uploads/2015/03/DNA_Denmark.pdf, last accessed 22 May 2018.

Guelke, J. and T. Sorell, 'Violations of Privacy and Law: the Case of Stalking', *Law, Ethics and Philosophy* 4 (2017): 32–60.

Husak, D., *Overcriminalization* (Oxford University Press, New York, 2008).

Independent, The, 'Top Judge: Put Everyone on DNA Database', *Independent*, 5 September 2007, available at: http://www.independent.co.uk/news/uk/crime/top-judge-put-everyone-on-dna-database-401447.html, last accessed 22 May 2018.

Joh, E., 'Policing by Numbers: Big Data and the Fourth Amendment', *Washington Law Review* 89 (2014): 35–68.

Kerr, O. S., 'The Fourth Amendment and New Technologies: Constitutional Myths and the Case for Caution', *Michigan Law Review* 102 (2004): 801–88.

Nagel, T., 'Concealment and Exposure', *Philosophy & Public Affairs* 27(1) (1998): 3–30.

Seringhaus, M. R., 'Forensic DNA Profiles: Database Expansion, Familial Search, and a Radical Solution', *Association for the Advancement of Artificial Intelligence*, 2009, 150–4, available at: https://www.aaai.org/ocs/index.php/SSS/SSS10/paper/viewFile/1187/1503, last accessed 22 May 2018.

Smith, M. E., 'Let's Make the DNA Database as Inclusive as Possible', *Journal of Law, Medicine and Ethics* 34 (2006): 385–89.

Solove, D., 'Digital Dossiers and the Dissipation of Fourth Amendment Privacy', *California Law Review* 75 (2002): 1083–167.

Sorell, T., 'Preventive Policing, Surveillance and European Counter-terrorism', *Criminal Justice Ethics* 30 (2011): 1–22.

Sorell, T., 'The Scope of Serious Crime and Preventive Justice', *Criminal Justice Ethics* 35 (2016): 163–82.

Sorell, T., 'Organized Crime and Preventive Justice', *Ethical Theory and Moral Practice* 1 (2018a): 137–53.

Sorell, T., 'Bulk Collection, Intrusion and Domination', in A. I. Cohen (ed.), *Essays in Philosophy and Policy* (Lanham, MD: Rowman & Littlefield, 2018b).

UK Government, 'Protections of Freedoms Act', 2012, available at: http://www.legislation.gov.uk/ukpga/2012/9/contents/enacted, last accessed 22 May 2018.

UK Government, 'National DNA Database: Annual Report 2015–2016', 2016, available at: https://assets.publishing.service.gov.uk/government/uploads/system/uploads/attachment_data/file/594185/58714_Un-Num_Nat_DNA_DB_Accessible.pdf, last accessed 22 May 2018.

US Supreme Court, *Maryland* v. *King*, 2013, available at: https://www.supremecourt.gov/opinions/12pdf/12-207_d18e.pdf, last accessed 22 May 2018.

Walsh, S., J. Curran and J. Buckleton, 'Modelling Forensic DNA Database Performance', *Forensic Sciences* 55 (2010): 1174–83.

Part Two

FIVE

Dark Advertising and the Democratic Process

Joe Saunders

Political advertising is changing. Dominic Cummings, Campaign Director for Vote Leave sums this up well in an article on how Brexit was 'won':

> We were urged by everyone to hire a big advertising agency and do tradi-
> tional posters. 'When can we discuss our posters?' I was asked constantly by
> people who would then try to explain to me their creative ideas ('we need
> another Labour Isn't Working, Dominic, I've got an idea for a picture of the
> globe and arrows . . .') . . . Instead of spending a fortune on an expensive
> agency (with 15% going to them out of 'controlled expenditure') and putting
> up posters to be 'part of the national conversation' weeks or months before
> the vote, we decided to . . . put almost all our money into digital (~98%) . . .
> (Cummings 2017)

Facebook also advertised its own 'success story' with the election of the Conservative Party in the UK in 2015. The advert claims:[1]

> In a tightly contested election, the UK political party combined powerful
> creative [advertising] with Facebook's targeting tools to achieve what the
> pollsters and media had universally predicted to be impossible: a win by
> outright majority.
> - 80.6% reach in key constituencies on Facebook
> - 3.5 million video views
> - 86.9% of all ads served had social context

This advertisement also contains the following quote from Craig Elder, Digital Director of the Conservative Party:

> The level of targeting we had available to us on Facebook – coupled with the research and data we produced internally – meant that we can say for the first time in a UK election that digital made a demonstrable difference to the final election result.

Political advertising is changing. In this chapter, I consider some of the implications of this for the democratic process.[2]

We are now aware that Cambridge Analytica, for instance, harvested data from Facebook and used it to create targeted online political advertisements in both the Brexit vote and the 2016 US Presidential Election.[3] This raises numerous ethical concerns, including issues of consent, privacy and respect for citizens' data and information. These are seriously important issues, but I will not explicitly address them here. In this chapter, I focus on online political advertisements.

I start my inquiry with the hunch that online political advertisements can undermine important parts of the democratic process. In what follows, I explore that hunch, looking to unpack what – if anything – is wrong with online political advertising.

I begin with recent reports of online political advertising. From this, two related concerns emerge. The first is that online political advertisements sometimes occur in the dark, and the second is that they can involve sending different messages to different groups. I consider these issues in turn. This involves an extended discussion of the importance of publicity and discussion in a democracy, and a comparison between dog whistles and dark advertisements. Through this, I look to outline some of the ways in which online political advertisements can undermine the democratic process.

What, if Anything, is Wrong with Online Political Advertising?

The ways in which advertising can be ethically problematic are relatively well understood. Advertising can involve deception, manipulation and puffery; it can also have negative consequences, such as contributing to the over-sexualisation of women. But advertising is not all bad. There are ethical problems with advertising, but it can play a useful role. For instance, it can help to raise awareness of matters in the public interest. At its most basic, advertising is a persuasive form of communication, and one that can inform and persuade people for the better.[4]

The same goes for both online and political advertising. Both can serve useful roles – raising awareness and informing and persuading people well. As with advertising in general, these forms can also be ethically problematic. Indeed, the ethical worries are presumably greater in political – rather than commercial – advertising, as the stakes are higher when we are electing a political party to govern us, rather than when we are buying a new phone charger online.

In this chapter, I want to consider whether online political advertising poses a new threat to the democratic process, over and above the traditional worries one might have with advertising, online advertising or political advertising in general. And for this, it helps to turn to recent reports about online political advertising.

Julia Carrie Wong, in an article titled '"It Might Work too Well": the Dark Art of Political Advertising Online', writes:

> Any candidate using Facebook can put a campaign message promising one thing in front of one group of voters while simultaneously running an ad with a completely opposite message in front of a different group of voters. The ads themselves are not posted anywhere for the general public to see (this is what's known as 'dark advertising') . . . That undermines the very idea of a 'marketplace of ideas', says Ann Ravel. [Ravel said that:] . . . 'The way to have a robust democracy is for people to hear all these ideas and make decisions and discuss . . . With micro-targeting, that is not happening.' (Wong 2018)

So, what, if anything, is wrong with online political advertising? Wong points towards two things:

1. online political advertising can occur in the dark; and
2. this creates the possibility of sending different messages to different groups.

In what follows, I unpack each of these worries in turn. In doing so, I look to articulate what exactly is worrying with online political advertising.

Dark Advertising

Dark advertising, as the name suggests, involves advertising in the dark, without sufficient light or illumination. These are advertisements that are not publicly aired, but sent to people privately, for them to view on their own. In this section, I consider the threat that dark political advertising might pose to the democratic process. To get this into focus, I begin by sharing three pieces of evidence from: (1) Dominic Cummings; (2) Ann Ravel; and (3) the LSE Media Policy Brief.

Let us start by returning to Dominic Cummings' own account of how he helped 'win' Brexit. Cummings did not put up posters 'to be part of the national conversation weeks or months before the vote', instead he put 'almost all our money into digital (~98%)'. Regarding this strategy, he remarks that:

> The world of advertising agencies and PR companies were sure we had screwed up because they did not see what we were doing . . . It is actually hard even for very competent and determined people to track digital communication accurately, and it is important that the political media is not set up to do this. There was not a single report anywhere (and very little curiosity) on how the official Leave campaign spent 98% of its marketing budget. There was a lot of coverage of a few tactical posters. (Cummings 2017)

He also notes that 'it is actually hard even for very competent and determined people to track digital communication accurately, and it is important that the political media is not set up to do this'.

Earlier, in the article by Julia Wong, Ann Ravel claimed that such a strategy undermines the marketplace of ideas:

> The way to have a robust democracy is for people to hear all these ideas and make decisions and discuss . . . With micro-targeting, that is not happening. (Ravel, in Wong 2018)

Echoing John Stuart Mill, Ravel claims that democracy requires a marketplace of ideas, people hearing political policies and proposals and discussing them together. I will return to unpack this shortly, but first I want to share one final piece of evidence.

The LSE Media Policy Project has released a report titled, 'The New Political Campaigning'. They make two points, the first being that targeted content can make elections less fair as potential voters are only exposed to limited information:

> Message targeting encourages contact and engagement only with those who are deemed worthy of political campaigning, for example those in marginal seats or judged to be undecided voters . . . Groups less likely to vote risk being further disenfranchised if they do not see campaign messages, and there is also a risk of a compounding effect . . . If democratic societies flourish through the free flow of information which in turn allows citizens to consider issues on balance, then any move to restrict information flow might exacerbate polarization. (Tambini et al. 2017: 19)

The second finding from the report is that targeted messaging can increase the focus on divisive issues:

The ability to micro-target political messages increases the likelihood that parties and candidates campaign on wedge issues, which are highly divisive in a public forum but also have the ability to mobilize voters such as matters on immigration and welfare. Research from the U.S. has shown that candidates are more likely to campaign on these wedge issues when the forum is not public . . . Because these messages are being played out largely in secret they cannot be challenged or fact checked. (Goodman et al. 2017: 19)

Pulling together these three sources of evidence, I can begin to answer my initial question of what, if anything, is wrong with dark advertising? The evidence considered here suggests five things. Dark advertisements:

(1) are not part of the national conversation;
(2) are difficult for the political media to track;
(3) undermine the marketplace of ideas;
(4) cannot be challenged or fact-checked;
(5) cause long-term issues, such as disenfranchisement and polarisation.

These all seem like important ways in which dark advertisements can undermine the democratic process. It is worth thinking whether a single general issue can be abstracted here, or whether that urge might be counter-productive; it might be that there are five distinct issues here, and any attempt to bring them together could distort this. Philosophers often tend towards abstraction, but we should not always scratch that itch.

So what can philosophy add? First, it is worth briefly saying something about point (5), the long-term issues involved with dark advertising. Here I want to note the second half of the phrase 'democratic process'; democracy is not an event, but a process. It occurs over time. In thinking about a healthy democracy, we should not exclusively focus on a single election (or referendum), but also longer-term trends. There is a difference between a group of people not voting in a particular election, and a group of people being disenfranchised over time.

Moving on, is there anything more general we can abstract from the above five claims? I think one general theme does seem to emerge. All five issues recall Ann Ravel's claim that, '[t]he way to have a robust democracy is for people to hear all these ideas and make decisions and discuss'. This seems right. The trouble with dark advertising is relatively simple: it happens in the dark, and thus involves less public discussion of political advertisements, policies and campaigns.

Here, I want to offer two general claims:

(1) the healthier the discussion of political policies, advertisements and campaigns, the healthier the democracy;
(2) the more dark advertisements there are, the less healthy the discussion, and so the less healthy the democracy.

The first of these puts forward a basic claim about democracy and discussion, and the second makes explicit how dark advertisements pose a threat to this.

Before we move on, I think it is helpful to say more about the exact formulation of these claims. In an initial attempt to formulate the first claim, I hypothesised that:

1.* The more discussion of political policies, advertisements and campaigns, the healthier the democracy.

While this seems vaguely correct, I have been persuaded that the phrase 'more discussion' does not quite capture the issue at hand.[5] For one, there are some general concerns about how helpful public discussions are. In a recent article, Raymond Guess criticises Habermas on this score:

Discussions, even discussions that take place under reasonably favorable conditions, are not necessarily enlightening, clarifying or conducive to fostering consensus. In fact, they just as often foster polemics, and generate further bitterness, rancor and division. (Guess 2019)

On a related note, it does not seem that it is just the sheer quantity of discussion that makes a democracy healthy. And this seems relevant to dark advertisements. Dark advertisements, for instance, could foster more discussion of a certain kind: micro-targeted citizens might comment on the same dark advertisement, confirming each other's prejudices on some topic, in an echo-chamber like fashion. (This could also be driven – or encouraged – by covert affiliates of the political party in question.) Here we have a relatively clear case of more discussion, but not a healthier democracy. For this reason, instead of claiming that the more discussion, the healthier the democracy, I now claim that the healthier the discussion, the healthier the democracy.

This raises a further question about what makes discussion healthy. When it comes to dark advertisements, we already have a relatively clear idea of what leads to unhealthy discussion, namely, that dark advertisements:

    (1)   are not part of the national conversation;
    (2)   are difficult for the political media to track;
    (3)   undermine the marketplace of ideas;
    (4)   cannot be challenged or fact-checked.

The flip-side of this suggests that healthy discussion would involve political advertisements being part of the national conversation, easy for the political media to track, part of the marketplace of ideas, and open to challenge and fact-checking.

The second issue of formulation that arose concerns the strength of these claims. In formulating the first claim, I was tempted to try for something stronger.[6] For instance, it is tempting to propose a very tight link between democracy and public discussion, and claim something like the following:

> 1.** Democracy requires public discussion of political policies, advertisements and campaigns.

One could even go further and make the connection explicitly stronger:

> 1.*** Public discussion of political policies, advertisements and campaigns, is essential for democracy.

While these claims might have more rhetorical force, I have to come to think that they are not quite true.[7]

To illustrate this, imagine a more digital, but also more equal world: Democracy 2.0. In this world are several political parties. They all have equal funding, and are proposing different, but informed, thoughtful and ethical policies. They also refrain from manipulation and deceit. So far, so good! The fanciful wrinkle is that in this world, all political campaigning is done online, and there is no public discussion of political policies (either online or off). Citizens go online, and privately receive information from each of the political parties there. Through this, the citizens are well-informed and vote in line with their information, interests and values.

What is the point of this thought-experiment? The basic idea is that we can imagine a democracy without public discussion of political policies (either online or off).[8] To get this basic idea to stick, though, I need to respond to some likely objections and offer some tweaks to the initial thought-experiment.

First of all, one might think that the above scenario is too passive.[9] Proper engagement with politics, so the thought goes, requires interaction; one cannot passively take in political information. But we can tweak the example to account for at least part of this. Teaching someone ethics typically involves interaction, but you can also teach ethics online. You can do so without public – or even group – discussions. Returning to Democracy 2.0, the political parties in question could put their platforms online, but then correspond with individual citizens one-on-one, in private. (We can further stipulate that this all occurs in good faith, and that it is monitored by suitable regulatory bodies.) Here we have what looks like an informed citizenship, actively engaging with proposed policies, without public discussion.

A second worry with the above thought-experiment concerns empathy.[10] Perhaps a crucial part of democracy is the ability to empathise with other individuals and groups, and to understand their perspectives and thoughts, and this requires public discussion. However, I suspect we can tweak the thought-experiment to accommodate this. Imagine that a significant part of the information that you are given online does convey the perspectives and thoughts of others.

Now, of course, none of this might be perfect. Perhaps public discussion fosters interaction and empathy in a richer way than can ever be done online. That might be true, but the point of the experiment is that we could have an informed, engaged and empathetic citizenship without public discussion. Perhaps we could do better on all these accounts with public discussion, but the point in question was whether public discussion of political policies is essential for democracy, and I suspect that the thought-experiment shows that it is not, strictly speaking, necessary.

A third worry is that Democracy 2.0 is too individualistic or atomistic. The thought is that a flourishing democracy involves shared understanding, which realises the idea of the collective autonomy of citizens.[11] Another related thought is that democracy requires horizontal engagement between citizens, rather than just vertical engagement between citizens and political parties.[12] This all seems to point towards a plausible ideal, which again might show that Democracy 2.0 is not an ideal democracy. This seems fair, but just because Democracy 2.0 is not an ideal democracy does not mean that it is not a democracy at all. In Democracy 2.0, we have an informed, engaged and empathetic citizenship voting in line with their information, interests and values, and this suggests that we can have democracy without public discussion.[13]

That being said, it is important to note that just because public discussion is not essential to democracy does not mean that is not extremely important to democracy; it also does not mean that public discussion is not extremely important to democracy now.

We do not live in Democracy 2.0. In our world, political parties do not have equal funding, they do not all pose informed, thoughtful and ethical policies, and they do not all refrain from manipulation and deceit. And we fall short too: citizens are not always engaged, informed or empathetic. In this world, our world, public discussion of political policies, advertisements and campaigns help to safeguard against these shortcomings.

In his work on democracy and public deliberation, Cristiano (2008: 190) notes that public deliberation embodies a number of fundamental values. These include:

> the process of public deliberation is a public realization of equality to the extent that the process is reasonably egalitarian. Citizens' abilities to receive hearings for their views are not undermined by a skewed distribution of wealth or power. (Cristiano 2008: 190)

We live in a world marked by gross inequalities of wealth and power; and public discussion (and deliberation) can help safeguard against this.

How exactly can it do this? Of course, this is a big question. However, there is something that we can say here. Earlier, I claimed that healthy discussion would involve political advertisements being part of the national conversation, easy for the political media to track, part of the marketplace of ideas, and open to challenge and fact-checking. The above discussion also suggested that an ideal democracy would involve an active citizenship, engaging with policies together, and these virtues can also help improve the democratic process in a non-ideal world.

Martin Moore writes that:

> Campaigning in secrecy is enormously destructive of the basic principle of democracy. If you are not engaging people openly, you cannot be challenged, and you cannot be held to account. It's not possible to hold politicians to their promises. The more this is done, the more democracy loses its legitimacy. It's already looking pretty unhealthy. Large numbers of people are questioning whether it's sustainable, and this just takes us further down that road. Democracy cannot function in darkness. (Moore in Cadwalladr (2017))

What then is the relationship between democracy and darkness?

Publicity might not be strictly necessary for democracy, but it is important. And here I want to return to endorse my previous two claims:

(1) the healthier the discussion of political policies, advertisements and campaigns, the healthier the democracy;

(2) the more dark advertisements there are, the less healthy the discussion is, and so the less healthy the democracy.

To summarise, dark advertisements pose a threat to democracy because they circumvent public discussion of political policies, advertisements and campaigns. One reason why this can be especially problematic is that dark advertisements can allow for the same political party to send different messages to different groups and individuals. This brings us to the next section and dog-whistle politics.

Different Messages to Different Groups

Actual dog whistles sound at a high frequency that can be heard by dogs, but not humans. Dog-whistle politics attempt something similar. At their most basic, they are an act of communication that contains two distinct messages: one that typically comes from taking the communication at face value, and another that does not. This can be used to say different things to two different groups of voters through one act of communication. An example is the use of 'inner city' in political discourse in the United States. As Saul notes:

> In the United States, 'inner city' has come to function as a dog-whistle for black. Thus, politicians who would be rebuked if they called for harsher measures against black criminals can safely call for cracking down on inner city crime. (Saul 2018: 367)

There is a lot of interesting work on dog whistles, and the subtle differences between different ways in which they operate, but here I consider the simple fact that they provide a way of politically campaigning through sending different messages to different groups.[14] In this, I find a helpful analogue to dark advertising.

> In a way, dog-whistle politics merely resurrects a practice common in the days of 'whistle-stop campaigns' and segmented news markets, when candidates could say different things to different audiences in complete confidence that no one would ever notice the discrepancies. Clever marketing techniques do for today's politicians what moving trains and localised newspapers did for those of a previous generation. (Goodin and Saward 2005: 471)

This suggests a curious history to political campaigning, with the following three stages:

(1) whistle-stop campaigns, segmented news markets, moving trains and localised newspapers;

    (2) national TV, national newspapers, posters and clever marketing techniques;

    (3) online dark advertisements.

In the first period, political campaigners could offer different messages to different groups, relatively in the dark. In the second period, political campaigners used clever marketing techniques (dog whistles) to offer different messages to different groups, also often in the dark. And now, online advertising allows political campaigners to offer different messages to different groups, again in the dark.

Seen in this light, online political advertisements do not pose a radically new threat to the democratic process. Offering different messages to different groups and advertising in the dark is not a new practice. Nevertheless, something new might be happening now, even if it is just a matter of degree (rather than a new kind of problem). The scale seems worse now, given the availability of information and scale of impact. As Wong notes:

> What did that money buy? . . . In the first instance, everything that any Facebook advertiser can get:[15] access to one of the most powerful databases of personal information that has ever existed, with insights into individuals' intimate relationships, political beliefs, consumer habits and internet browsing. (Wong 2018)

This level of information seems to amplify the ways in which advertising can go wrong. At the beginning of the chapter, I noted that, amongst other ethical problems, advertising can involve deception and manipulation. Unfortunately, this will be made easier the more information is available about voters, and the easier it is to micro-target voters.

The good news is that the analogue with dog whistles provides us with an excellent resource, in that we can draw upon recent work on dog whistles to help to illuminate what is wrong with sending mixed messages to different groups.

In what follows, I do just this, beginning with Goodin and Saward and moving on to Saul.

Goodin and Saward (2005: 472) distinguish between the mandate to rule and a policy mandate:

> The mandate to rule is 'the right to govern, to occupy offices of the state and [so on]'
>
>   The policy mandate is 'a right to implement a specific set of policies explicitly stipulated during the election and explicitly endorsed by the electorate at that election'.

Goodin and Saward (2005: 473) argue that dog-whistle politics do not undermine the right to rule, but that, 'insofar as the winner's victory was tainted by dog-whistle politics, the second sort of mandate proves more elusive'.

They offer the following example:

> A conservative party dog-whistles an encouraging message to racists that its own traditional supporters would instantly repudiate. It wins the ensuing election. Half its voters voted for it purely because of its (coded) support for racist policies, half voted for it purely because of its traditionally decent policies on race. Clearly, the party won a majority; clearly, it has a mandate to rule. But under those circumstances, it equally clearly could not claim a policy mandate to pursue either of the two contradictory policies that won it its votes (Goodin and Saward 2005: 475)

They note that:

> In order to secure a mandate to implement any policy in particular, candidates must first tell people what specific policy or policies they propose to implement if elected. Only then can they claim to have some special mandate to implement that policy in particular (as opposed to 'rule' more generally) . . .
> Politicians engaging in dog-whistle politics are doing almost the opposite of that. They are not telling everyone what specific policies they propose to implement if elected. Instead, they tell one group of voters one thing, while allowing (and indeed, encouraging) another group to believe another. If they win the election on the basis of such mixed messages, what does their victory add up to in substantive policy terms? Nothing, we suggest. (Goodin and Saward 2005: 473)

This seems right to me. And the same concerns apply, *mutatis mutandis*, to online political advertisements. If a political party uses dark advertisements to propose different (incompatible) policies to different groups, that thereby undermines their policy mandate.

Saul (2018: 379) claims that Goodin and Saward 'do not go quite far enough' here. She argues that:

> If they are right about the policy mandate, then the mandate to rule may also often be undermined. This will happen, for example, in the case of single-issue voters, of which there are likely to be many. If a voting decision is based

on abortion policy, and different messages are sent about this to different groups of voters, then surely the mandate to rule is also – in any meaningful sense – undermined. (Saul 2018: 379)

Neither Goodin and Saward nor Saul are claiming that every case of sending different messages to different groups undermines democratic mandates. What they show is how sending different messages to different groups can undermine democratic mandates. They focus on how this can – and does – occur through dog whistles, but given that dark advertisements allow for the same phenomenon, we should also be wary of the threat that they can pose to the democratic process.

Online political advertising does not pose any radically new threat here, but it is still a new tool. And as with any tool or source of information, part of its ethical status will depend on who has access to it, the power to use it, how they use it, and what ends they use it for.

This seems especially important for the issue at hand, for two reasons. First, we are talking about democracy, which does not just concern the ends or outcomes of elections, but also the democratic process itself. And sending different messages to different groups can undermine this, both in terms of the mandate to rule and specific policy mandates.

Secondly, this new tool is very powerful. As Wong notes, we are now dealing with a situation where Facebook advertisers have access to:

. . . one of the most powerful databases of personal information that has ever existed, with insights into individuals' intimate relationships, political beliefs, consumer habits and internet browsing. (Wong 2018)

This is more information than we have ever had access to before, and it is up for sale. If we want to seriously safeguard against inequalities in wealth translating into inequalities in political power, we should tread carefully here.

We are seeing some progress on this front. After the recent public outcry about Cambridge Analytica, Facebook has promised to make political advertisements more transparent in the future.[16] This is an important development, and it could help to curb the threat of dark advertisements.

However, we still need to remain on guard. One serious underlying threat to the democratic process originates from vast inequalities in wealth, and the ways in which this can translate into vast inequalities in political power. We have seen this in the past (think of Rupert Murdoch, for instance, who has had more political power than you, me, and probably everyone we know). We see it now, in how vast sums of money have been able to influence elections through dark advertisements, and I suspect we will see it again in the future. What are we to do in response? That question is too big to answer in this chapter. But one thing we can say here is that public discussion of political policies, advertisements and campaigns can help safeguard against this.

Conclusion

I began this chapter with a hunch that online political advertising could undermine important parts of the democratic process. Through looking at the available evidence, and the literature on dog whistles, I am now able propose two things that are wrong with online political advertising. First, public discussion is an important part of a healthy democracy; and dark advertisements circumvent this. Secondly, mixed messages can undermine democratic mandates; and dark advertisements make this easier.

Notes

1. This advertisement can still be found online, available at: https://www.face-book.com/business/success/conservative-party#u_0_p, last accessed 24 September 2019.
2. I would like to thank the audience at the IDEA Centre for a very helpful discussion of this topic, and Cezara Nicoara, Natasha McKeever, Kevin Macnish and Martin Sticker for reading drafts of the chapter.
3. For an overview of these issues, see Greenfield (2018).
4. For a helpful overview of the ethics of advertising, see Dow (2013).
5. I am grateful to Cezara Nicoara for helping me with this point, and talking me through how more discussion online can be unhelpful.
6. I suspect that it is not just an idiosyncratic intuition that drove this. Indeed, as we will see over the course of this chapter, other people have characterised the relationship between democracy and discussion in strong terms. Martin Moore, for instance, writes that 'Campaigning in secrecy is enormously destructive of the basic principle of democracy . . . Democracy cannot function in darkness' (Moore in Cadwalladr (2017)).
7. I want to thank Thomas Hancocks for pushing me on this point.
8. Machin (2012: 107) briefly considers two other ways in which democracy and publicity are importantly connected, namely, that (1) 'citizens are entitled to some account of why their legislature passed law f rather than law g', and (2) 'the requirements of publicity are better satisfied where citizens elect and remove their legislators than when citizens do not have this power'.

9. I am grateful to Nathan Wood and Sean Sinclair for prompting me to think about this.
10. Thanks to Natasha McKeever for suggesting this.
11. Thanks to Megan Kime and Andrew Stanners for this suggestion.
12. Thanks to Lea Salje for this suggestion.
13. Of course, there are other additional issues with Democracy 2.0 that I have not discussed here. One set of issues concerns how these political parties and their policies are formed *in the first place*. This, it might be thought requires public discussion. As with the other worries about Democracy 2.0, that seems vaguely right, but still does not entirely count against the thought that Democracy 2.0 is some form of democracy.
14. For a full account of how dog whistles function, see Saul (2018).
15. It should be noted that it is Facebook that has these insights, not the advertisers themselves. Thanks to Kevin Macnish for spotting this.
16. See Hern (2018).

References

Cadwalladr, C., 'Revealed: Tory "Dark" Ads Targeted Voters' Facebook Feeds in Welsh Marginal Seat', *The Guardian*, 27 May 2017, available at: https://www.theguardian.com/politics/2017/may/27/conservatives-facebook-dark-ads-data-protection-election, last accessed 24 September 2019.

Christiano, T., *The Constitution of Equality* (Oxford: Oxford University Press. 2008).

Cummings, D., 'Dominic Cummings: How the Brexit Referendum was Won', *The Spectator*, 9 January 2017, available at: https://blogs.spectator.co.uk/2017/01/dominic-cummings-brexit-referendum-won, last accessed 24 September 2019.

Dow, J., 'Ethics of Advertising', in Hugh LaFollette (ed.), *International Encyclopedia of Ethics* (Oxford: Wiley-Blackwell, 2013).

Goodin, R. and M. Saward, 'Dog Whistles and Democratic Mandates', *Political Quarterly* (2005): 471–6.

Greenfield, P., 'The Cambridge Analytica Files: the Story So Far' *The Guardian*, 26 March 2018, available at: https://www.theguardian.com/news/2018/mar/26/the-cambridge-analytica-files-the-story-so-far, last accessed 24 September 2019.

Guess, R., 'A Republic of Discussion', *The Point*, 2019, available at: https://the-pointmag.com/2019/politics/republic-of-discussion-habermas-at-ninety, last accessed 24 September 2019.

Hern, A., 'New Facebook Controls Aim to Regulate Political Ads and Fight Fake News', *The Guardian*, 6 April 2018, available at: https://www.theguardian.com/technology/2018/apr/06/facebook-launches-controls-regulate-ads-publishers, last accessed 24 September 2019.

Machin, D. J., 'Political Legitimacy, the Egalitarian Challenge, and Democracy', *Journal of Applied Philosophy* 29 (2012): 101–17.

Saul, J., 'Dogwhistles, Political Manipulation, and Philosophy of Language', in D. Fogal, D. W. Harris and M. Moss (eds), *New Work on Speech Act* (Oxford: Oxford University Press, 2018), pp. 360–83.

Tambini, D., S. Labo, E. Goodman and M. Moore, M., 'The New Political Campaigning', LSE Media Policy Project Policy Brief, (19), 2017.

Wong, J. C., '"It Might Work too Well": the Dark Art of Political Advertising Online', *The Guardian*, 19 March 2018, available at: https://www.theguardian.com/technology/2018/mar/19/facebook-political-ads-social-media-history-online-democracy, last accessed 24 September 2019.

SIX

Twitter and Electoral Bias

Wulf Loh, Anne Suphan and Christopher Zirnig

Introduction

The recent general elections in Germany were anticipated with some anxiety. Fake accounts and social bots, filter bubbles and echo chambers, foreign propaganda machineries and campaign micro-targeting called the neutrality, inclusiveness and permeability of the digital public spheres into question. In this chapter, we argue that these qualities of public spheres are important to enable and support three functional dimensions of democracies: the aggregation, control and social integration dimension. Without neutral, inclusive and open public spheres, the aggregation of individual interests or beliefs about the common good are likely to be distorted, the control of political institutions loses effectiveness, and the solidaristic commitments of the citizens may deteriorate.

While most of the worries in the run-up to the elections were exaggerated, fragmentations between online and offline public spheres remain. In distinguishing between first-, second- and third-order digital divides, we are able to analyse these fragmentations and show their prevalence in the general election. We interpret electoral biases in social media as manifestations of inequalities on information access and online political participation.

By comparing Twitter information streams and trends with media coverage in traditional media (especially the online presence of nationwide newspapers and TV/radio), we demonstrate three perspectives of electoral bias influenced by Twitter: the relevance of (1) Twitter as an arena for political debates; (2) manipulation by automated social media accounts on Twitter; and (3) differences on the topic agenda between Twitter and traditional media.

We conclude that, first, one-to-many communication forms are still the main arenas for agenda-setting, information allocation, editing and gate-keeping; secondly, that automated accounts are not yet a dominant issue in German election campaigns; and finally, the data suggest that social media debates are not representative of public opinion.

Participation in Democracy

Democratic theories do not typically value democratic institutions for their own sake, but assign them an instrumental function for achieving other values, such as human rights (Christiano 2011), individual self-determination and autonomy (Christiano 2011), fundamental equal status (Rawls 2001: 18–21), or even an epistemic value for political decision-making (Habermas 1989). In order to fulfil these functions, democracies have to be able to (a) aggregate individual interests and/or individual political beliefs, (b) provide for effective control of political power, and (c) accomplish at least a basic form of social integration.

Democracies do not only need to elect government officials from amid their own constituencies, but also come to terms with which policies these officials should pursue. This is what the aggregation dimension captures. Depending on the normative democratic theory, what it is that is to be aggregated may differ. We distinguish between liberal, republican and deliberative notions of democracy (Habermas 1989).[1] While liberal democratic theories focus on the aggregation of individual interests, which are to be balanced against each other according to majority rule and minority provisions (Rawls 1993), republican ideals of democracy assume that what should be aggregated are individual beliefs about the common good (Pettit 1999). Deliberative democratic theories do not postulate an aggregation, but focus on exchanging arguments in public debates with regard to topics, policies and ends.

Democracies must also hold elected officials accountable, the aforementioned control dimension. The media is commonly called upon to spark, foster and guide public debate. Civil society is also charged with the responsibility of controlling political power (Cohen and Arato 1994). This may occur in the form of associations, movements and demonstrations up to and including civil disobedience, or in the form of artistic endeavours, such as political performance. The more active and vibrant a civil society, the more it serves as a counterweight to political power.

Finally, democracies must ensure a minimum civic solidarity. Only if democratic institutions are seen by most of their constituents as an 'expression of common goals, shared projects or a common fate' (Jaeggi 2001:

291), will these institutions be stable 'for the right reasons' (Rawls 1993: lecture IV). This is crucial in order to provide the goods and services determined desirable by the aggregation dimension. Adherence to law, active involvement and participation, and the willingness to make compromises are preconditions for effectively functioning democracies (Habermas 1997: ch. 2). This third dimension of social integration is usually achieved by civic education.

Hence, there are at least three reasons as to why active participation is necessary for any democratic order. First, participation is crucial for obtaining the most complete picture possible with respect to the aggregation of interests and/or convictions about the common good. Even if the sole purpose of democratic government were to aggregate the individual interests of its subjects, the more citizens engage, the more accurate will be the results.

Secondly, with respect to the control dimension, democracies also rely on the active participation of their citizens. As democratic control is exercised through media, public contestation and civil society institutions, citizens should become involved in these structures. Participation cannot just be an ad hoc reaction to grave injustices. It involves ongoing efforts, which yield some opportunity costs and can even be a high-risk endeavour.

Thirdly, active participation is important to shape civic solidarity among citizens. This pertains to the social integration dimension. Even though solidarity within a society may have sources other than 'democratic-legitimatory' ones (Loh and Skupien 2016), democratic institutions are capable of generating civic solidarity (Habermas 1989). To do so, democracies must teach civic virtues as well as the value of democracy.

Participation therefore plays a crucial role in realising the three dimensions of democracy. To give citizen participation a space distinct from (and sometimes in opposition to) the state, democracies must ensure public spheres are platforms for discussion. Historically these arenas were confined to the relatively closed space of literary salons and coffee houses, but with the advent of the free press they widened to include newspapers, radio and television. However, there was never one single public sphere in which the whole constituency would be present. Rather, 'the' public sphere has always been fragmented. The Internet gave hope for unifying these fragmentations through an inclusive and egalitarian digital public sphere (Gil de Zuniga 2015). However, half of the globe still lacks Internet access (ITU 2015), and even within the OECD, certain demographic groups are predominantly excluded from participating online in some states. Furthermore, social media can be manipulated through fake accounts and social bots; newsfeed algorithms encourage 'echo chambers' (Bozdag 2013); fake news sites and foreign propaganda spread disinformation and cause confusion (Papenfuss

2017); and the Cambridge Analytica scandal underscores the importance of campaign micro-targeting (Cadwalladr and Graham-Harrison 2018).

Instead of reducing fragmentation, the Internet and especially social media platforms merely replaced old fragmentations of public spheres with new ones. In the next section, we look at these fragmentations that have been subsumed under the term 'digital divide', in order to single out specific biases attributed to Twitter.

The Twenty-first-Century Divide

The 'digital divide' initially distinguished between users and non-users of ICT (Attewell 2001). However, within this divide can be seen two layers identified by Dewan and Riggins (2005): the first layer refers to the digital divide based on material access, which requires hardware and connection to the Internet. The second layer refers to the cognitive skills required to use the technology (hardware, software and connection), such as operational Internet skills, formal Internet skills, information Internet skills and strategic Internet skills. Both material and cognitive access are crucial factors for inclusion on the Internet. Thus, we refer to these two layers as the first-order digital divide.

The first-order digital divide is becoming less relevant in Western countries (Hargittai 2010). For those who have grown up with the Internet, ICT usage is hardly a question of material access or skills. Recent studies focus on differences in usage behaviour as forms of a second-order digital divide by adding various further layers: Hargittai and Walejko (2008) describe a gap of willingness between users who want to use the Internet and non-users who do not want to use it. Van Dijk and Hacker (2003) see a further level of the digital divide between those who do and those who do not participate in the use of the Internet. In general, the second-order digital divide is based on the assumption that there are multiple and multifaceted patterns of usage behaviour (Livingstone and Helsper 2007).

Recent literature has introduced further dimensions as a *third-order digital divide*. Ragnedda (2017) refers to the offline life changes that can be derived from using the Internet. Klinkisch and Suphan (2017) argue that the digital divide is related to experiences of (mis-)recognition which are crucial to identity formation and social participation. Using the Internet increases economic, cultural and social benefits. By the same token, being excluded from the Internet means being excluded from society in several ways. However, to analyse political participation we focus on a framework based on the differentiation between first-order access and second-order usage digital divide only.

While online participation can have important social consequences, studies also show that inequalities in using the Internet are traced back to users' socio-economics, cultural, political and personal capital. Many studies document the impact of socio-demographic variables on both dimensions of the digital divide: individuals' access to the Internet and usage behaviour (for example, van Deursen and van Dijk 2011; Zillien and Hargittai 2009). Therefore, the digital divide should be seen as a social rather than a technological issue (Ragnedda 2017).

The twenty-first-century digital divide is also helpful in analysing social media usage. Based on the first-order digital divide we can ask who is included in specific social media applications. While 81 per cent of Germans use the Internet (Initiative D21 2018), only half (51 per cent) use any type of social media (Eurostat 2017). To describe the socio-demographic variables of social media users, we differentiate between applications. For example, on Snapchat and Instagram women are slightly over-represented (Koch and Frees 2017), while Twitter is more popular with men. In Germany, social media usage is inversely correlated with the age of users. In the US, although it is mainly young Americans who are active on Facebook, older adults are joining in increasing numbers: 62 per cent of Internet users aged 65 and above use Facebook, which is the most popular social media network. In contrast, Twitter is more popular among the highly educated with higher incomes (Greenwood, Perrin and Duggan 2016). YouTube is the most popular social media application in Germany: 69 per cent of Internet users used YouTube in 2017 (We Are Social 2017). But the majority of users use YouTube exclusively for entertainment purposes. Relatively few users create and share content. In contrast, on Facebook half of German users do participate actively (Faktenkontor, IMWF and Toluna 2017). The remaining users passively 'listen to the buzz'. On Twitter only one-third of users participate actively (Statista DMO 2016).

The Digital Divide and Online Political Participation

Research has not so far focused on inequalities in political participation as a social phenomenon of the social media digital divide. However, it is useful to analyse electoral bias in social media from the perspective of access and usage inequalities. Thus, our first purpose is to redevelop the social media digital divide framework in the context of online political participation.

We can describe the first-order digital divide as an access gap to political information. Depending on the degree of formal inclusion in social media, we can differentiate between 'information-rich' and 'information-poor' (Ragnedda 2017). While the former gains access to political information sooner, which again comes with advantages in shaping public opinion and decision-making processes, the information-poor acquire this crucial information and knowledge at a slower rate. This information gap is again closely related to socio-economic status, as material and cognitive access increase with higher socio-economic status (Ragnedda and Muschert 2016).

However, information access does not automatically result in political participation. The degree of online political participation is more adequately described by the second-order digital divide. From that perspective, various levels of active social media behaviour can be defined. Lutz, Hoffmann and Meckel (2014) identified three perspectives on participatory practices: (1) optimists see online political participation as an enhancement of democratic processes and political engagement; (2) pessimists see time spent online on social media applications as time unavailable for political engagement; and (3) realists represent the normalisation hypothesis, seeing little effect from social media applications on online political participation.

Several studies document the relevance of demographics and socio-economic status for differences in both online and offline political participation (Best and Krueger 2005). For example, men show higher rates of online political participation than women. The positive effects of political interest on online participation are mediated through educational level and income, which in turn have a positive effect on online political participation that is influenced by online experiences and skills. For young citizens and marginalised groups, less institutionalised forms of online political participation offer accessible opportunities to participate (Lutz, Hoffmann and Meckel 2014). Differences in participation will lead to a democratic gap, as being excluded from the digital realm goes hand-in-hand with exclusion from democratic processes (Norris 2001).

We follow with analysing the role of Twitter and the digital divide in the German general election campaign 2017. The following cases include three perspectives on electoral bias influenced by Twitter, including the relevance of: (1) Twitter as an arena for political debates; (2) manipulation by automated social media accounts on Twitter; and (3) differences on the topic agenda between Twitter and traditional media. We selected Twitter as one specific social media application as the platform enables two means of political participation (Kim and Park 2012). First, it allows direct communications between politicians and citizens; and, secondly, tweets and retweets are alternative means of political communication and mobilisation. Thus, it is not surprising that both parties and members of the German parliament are more active on Twitter. The Twittersphere was used especially by non-major parties for general election campaigning in 2017: overall, the right-wing party Alternative für Deutschland (AfD) has the largest number of followers and fans across all social media channels (n = 385,695). More than 15,000 tweets were posted from the official account @AfD, which is followed by 110,000 Twitter users. In contrast, major parties like the SPD (n = 184,413) or the CDU (n = 173,609) have less than half of this (Pluragraph 2018).

Twitter and the German General Election Campaign 2017

In this section, we look at the significance of Twitter as an arena for political debates. It is often stressed that social media can change political debates (Kim and Park 2012). However, the data of Twitter activities during the general election campaign in 2017 show that the Twittersphere in Germany was not the place for agenda-setting. Although traditional newspapers have declined in their relevance as an information provider among people of all ages and struggle to keep up with online information, TV still remains the most widely used channel for news consumption in Germany (Hölig and Hasebrink 2017). Looking at the topics discussed on Twitter in the forecast of the 2017 general election in Germany shows that virtually all major topics were triggered by events that took place outside social media.

Topics related to the elections that were followed by a peak in election-related tweets were the 'TV-Duell', a debate on television between the two most important candidates Martin Schulz and Angela Merkel (Infratest dimap 2017); the publication of the electoral rankings of the parties' candidates within their respective party (the so-called 'Landeslisten'); a TV debate between Christian Lindner (FDP) and Alice Weidel (AfD); and the start of the online election tool Wahl-o-Mat, which makes voting suggestions based on a questionnaire (Ross 2017). None of those peaks reached the intensity of the TV-Duell. They show, however, how the social media debate is influenced, if not led, by outside events, thereby becoming primarily a reaction to more traditional media. This is in line with the results from Kratzke (2017), which show that only 5 per cent of the tweets using the hashtag #btw2017 were status messages containing political content or statements, while the majority were retweets, replies and quotes. The most retweeted post during the TV debate was the link to an article in the German newspaper *Welt*, which listed contradictions between statements the candidates had made in the past and what they had stated during the television debate (Ross 2017).

This being said, Grimme et al. (2017) show specific strategies that use the advent of an event like the TV-Duell to actively influence the political agenda. Right-wing activists tried to undermine the hashtag #kanzlerduell with their own hashtag #verräterduell (Schmehl 2017). This is a strategy called 'misdirecting' (Abokhodair, Yoo and McDonald 2015), as it tries to flood a certain hashtag with unrelated content and reinterpret it in this way. Usually botnets are used to execute this strategy. In this case, there is no certain proof of the use of botnets. All that Grimme et al. (2017) can show is that a large amount of young Twitter accounts were responsible and that after an hour the attempt to undermine the hashtag #kanzlerduell stopped, as it remained largely unsuccessful. However the example shows how important bots can potentially become in the shaping of debates, the trending of topics and forming Twitter as a public sphere. The next section will therefore take a closer look at automated accounts, so-called social or political bots and evaluate their importance for the German political online debate.

The (Ir-)relevance of Twitter Bots

According to Abokhodair, Yoo and McDonald (2015), social bots are automated social media accounts which try to mimic human behaviour. Neudert (2017) claims that these technologies could play a major role in elections. She stresses that 'the implications of the outcomes of the elections in September 2017 far exceed the German and even European sphere, making Germany a vulnerable target for the manipulation of public opinion' (ibid.: 4–5). In her study, Neudert monitored two German elections that took place shortly prior to the general election: the federal presidency election in February 2017 and the Saarland state parliament election in 2017. While her results show that the use of social bots was 'marginal', she claims that 'misinformation and junk news content play a substantial role on German social media, accounting for roughly 20 percent of all political news and information on Twitter' (ibid.: 23). If this is true, misleading information rather than social bots seems to be the more urgent problem of online political debates. Furthermore, her results show that conspiracy stories 'originate from individuals who see themselves as activists and minor, semi-professional media organisations, a handful of major professional media corporations or Russian media outlets' (ibid.: 18). Brachten et al. (2017) have found similar results for the 2017 state election in North Rhine Westfalia, where out of 33,481 accounts 'only 61 were classified as social bots' (ibid.: 8). Brachten (2017) claims that during the general election there were some automated accounts tweeting about the different parties. However, those accounts were not necessarily social bots that tried to distort public debates, but rather an efficient way of organising professional social media accounts. It is worth mentioning that in the forecast of the German general election and in the light of the US presidential election there had been a broad debate among German politicians about the use of social bots in campaigning. It had been mostly agreed not to use this technology, as it was considered a danger to the democratic process (Reinsch 2016).

The above analyses show that social bots do not yet play a significant role in German elections. Misinformation and the spread of fake news via social media seem to be a greater problem for online political debates in Germany. As seen above, both retrieval and processing of information are linked to socio-economic status. It can be argued that through the spread of misinformation on social media this social divide is extended. Next we look at how online debates are influenced by a digital divide that exists on Twitter.

In the Middle of an Information Elite

The political debate on social media is different from other forms of political debate, mainly because the social composition of the participating subjects differs. This is especially true for Twitter users in Germany. 'The German Twittersphere is populated with politicians, journalists and highly educated users' (Neudert 2017: 17). This becomes obvious when one takes a look at the topics discussed on Twitter in comparison with topics elsewhere.

Koethe (2018) demonstrates a bias between topics discussed in the online versions of traditional media and social media. For example, on 20 June 2017 the three most discussed topics in online traditional media were the economy, taxes and the European Union, whereas on social media the three most important topics that day were taxes, the economy and terrorism. This was one day after Social Democrat candidate Martin Schulz published the tax plan of his party. It is clear that a different public on social media has a different agenda from that on traditional media. These results are in line with another example by Koethe (2018), which shows a Twitter comment by Christian Democrat Peter Tauber. On 3 July 2017, he shared an article from the German newspaper *Welt* adding the comment: '"full employment" is much better than "justice"'. After one of his followers asked whether this meant he should take on three jobs rather than receiving welfare, Tauber answered that if one had a proper education one would not need three jobs. This was followed by a storm of outrage, but solely on Twitter. Koethe's results show that hardly any other media referred to the debate. These examples suggest that the Twittersphere is sensible to social injustice but remains largely closed from impacting media coverage and the broader public debate. Agenda-setting on social media and especially on Twitter therefore differs from traditional media, and debates on social media remain largely within the confines of a relatively closed public space.

This shows that social media debates are hardly representative of public opinion. Because the results seem to point to the fact that as the social background differs so does the agenda. It is important to consider that with the different social background of Twitter users different topics will come into public focus. Concepts like Big Data make the promise that political debates can be observed in real-time. Some authors even go as far as to try to predict election outcomes with data retrieved from social media (for example, Kalampokis et al. 2017). While social media can be a valuable source for policymakers, it should always be interpreted considering social inequality, digital divide and exclusion.

Discussion and Conclusion

Even though the German general election of 2017 was not riddled with outside manipulation, significant electoral biases between offline and online public spheres remain. These biases amount to fragmentation and polarisation, which can be attributed to different dimensions of a digital divide.

In our case study, it became obvious that (1) one-to-many communication forms are still the main arena for agenda-setting, information allocation, editing and gate-keeping. At the same time, social media plays an important role in the distribution of information and should therefore be analysed as a distinct public sphere. As we were unable to find a significant distorting impact on political debates, we conclude that (2) automated accounts are not yet a dominant issue in German election campaigns. However, misinformation and fake news seem to be increasing through the easy access to and fast spread of social media. Finally, the data suggest that (3) social media debates are not representative of public opinion. With the different social background of Twitter users, different topics will come into public focus. As a result, a prediction or even approximation of the election outcome via Twitter is – especially in Germany – impossible.

As the different dimensions of the digital divide remain prevalent with respect to Twitter and other social media, the fragmented public sphere remains manifest. The support function of public spheres for the three functional dimensions of democracy is hence impaired. First, the aggregation of interests or convictions about the public good becomes more difficult, as voting behaviour is highly influenced by the public spheres in which a voter takes part. As we have shown, the topics on Twitter often diverge wildly from other public spheres. When fragmentation reaches a certain threshold, it tends to turn into polarisation, where people vote for their camp rather than for their interests or convictions about the public good (Frank 2004). At the same time, public deliberation is limited, since polarisation often leads to immunisation against the arguments of the other camp. At this point, communicative action is likely to lapse into strategic action (Habermas 1984). This manifests itself in our examples of the strategic use of automated social media accounts or the attempt at misdirecting hashtags.

Secondly, public control is weakened, since misuse of authority is more likely to be disregarded as a result of this immunisation process. When public debates are highly fragmented, minor power abuses will not reach the threshold of public attention, as it remains within the confines of specific public arenas. In our examples, we can see that topics on Twitter often have little or no repercussion in other public spheres. In addition, it is more likely that political scandals will be attributed to a media war.

While our findings support a cautious optimism with respect to the active manipulation and distortion strategies currently employed within social media, we notice that these digital arenas are still separated from other public spheres by a digital divide. Although the reasons for this divide have changed over the last decade, from technological and literacy gaps to more intricate forms of misrecognition, the divide is still palpable and may thereby result in the abovementioned negative effects for democratic aggregation, control and integration. For this reason, we have to closely monitor recent as well as up and coming developments in order to safeguard democratic participation.

Note

1. Many other distinctions are possible, such as with regard to the system of representation (representative, direct or radical democracy), or with regard to the type of political competition (competitive, consociational or consensus democracy). Since here we are interested in the role of citizen participation for democracy, Habermas' distinction fits well as it covers the different ways that participation may come into play with regard to will formation and political decision-making.

References

Abokhodair, N., D. Yoo and D.W. McDonald, 'Dissecting a Social Botnet: Growth, Content and Influence in Twitter', in *ACM Press*, 2015, pp. 839–51, available at: http://dl.acm.org/citation.cfm?doid=2675133.2675208, last accessed 15 May 2018.

Attewell, P., 'Comment: the First and Second Digital Divides', *Sociology of Education* 74(3) (2001): 252–9.

Best, S. J. and B. S. Krueger, 'Analyzing the Representativeness of Internet Political Participation', Political Behavior 27(2) (2005): 183–216.

Bozdag, E., 'Bias in Algorithmic Filtering and Personalization', Ethics and Information Technology 15(3) (2013): 209–27.

Brachten, F., 'Automatisierte Kommunikation im Datensatz', 2017, available at: https://social-media-analytics.org/2017/08/automatisierte-kommunikation, last accessed 16 May 2018.

Brachten, F., S. Stieglitz, L. Hofeditz, K. Kloppenborg and A. Reimann, 'Strategies and Influence of Social Bots in a 2017 German State Election – a Case Study on Twitter', Australasian Conference on Information Systems, 2017, 12.

Cadwalladr, C. and E. Graham-Harrison, 'Revealed: 50 million Facebook Profiles Harvested for Cambridge Analytica in Major Data Breach', The Guardian, 17 March 2018, available at: https://www.theguardian.com/news/2018/mar/17/cambridge-analytica-facebook-influence-us-election, last accessed 27 September 2018.

Christiano, T., 'An Instrumental Argument for a Human Right to Democracy', Philosophy & Public Affairs 39(2) (2011): 142–76.

Cohen, J. L. and A. Arato, Civil Society and Political Theory (Cambridge, MA: MIT Press, 1994).

van Deursen, A. and J. van Dijk, 'Internet Skills and the Digital Divide', New Media & Society 13(6) (2011): 893–911.

Dewan, S. and F. J. Riggins, 'The Digital Divide: Current and Future Research Directions', Journal of the Association for Information Systems 6(12) (2005): 298–337.

Dijk, J. van and K. Hacker, 'The Digital Divide as a Complex and Dynamic Phenomenon', The Information Society 19(4) (2003): 315–26.

Eurostat, Anteil der Personen, die das Internet zur Teilnahme an sozialen Netzwerken genutzt haben in ausgewählten Ländern in Europa im Jahr 2017, 2017, available at: https://de.statista.com/statistik/daten/studie/214663/umfrage/nutzung-von-social-networks-in-europa-nach-laendern, last accessed 24 September 2019.

Faktenkontor, IMWF and Toluna, Verteilung der aktiven und passiven Nutzer von Facebook in Deutschland in den Jahren 2012 bis 2016, 2017, available at: https://de.statista.com/statistik/daten/studie/505508/umfrage/aktive-und-passive-nutzer-von-facebook-deutschland, last accessed 24 September 2019.

Frank, T., What's the Matter with Kansas?: How Conservatives Won the Heart of America (New York: Owl Books, 2004).

Gil de Zuniga, H., 'Toward a European Public Sphere? The Promise and Perils of Modern Democracy in the Age of Digital and Social Media', International Journal of Communication 9 (2015): 3152–60.

Greenwood, S., A. Perrin and M. Duggan, Social Media Update 2016, Pew Research Center, 2016.

Grimme, C., D. Assenmacher, M. Preuss, L. Adam and J. F. H. Lütke-Stkdiek, Bundestagswahl 2017: Social-Media-Angriff auf das #kanzlerduell?, 2017, available at: https://www.researchgate.net/profile/Christian_Grimme/publication/319746740_

Bundestagswahl_2017_Social-Media-Angriff_auf_das_kanzlerduell/
links/59bb85570f7e9b48a28b97fb/Bundestagswahl-2017-Social-Media-Angriff-
auf-das-kanzlerduell.pdf, last accessed 15 May 2018.

Habermas, J., *The Theory of Communicative Action, Vol. 1: Reason and the Rational-
ization of Society* (Boston, MA: Beacon Press, 1984).

Habermas, J., *The Structural Transformation of the Public Sphere: an Inquiry into a Category of Bourgeois Society* (Cambridge: Polity Press, 1989).

Habermas, J., *Between Facts and Norms: Contributions to a Discourse Theory of Law and
Democracy* (Cambridge: Polity Press, 1997).

Hargittai, E., 'Digital Na(t)ives? Variation in Internet Skills and Uses among
Members of the "Net Generation"', *Sociological Inquiry* 80(1) (2010): 92–113.

Hargittai, E. and G. Walejko, 'The Participation Divide: Content Creation and Sharing in the Digital Age', *Information, Communication & Society* 11(2) (2008): 239–
56.

Hölig, S. and U. Hasebrink, 'The Role of Social Media in Promoting Hate Speech
and So-called "Fake News" has Become a Key Issue Ahead of Federal Elections,
but Most Germans Continue to get Their News from Traditional Media, with
Television Still Preferred', 2017, available at: http://www.digitalnewsreport.org/
survey/2017/germany-2017, last accessed 15 May 2018.

Infratest dimap, 'TV Duell 2017: Merkel überzeugender als Schulz', 2017, available at: https://www.infratest-dimap.de/umfragen-analysen/bundesweit/ard-
deutschlandtrend/2017/blitz-tv-duell, last accessed 31 May 2018.

Initiative D21, *Anteil der Internetnutzer nach Nutzertypen in Deutschland in den
Jahren 2001 bis 2017*, 2018, available at: https://de.statista.com/statistik/daten/
studie/3500/umfrage/internetnutzung-in-deutschland-seit-2001-nach-art-der-
nutzung, last accessed 24 September 2019.

ITU, 'ICT Facts and Figures', International Telecommunication Union, 2015.

Jaeggi, R., 'Solidarity and Indifference', in R. ter Meulen, W. Arts and R. J. A. Muffels
(eds), *Solidarity in Health and Social Care in Europe* (Dordrecht: Kluwer Academic,
2001), pp. 287–308.

Kalampokis, E., A. Karamanou, E. Tambouris and K. Tarabanis, 'On Predicting Election Results Using Twitter and Linked Open Data: the Case of the UK 2010
Election', *Journal of Universal Computer Science* 3 (2017): 24.

Kim, M. and Park, H. W., 'Measuring Twitter-based Political Participation and Deliberation in the South Korean Context by Using Social Network and Triple Helix
Indicators', *Scientometrics* 90(1) (2012): 121–40.

Klinkisch, E. and A. Suphan, 'A "Recognitional Perspective" on the 21st Century
Digital Divide', in M. Ragnedda and G. W. Muschert (eds), *Theorizing Digital
Divides* (London: Routledge, 2017).

Koch, W. and B. Frees, 'ARD/ZDF-Onlinestudie 2017: Neun von zehn Deutschen
online - Ergebnisse aus der Studienreihe "Medien und ihr Publikum" (MiP)',
Media Perspektiven 9 (2017): 434–46.

Koethe, D., 'Politik im Social Web – Diskussionen und Trends', *Talkwalker.com*, 2018, available at: https://www.talkwalker.com/de/blog/bundestagswahl-2017#, last accessed 16 May 2018.

Kratzke, N., 'The #BTW17 Twitter Dataset – Recorded Tweets of the Federal Election Campaigns of 2017 for the 19th German Bundestag', *Data* 2(4) (2017): 34.

Livingstone, S. and E. Helsper, 'Gradations in Digital Inclusion: Children, Young People and the Digital Divide', *New Media & Society* 9(4) (2007): 671–96.

Loh, W. and S. Skupien, 'Die EU als Solidargemeinschaft', *Leviathan* 44(4) (2016): 578–603.

Lutz, C., C. P. Hoffmann and M. Meckel, 'Beyond Just Politics: a Systematic Literature Review of Online Participation', *First Monday* 19(7) (2014), available at: http://www.ojphi.org/ojs/index.php/fm/article/view/5260, last accessed 24 April 2018.

Neudert, L-M. N., *Computational Propaganda in Germany: a Cautionary Tale* (Oxford: Oxford Internet Institute, 2017), available at: http://comprop.oii.ox.ac.uk/wp-content/uploads/sites/89/2017/06/Comprop-Germany.pdf, last accessed 15 May 2018.

Norris, P., *Digital Divide: Civic Engagement, Information Poverty, and the Internet Worldwide* (Cambridge: Cambridge University Press, 2001).

Papenfuss, M., '1,000 Paid Russian Trolls Spread Fake News on Hillary Clinton, Senate Intelligence Heads Told', *The Huffington Post*, 31 March 2017, available at: https://www.huffingtonpost.co.uk/entry/russian-trolls-fake-news_us_58dde6bae4b08194e3b8d5c4?, last accessed 28 September 2019.

Pettit, P., *Republicanism: a Theory of Freedom and Government* (Oxford: Oxford University Press, 1999), available at: http://www.oxfordscholarship.com/view/10.1093/0198296428.001.0001/acprof-9780198296423, last accessed 31 May 2018.

Pluragraph, 'Beliebteste politische Parteien in sozialen Netzwerken in Deutschland im Januar 2018', 2018, available at: https://de.statista.com/statistik/daten/studie/172474/umfrage/politische-parteien-nach-anzahl-der-fans-bei-facebook, last accessed 17 May 2018.

Ragnedda, M., *The Third Digital Divide: a Weberian Approach to Digital Inequalities* (London: Routledge, 2017).

Ragnedda, M. and G. W. Muschert, 'Theorizing Digital Divides and Digital Inequalities', in J. Servaes and T. Oyedemi (eds), *Social Inequalities, Media, and Communication: Theory and Roots* (Lanham, MD: Lexington Books, 2016), pp. 23–35.

Rawls, J., *Political Liberalism* (New York: Columbia University Press, 1993).

Rawls, J., *Justice as Fairness: a Restatement* (Cambridge, MA: Harvard University Press, 2001).

Reinsch, M., 'Social Bots Parteien in Deutschland wollen auf technische Wahlkampfhelfer verzichten – Quelle', *Berliner Zeitung*, 2016, available at: https://www.berliner-zeitung.de/politik/social-bots-parteien-in-deutschland-wollen-auf-technische-wahlkampfhelfer-verzichten-25278052, last accessed 18 May 2018.

Ross, B., 'Zu welchen Ereignissen diskutieren Twitternutzer zur #btw17?', *Social Media Analytics*, 2017, available at: https://social-media-analytics.org/2017/09/zu-welchen-ereignissen-zur-btw17-diskutieren-twitternutzer, last accessed 15 May 2018.

Schmehl, C., 'Diese geheimen Chats zeigen, wer hinter dem Meme-Angriff #Verräterduell aufs TV-Duell steckt', *Buzz Feed*, 2017, available at: https://www.buzzfeed.com/de/karstenschmehl/willkommen-in-der-welt-von-discord-teil1?utm_term=.qf34z6lVM#.fcOb3jkqB, last accessed 15 May 2018.

Statista DMO, 'Anzahl der monatlich aktiven Nutzer von Twitter in ausgewählten Ländern weltweit im Jahr 2015 (in Millionen)', *Statista*, 2016, available at: https://de.statista.com/statistik/daten/studie/554459/umfrage/anzahl-der-monatlich-aktiven-twitter-nutzer-in-ausgewaehlten-laendern-weltweit, last accessed 15 May 2018.

We Are Social, 'Ranking der beliebtesten Social Networks und Messenger nach dem Anteil der Nutzer an der Bevölkerung in Deutschland im Jahr 2017', *Statista*, 2017, available at: https://de.statista.com/statistik/daten/studie/505947/umfrage/reichweite-von-social-networks-in-deutschland, last accessed 15 May 2018.

Zillien, N. and E. Hargittai, 'Digital Distinction: Status-Specific Types of Internet Usage', *Social Science Quarterly* 90 (2009): 274–91. doi.org/10.1111/j.1540-6237.2009.00617.x.

SEVEN

Gated Communities of the Digitised Mind

Thorsten Brønholt

Introduction

Web services and sites increasingly filter and adapt their content to the individual user. Prior to this project, the research on echo chambers and filter bubbles failed to answer an elusively simple question: are the worlds viewed online by people of different political convictions and/or affiliations notably different from one another, and, if yes, what are the implications for deliberative democracy?

In this chapter, I summarise the research, and the results of the Gated Communities of the Digitised Mind project, exploring further the state of contemporary digital societies in the light of current developments in social media and politics. First, the discussion about echo chambers and filter bubbles is situated in the broader fields of political science and media studies. Secondly, these central concepts and their origins are detailed, and the extant literature on them reviewed. Thirdly, the study carried out to build more knowledge about echo chambers, filter bubbles and their effects on societies is summarised. Then, as a tool to interpret the results and what they imply about current societies, the concept of gated communities of the digitised mind is proposed. This leads into an exploration of the implications of the results for would-be deliberative democracies. Finally, possible answers to what could be done to counter these effects are considered, as are the effects on societies.

Structures of the Online Realm

At the beginning of this millennium, the Internet was starting to penetrate the life-worlds of more and more individuals, particularly in Western societies. As a result, scholars of different creeds and breeds were starting to ponder what this new medium, this new digital 'Cyberspace' (Barlow 1996), meant for individuals and societies. An early entry that would come to shape this debate was the 2001 book by Cass R. Sunstein, *Republic.com*.[1] Sunstein (2007) was perhaps the first academic to voice concerns about the implications of online 'echo chambers' for the digitised individuals and societies in which he is situated, and sees in the future. As Sunstein presents it, users embedded in an ideal-typical echo chamber will see and interact only with content that originates from and/or targets users inhabiting the same metaphysical social space as themselves. Echo chambers are perhaps best exemplified to the contemporary audience by Facebook groups devoted to a particular cause or opinion. Imagine that I were to join a Facebook group titled 'Trump is unfit to be president', and write on the 'wall' of the group that 'Donald Trump has little or none of the skills required to run a country!'. The responses I would get to this statement, in such a group, would most likely echo my own stated considerations and opinions. If I go further and join many Facebook groups expressing similar sentiments, subscribe to news outlets who hold the same belief, and befriend and interact online solely with people who also agree with these opinions, then my Facebook 'News Feed' will start containing content from these sources only, and Facebook will have become to me an echo chamber for these messages and opinions (Bakshy, Messing and Adamic 2015). Sunstein argues, with reference to Habermas, that common beliefs and experiences are the basis of meaningful deliberation. Thus, if citizens of a liberal democracy increasingly occupy echo chambers online – especially ones that are grouped at least partly around difference from the respective other ones, then they are likely to lose the ability to meaningfully deliberate, since their social and informational life-worlds will be increasingly dissimilar.

Where echo chambers imply at least a degree of choice on the part of the user, a 'filter bubble' is a personal, invisible virtual space that users are embedded into. Proposed by Eli Pariser (2011) in his Ted talk and book of the same name, filter bubbles refers to an effect of what is popularly called Web 2.0 – the personalised internet. On almost all web pages we visit today, the page is personalised according to what the server for the page is set to 'see' as fitting for us. Some pages do this more than others, but, essentially, everything we see online is filtered to our individually assigned preferences: we see the web from within our own personal bubble – our filter bubble – tailored by computer programs, employing machine learning and statistical correlation to come ever closer to creating what is, according to the assigned metrics, the optimal experience for the user. This, Pariser argues, ultimately changes the way we encounter and process 'ideas and information' (Pariser

2011: 10). Each user is encapsulated in his or her own bubble, and thus has a unique outlook on the Internet. Users can access most of the same things, but they will see them through their personal prism. Pariser's warning is akin to Sunstein's, but where Sunstein cautions against potential dangers as a consequence of unreflected choice, Pariser emphasises the psycho-social effects of the automated, unchosen filtering of content. If queries on Google and other search engines emphasise results confirming rather than challenging existing beliefs, and if the opinions and comments one encounters from other users are mainly akin to the those the user would write him- or herself, then one may come to see held beliefs as objective truths. This caution is similar to the above, as it relates to a possible entrenching of beliefs, but it is more focused on the lack of consent, and the all-encompassing quality of the filter bubble, as a condition for using the contemporary web.

Truth and Theory

Most of the research into online echo chambers and filter bubbles is quantitative and based on large n data and/or surveys (Bakshy, Messing and Adamic 2015; Boutyline and Willer 2016; Flaxman, Goel and Rao 2016). While this is not problematic in itself, it suggests that there is a deficit of qualitative data. Quantitative studies into this have answered many questions about prevalence, and about the empirical, statistical reality of the quantified effects. When researching theoretical phenomena, though, an exploration into their qualitative nature can add salience to the interpretations of the quantitative results: if we know more about what a phenomenon is, we can say more about how (much) it affects those people influenced by it, as told by the numbers.

In an innovative application of statistical correlation on Facebook data Bessi (2016) was able to quantify and track developments in the psychological profiles of users. Bessi found evidence that psychologically similar users tend to seek and interact in similar groups and, perhaps more importantly, that users are socialised by the groups they are in, adapting (more) psychological traits of fellow group members. Also, several studies have confirmed that Facebook and Twitter (and, by extension, YouTube, Weibo and other social media platforms) are indeed prone to creating echo chambers and exacerbating the filter bubble effect (exacerbating the heterogeneity of content based on preferences assigned to the individual user) (Williams et al. 2015; Boutyline and Willer 2016; Flaxman, Goel and Rao 2016). Adding more salience to the anthropological and psychological studies brought in by Sunstein and Pariser to validate their claims, other researchers have confirmed that users are indeed prone to seek confirmation of their own beliefs (Garrett 2009; Farrell 2015). Furthermore, research has shown that users were largely unaware of terms, conditions and the therein mentioned filtering of content taking place on news feeds and search engines across the web (2.0) (Eslami et al. 2015: 157).

On the other hand, this subject matter is hardly static. The Facebook in-house researchers Bakshy, Messing and Adamic (2015), have claimed that the nature of one's filter bubble and whether Facebook became an echo chamber was based on user choices rather than the (nefarious) aims of the company. They suggested that, all other things being equal, the algorithms used by Facebook were in fact designed to counteract such filtering and grouping, weighing politically adverse content slightly higher than content corresponding to the political standpoint of the majority of a user's Facebook friends. This is argued to boost minority views among the potential sources of items for the news feed.[2] According to Bakshy et al. (2015), Facebook's filtering is mainly based on the users' own choices in terms of friends and interests, and actively works to 'pop' rather than strengthen echo chambers and filter bubbles. With the changes to the news feed algorithm in 2018, this narrative is further reinforced (Hardiman and Brown 2018; Mosseri 2018). Following up on this, recent research has suggested that on social media, a majority of users actually see much content from sources categorised to differ from their ideological standpoint – and much more so than they do in other (older) media sources (Flaxman, Goel and Rao 2016; Roliggård 2017; Chakrabarti 2018). Furthermore, there is evidence that social media creates increased interaction and engagement with, and about, political content (Williams et al. 2015; Chakrabarti 2018). Finally, due to the increased media attention, users and politicians are increasingly aware of these issues, even if not all users will be affected by initiatives like the General Data Protection Regulation (GDPR) (EU 2018; Hern 2018).

Seeing is Believing

The aim of my project was to assess, qualitatively, the empirically observable differences in the filter bubbles and echo chambers of users with differing political affiliations in Denmark. I found three to four respondents from the four Danish parties that were deemed furthest apart ideologically,[3] and conducted semi-structured interviews with them, before gathering and analysing screenshots of their Facebook news page, Twitter feed and a Google search conducted on their personal device. The study was inspired and supported by the general precepts and considerations for carrying out qualitative case studies by Robert K. Yin (2015), but the methods used were designed for the purpose (Brønholt 2017).[4] These methods involved a test of the ideological group coherence of the respondents, employing Computer Assisted Qualitative Digital Analysis (CAQDAS).

The data gathered from the two social media platforms, Facebook and Twitter, was quite similar in form, if not always in content. I sorted and anonymised the screenshots, and looked at the feeds individually and grouped, assessing whether the group cohesion mentioned above translated into similar content and rhetoric on Facebook and Twitter – and whether there were clear dissimilarities between the different groups/parties. Clear patterns emerged, though with some exceptions. Twitter feeds in particular were very much either/or, but on the whole, the Facebook news feed and Twitter home page showed all but ideal-typical echo chambers. The content featured was either partisan, supported the partisan ideology, and/or had narratives or comments supporting the agenda of the party. In part, the type of content and the narratives and assumptions inherent in the items appearing in each individual's news feed was so consistent with the party ideology that even when completely anonymised, the political adherence of the originator of each feed was easily identifiable, as was the grouping according to party affiliation. The filter bubble effect, as described by Pariser, was substantiated, and the echo chamber condition warned of by Sunstein was confirmed. Testing the salience of the filter bubble theory, I measured the differences in individual Google searches. I did this by devising a list of ten potentially contentious Google search terms, and searched for them on each respondent's device. To make sense of the resulting screenshots, I employed CAQDAS. For the Google search, the picture was less clear than for the Facebook and Twitter results. Some filtering was clearly taking place, but there was no evidence to suggest similar results for those of similar political leanings. This could have been due to the design of the study,[5] but there was no evidence to support echo chambers being created or perpetuated by the Google Search engine. Filtering was taking place, and assuming different search queries and interests on the part of the users, Google Search does build their part of the filter bubble. But according to these findings, the individual filtering observed in this case was negligible. Evidence was found to support the filter bubble theory, but it was weak.

On completing the study of echo chambers and filter bubbles in Danish politics, the picture I was left with was more complex than anticipated. While echo chambers could be identified for respondents from the same party, there were still some differences and apparent overlaps with those from other parties. This suggested that while the echo chamber hypothesis certainly was confirmed, there was, as they say, more to the story: the

echo chambers had fuzzy edges and, in some cases, there was sudden overlap with various issues other than those of the party news or ideology. For
instance, two respondents had the same posts about an (apolitical) Facebook group devoted to historic buildings in Copenhagen. This also suggested that though the filter bubble theory stood confirmed, each user's
content was not equally different from all the others'. Those of the same
party appeared to be shown much of the same content as each other, but
also shared some commonalities with those of people who shared some,
but not all, political agendas and opinions with them. It was evident that
similar users had more content in common with each other than with those
of starkly different political leanings, but there were degrees of difference,
far more complex than what could be assigned to discrete echo chambers.
This was particularly clear for the respondents of the two left-wing parties,
the Unity List, and the Alternative. But there was also more common overlap, such as various pictures of a particularly stunning Copenhagen sunrise,
and contacts' similar holiday photos. Though each user had their personal
filter bubble, there were varying degrees of similarity between them. These
findings merited further consideration. Clearly, both theories had been confirmed – but results were enriched with findings that fit outside the frame of
the theories. The existing concepts lacked the explanatory power to analyse
the empirical reality I was seeing. To fully express what I found, I needed to
find a more sophisticated concept than those that I had. A conceptual frame
that could fathom the complex reality that I was seeking to make sense of.

Gated Communities of the Digitised Mind

To explain more fully the digital social phenomena I encountered, I have
proposed a new analytical position, the Gated Communities of the Digitised Mind. In the extreme decentralisation of context creation and distribution enabled by social networks, there are as many sources as there are
users, let alone news media. Content gets created, changed, contradicted,
reused and shared from multiple and varying sources. On social network
sites such as Facebook, the amount of content that could principally be
shown to any given user is staggering. All that is shared publicly, all that is
shared by friends, to friends could appear on one user's news feed – not to
mention advertisements and other content from around the web. To decide
what to show the user, Facebook employs various sorting algorithms, powered by machine learning (Bakshy, Messing and Adamic 2015). The aim
is to show ever more content of interest to the user (or, perhaps, rather, to
keep the user on the site, engaging with content). To a degree, and as my
research has shown, this content can be associated with the user's political

profile, but few users are as thoroughly defined by their political leanings as are politicians, and even their interests overlap.

Users have varied and differentiated tastes and interests, and their media consumption reflects this. This means that most users will occupy several echo chambers concurrently. These various echo chambers are of different sizes and strengths, have different degrees of influence on the user, and they overlap. The computational drive towards convergence will mean that the more data points on which two users correlate, the higher the likelihood that user A will be shown something user B has been recorded to halt their scrolling at or react to.[6] Aggregated, the patterns that would emerge if data was collected on all content enveloping a user can be seen to coalesce into a larger virtual, social structure. The dividing lines between the various groupings that can be made correlate and create separate social spaces. This is what I call the Gated Communities of the Digitised Mind.

In the same way that different people can occupy different physical spaces in a (gated) community, the data doubles/digital personas (Palmås 2011: 342) of the users in the gated communities of the digitised mind share varying degrees of similitude. A new user might be placed in the community by happenstance – a chance click on a Facebook group; a break from scrolling on an advertisement, simply because the user was distracted by a cat in the offline world might be enough for the algorithms to start building their metaphorical walls. The next time the user logs in, he or she is then met with content that corresponds broadly to the data points registered, and if the user interacts with that, he or she gets walled in further. These metaphysical walls are to some degree based on good intentions – a wish to serve the user's needs – but they are walls nonetheless. Over time, if a user enmeshed deeply in a gated community of the digitised mind is confronted with content from 'outside the wall', it can seem foreign, even disturbing. If the development is as described by Pariser and others, then the more the formulation of Google Search suggestions, and the results of said search are adapted to the statistically determined interests of the user, the more likely that user is to get caught in a series of cognitive loops – loops from which it can be hard to break free. In this way, the algorithms act as both gatekeepers and walls in each gated community of the digitised mind. What is important to realise is that even when these communities start out disparate and heterogeneous the bias towards convergence inherent in the application of statistical correlation to determine interests, will homogenise the online worlds of individuals (Fieseler and Fleck 2013). The shaping of individuals is implicit and as the process goes on these communities become more and more salient from a psycho-social point of view.

Communities of the Online Realm

As the social salience of the digital gated communities rise, the prospect of imagined communities across offline borders is enhanced. Nationality and language are still relevant data points for the algorithmic sorting, but as automated translation gets ever better, so the reason for putting weight on those points wanes. In my research, I saw this exemplified by how one nationalistic politician had content from US American content creators, relevant to his interest since he and the originators shared a fear and/or dislike of Muslims. Similar to how religious or nationalistic communities and political movements have often gone across state borders (Anderson 2006), the gated communities of the digitised mind are limited only by the virtual borders drawn for them online. In a sense, this could herald the era of the world citizen. If social media and digital platforms become an organising principle akin to that of internally heterogeneous states of the past, then it seems a natural development that layers of shared identity should form within this frame. These world citizens, however, would be starkly divided into increasingly estranged, sometimes antagonistic communities.

Recent studies have shown how, through social media, many news sources reach a wide breadth of the population, across ideological divides. For this majority, wide gated communities might be forged that overlap to an extent that furthers rather than impedes deliberative democracy both nationally and internationally – that, at least, is what Facebook themselves suggest (Chakrabarti 2018). Still, the problem persists that the citizens situated in social spaces outside this area, the digitised minority communities, remain. Like the others, these users are met with 'facts' in the form of Facebook news, YouTube videos and Google searches that confirm or exacerbate their beliefs. And each click, each view, builds the wall ever higher, making the isolation greater. In this social structure users can unwittingly get caught in a radicalising social environment where often mistrust of mainstream narratives is part and parcel of the common group identifiers (Marwick and Lewis 2017).

The Weaponised Digital Social Reality

Algorithms shape our social reality, and there are actors who utilise this to their own ends, disrupting and affecting group formation and the attitudes of electorates both near and far. The structure around the digital social animal has been weaponised (Allenby 2017). In a globalised world, foreign state powers and independent actors can influence elections and social movements with relative ease, as Russia has done with the US (Howard et al. 2017), and as the now insolvent private firm Cambridge Analytica has done for various state and non-state customers (Cadwalladr 2018). Further, in a globalised society, fringe groups, even if relatively smaller in their national context, can in real numbers grow to be much bigger than their local counterparts could have been in a pre-digital world, and exercise influence accordingly. The most well-known current examples of this are (neo-)Nazis (now, successfully rebranded as 'alt-right'), and DAESH (aka IS/ISIL/ISIS). The latter has for many years been given a great deal of focus in the US, the EU and elsewhere, not least due to the impact and nature of terrorist attacks linked to DAESH. The US has famously invested massively in surveillance to combat this and other perceived threats (Cayford and Pieters 2018). The former, however, has long attracted some attention in the scholarly community (see Marwick and Lewis 2017), but not much in the political, though media coverage has increasingly linked the 'alt-right' movement to President Trump (Gramlich 2016). In 2019, due to terrorist attacks by people associated with this political movement, this shifted, most prominently with the prime minister of New Zealand, Jacinda Ardern, putting renewed focus on racist ideologies offline and online in the wake of a right-wing terrorist attack in her country (BBC News 2019). In March 2018, the European Commission released guidelines requiring social media platforms to remove 'terrorist content' within an hour of it being 'flagged' by users or algorithms, as their latest in a long line of steps to combat digital threats (European Commision 2018). Such steps, both overt and covert, have been taken by most states, but they do not address the problems emphasised here. These interventions are aimed at moderating specific user actions after the fact, or, more to the point, they are aimed at enforcing a governance or structural change aimed at detecting, deleting and potentially punishing and reporting users who take particular actions. In encouraging networks to detect and respond to 'hate speech', they address the digital equivalent of catching a small group of children who are spreading nasty rumours, curse words and all, but never addressing the structural reasons why these children are invariably put in the same room together and presented with rhetoric that confirms their alienation from the outside world (and learn curse words).

These children believe they know the truth that everyone outside the room seems to deny. It feels as if they are in the room by their own choice and volition, and they certainly feel at home there, surrounded by their peers. The children have reason to assume that the people around them are representative of society at large – or at least the part of society that, to their mind, belongs in their group. White supremacists can get the impression that any 'white' stranger, really – or at least most of them – would support their narrative. Islamist extremists can get the impression that most Muslims – all 'true' Muslims – will agree with them. Meanwhile, left-leaning academics will see how thousands agree with whatever is posted by *The Guardian*, and how the comments shown to them are in support of their own views. This is the essence of the problem: the individualised reinforcing of narratives and content one is likely to like. Even if most users are exposed to varied content, the social experience they will have in the current design is one where they are either reinforced in their views or meet with stark opposition, equally likely to make them feel validated in their views. Whatever the case, that still leaves the fringe cases, and the minority groups. Tens of thousands of users, clustered in social spaces where none from the outside are to be trusted. The walls of doubt and mistrust colonises the user, and when he or she logs out, he or she is still embedded in the gated community of the digitised mind.

Supply, Demand and the Happy Consumer

Assuming that we, as citizens and consumers, still want to be users of social media and search engines, these challenges are hard to resolve. When we log in to these sites, we arguably want to be met with content that is interesting and relevant to us – with other users to whom we feel comfortable 'talking'. If we did not feel interested and safe, we would log out – or rather, choose a different site that seemed more attuned to our interests. The GDPR and internal regulation changes have increasingly made our personal filtering a matter of choice; of meaningful consent, and of differentiation. Users are invited to opt-out of the micro-targeted advertising that has been given such a bad 'rep' through the Cambridge Analytica scandal. While this is ethically sound from an individualist, rational choice perspective, it does not respond to the issues raised here.

There are still some citizens who have not made a profile on Facebook, who do not use Google or Apple news and web services. Such persons have perhaps succeeded in insulating themselves from the direct influence of the shaping algorithms. The secondary influence, however, is hard to avoid. Humans are social animals, and whatever changes come to the people and media with whom one interacts in daily life will inexorably bleed over into the shaping of even the consciously analogue individual. Some users opting-out from various degrees of individualisation might indirectly curb the development, but it will not work counter to it. The same can be said for most suggestions that have been raised by Facebook management and others. Still, pulling the brakes and curbing effects might be better than doing nothing. Furthermore, educating and informing users and citizens can arguably go a long way to insulate them from inadvertently shutting themselves into minority gated communities of the digitised mind. Other approaches could also be imagined. Mark Zuckerberg famously stated that there are 10,000 versions of Facebook running at any given time (Huspeni 2017). Assuming the personalisation algorithm, the truth is that, in principle, there are as many different versions as there are users, and even those individual versions change time and again. One could imagine, then, a randomised change that could happen every time one logs into the platform, subtly changing not only the current version, but also the assumptions of the algorithms. If one logs in and sees content one is not currently inspired by, then one simply refreshes and gets content sorting done based on a different node. Given the multitude of content available, this could give a completely different experience altogether, and would cycle the filter bubbles and communities the user is ushered into and confronted with. Perhaps this too could help to stave off what seems inevitable.

Alternatively, it has been suggested that we decouple the company and the social network (McNamee 2018). It would be technically possible to separate the social connections – the literal social network – from the actual company and interface(s) of Facebook. The suggestion is that various companies could compete on different ways of sorting and presenting content on the same platform. Market logic and monopoly laws could thus be applied in the digital realm to ensure competition (McNamee 2018). The idea seems similar to that fuelling the then ground-breaking ban on specific internet browsers being native on an operating system. However, while this might lead to different sorting of data, it might just as well lead to the opposite: the grouped sorting of data being even stronger, once minority groups such as the aforementioned migrate to the same platform – or create their own.

It can be argued that the concept introduced here – the Gated Communities of the Digitised Mind – is simply a reflection, a digitalisation, of human beings as social actors. A person from a given social and political background shares traits with others who come from a similar social space, and it is to be expected that they carry these similarities with them into the digital sphere. In a supply/demand-based economy, market shares fall to those actors who can best match the individual consumers. In this view, this is all just the digital version of social (and market) forces we have long observed in other contexts. This is a perfectly reasonable critique, but I argue that the main difference is exactly that: it is digital – and the creation and continuation of these social spaces is largely happening automatically. It is a development steered by – governed by – algorithms. While humans have been said to be shaped by the social structures in which they are enveloped (Foucault 1978), these social structures are now being re-shaped by machines.[7] This matters, especially, because the digitalisation decouples the subjects from the physical limitations to these effects that are present in a pre-digital world. The development explored in this chapter is inherent to the social changes in the digital age and cannot (and perhaps should not) be stopped. But it can be mediated, possibly even controlled.

Conclusion

This chapter has discussed the key concepts of echo chambers and filter bubbles, and reviewed the literature on them. It has outlined new research, leading to introducing the concept of gated communities of the digitised mind. Finally, it has discussed possible implications to deliberative democracies and touched upon various avenues for addressing the issues raised.

Notes

1. Re-published in an updated version, *Republic.com 2.0*, in 2007.
2. Said article and its narrative has been heavily criticised, especially by Tüfekçi (2015).
3. Alternativet (the Alternative), Liberal Alliance, Enhedslisten (the Red–Green Alliance) and Dansk Folkeparti (Danish People's Party).
4. I originally intended to carry out the study in Germany. After sound advice from Dr Julia Schwanholz of the University of Göttingen, I realised that this was not feasible. I owe her a debt of gratitude for this caution and for her valuable feedback.
5. See Brønholt (2017) for further details and discussion of the methodology.
6. See per example Velickovic et al. (2018) (Facebook Research).
7. Machines that are under the control of a small elite management team – a theme further explored in my doctoral thesis (Brønholt (forthcoming)).

References

Allenby, B., 'White Paper on Weaponized Narrative', *Semantic Scholar*, 2017, available at: https://pdfs.semanticscholar.org/7527/190033941138ec9a1939d6f4030fd3c6e3dc.pdf, last accessed 24 September 2019.

Anderson, B., *Imagined Communities*, 2nd edn (London: Verso, 2006).

Bakshy, E., S. Messing and L. A. Adamic, 'Exposure to Ideologically Diverse News and Opinion on Facebook', *Science* (2015): 1130–2.

Barlow, J. P., 'A Declaration of the Independence of Cyberspace', *The Humanist* (1996): 18–19.

BBC News, 'Christchurch Shootings: Jacinda Ardern Calls for Global anti-Racism Fight', *BBC News*, 20 March 2019, available at: https://www.bbc.com/news/world-asia-47634132, last accessed 24 September 2019.

Bessi, A., 'Personality Traits and Echo Chambers on Facebook', *Computers in Human Behavior* 65(C) (2016): 319–24.

Boutyline, A. and R. Willer, 'The Social Structure of Political Echo Chambers: Variation in Ideological Homophily in Online Networks', *Political Psychology* 38(3) (2016): 551–69.

Brønholt, T., 'Gated Communities of the Digitised Mind', Master's thesis, Københavns Universitet, 2017.

Brønholt, T., *Governed by Algorithms* (Paisley: University of the West of Scotland, forthcoming).

Cadwalladr, C., 'Revealed: Graphic Video used by Cambridge Analytica to Influence Nigerian Election', *The Guardian*, 4 April 2018, available at: https://www.theguardian.com/uk-news/2018/apr/04/cambridge-analytica-used-violent-video-to-try-to-influence-nigerian-election, last accessed 24 September 2019.

Cayford, M. and W. Pieters, 'The Effectiveness of Surveillance Technology: What Intelligence Officials are Saying', *The Information Society* (2018): 88–103, doi:10.1080/01972243.2017.1414721.

Chakrabarti, S., 'Hard Questions: What Effect Does Social Media Have on Democracy?' *Newsroom.FB*, 22 January 2018, available at: https://newsroom.fb.com/news/2018/01/effect-social-media-democracy/?frame-nonce=bd5e374778, last accessed 30 January 2018.

Eslami, M., A. Rickmany, K. Vaccaro, A. Aleyasen and A. Vuong, '"I Always Assumed that I Wasn't Really that Close to [Her]": Reasoning about Invisible Algorithms in the News Feed', *CHI '15 Proceedings of the 33rd Annual ACM Conference on Human Factors in Computing Systems* (New York: ACM New York, 2015), pp. 153–62.

EU, 'GDPR Key Changes', *EU GDPR Portal*, 2018, https://www.eugdpr.org/key-changes.html, last accessed 3 May 2018.

European Commision, 'A Europe that Protects: Commission Reinforces EU Response to Illegal Content Online', *European Commission – Press Release Database*, 1 March 2018, available at: http://europa.eu/rapid/press-release_IP-18-1169_en.htm, last accessed 4 May 2018.

Farrell, J., 'Echo Chambers and False Certainty', *Nature* 5 (2015): 719–20.

Fieseler, C. and M. Fleck, 'The Pursuit of Empowerment through Social Media: Structural Social Capital Dynamics in CSR-Blogging', *Journal of Business Ethics* (2013): 759–75.

Flaxman, S., S. Goel and J. M. Rao, 'Filter Bubbles, Echo Chambers and Online News Consumption', *Public Opinion Quarterly* (2016): 298–320.

Foucault, M., *The History of Sexuality, Vol. 1: The Will to Knowledge* (New York: Pantheon, 1978).

Garrett, R. K., 'Echo Chambers Online?: Politically Motivated Selective Exposure Among Internet News Users', *Journal of Computer-Mediated Communication* (2009): 265–85.

Gramlich, J., 'Most Americans Haven't Heard of the 'Alt-Right'.' *Pew Reasearch Center*, 12 December 2016, available at: http://www.pewresearch.org/fact-tank/2016/12/12/most-americans-havent-heard-of-the-alt-right, last accessed 4 May 2018.

Hardiman, A. and C. Brown, 'FYI: More Local News on Facebook', *Newsroom.FB*, 2018, available at: https://newsroom.fb.com/news/2018/01/news-feed-fyi-local-news, last accessed 26 February 2018.

Hern, A., 'Facebook Refuses to Promise GDPR-style Privacy Protection for US Users', *The Guardian*, 4 April 2018, available at: https://www.theguardian.com/technology/2018/apr/04/facebook-gdpr-stronger-privacy-protections-eu-data-protection-law-mark-zuckerberg, last accessed 3 May 2018.

Howard, P. N., B. Kollanyi, S. Bradshaw and L-M. Neudert, 'Social Media, News and Political Information during the US Election: Was Polarizing Content Concentrated in Swing States?' *The Computational Propaganda Project*, 28 September 2017, available at: http://comprop.oii.ox.ac.uk/research/working-papers/social-media-news-and-political-information-during-the-us-election-was-polarizing-content-concentrated-in-swing-states, last accessed 4 May 2018.

Huspeni, A., 'Why Mark Zuckerberg Runs 10,000 Facebook Versions a Day', *Entrepeneur* (2017), available at: https://www.entrepreneur.com/article/294242, last accessed 8 May 2018.

Marwick, A. and R. Lewis, 'Media Manipulation and Disinformation Online', *Data & Society* (2017).

McNamee, R. 'How to Fix Facebook – Before It Fixes Us', *Washington Monthly*, (2018), available at: https://washingtonmonthly.com/magazine/january-february-march-2018/how-to-fix-facebook-before-it-fixes-us, last accessed 25 September 2019.

Mosseri, A., 'FYI: Bringing People Closer Together', *Newsroom.FB*, 2018, available at: https://newsroom.fb.com/news/2018/01/news-feed-fyi-bringing-people-closer-together, last accessed 26 February 2018.

Palmås, K., 'Predicting What You'll Do Tomorrow: Panspectric Surveillance and the Contemporary Corporation', *Surveillance and Society* (2011): 338–54.

Pariser, E., *The Filter Bubble: What the Internet is Hiding from You* (London: Penguin, 2011).

Roliggård, S., 'Fordom om ekkokamre aflives: Store medier forhindrer meningsbobler', *Politiken*, 28 April 2017, available at: http://politiken.dk/kultur/medier/art5927116/Store-medier-forhindrer-meningsbobler, last accessed 25 September 2019.

Sunstein, C. R., *Republic.com 2.0* (Princeton, NJ: Princeton University Press, 2007).

Tüfekçi, Z., 'Facebook Said Its Algorithms Do Help Form Echo Chambers, and the Tech Press Missed It', *New Perspectives Quarterly* (2015): 9–12.

Velickovic, P., G. Cucurull, A. Casanova, A. Romero, P. Lio and Y. Bengio, 'Graph Attention Networks', *Conference Paper at ICLR 2018*, Facebook research, 30 April 2018.

Williams, H. T. P., J. R. McMurray, T. Kurz and F. H. Lambert, 'Network Analysis Reveals Open Forums and Echo Chambers in Social Media Discussions of Climate Change', *Global Environmental Change* (2015): 126–38, available at: http://www.sciencedirect.com/science/article/pii/S0959378015000369, last accessed 25 September 2019.

Yin, R. K., 'Case Studies', in James D. Wright (ed.), *International Encyclopedia of the Social & Behavioral Sciences*, 2nd edn (Oxford: Elsevier, 2015), pp. 194–201, doi:10.1016/B978-0-08-097086-8.10507-0.

EIGHT

The Network and the Demos: Big Data and the Epistemic Justifications of Democracy

Dave Kinkead and David M. Douglas

A stable democracy requires a shared identity and political culture. Its citizens need to identify as one common demos lest it fracture and balkanise into separate political communities. This in turn necessitates some common communication network for political messages to be transmitted, understood and evaluated by citizens. Hence, what demarcates one demos from another are the means of communication connecting the citizens of those demoi, allowing them to debate and persuade each other on the proper conduct of government and on issues of common interest.

For the ancient Athenians, their public sphere was the agora (marketplace); for the Federalists in the American colonies, the newspaper; for us today, it is the Internet. Until now, the physical nature of these communication networks has resulted in a trade-off between the reach of political messages (the numeric and geographic composition of the demos who receive political messages and may participate in the public sphere) and the ability to target the content of a message on that network towards individual citizens.

One-to-one interpersonal conversation in the agora was highly targeted but could reach only as far as a voice could carry. The speakers and audience were well known to each other through personal interaction. As the printing press and later television allowed for greater and greater reach, the content of these messages became more generic as the speakers became more distant from their audience. The wider the audience grew, the less a message could be targeted at a particular audience segment without alienating others. The risk to reputation and credibility that came with making false claims and conflicting promises to different groups increased as more people could receive messages and identify contradictions and errors to the rest of the audience.

The Internet and big data analytics have changed the nature of political communication by decoupling message reach from message targeting. It allows individually tailored content to be distributed on a global scale without fear that the content of those messages will be overheard by others who may contest or reject it. Politicians are freed from the constraints imposed on what they say by the public presentation and discussion of arguments and claims. It frees political actors to engage in sophistry and demagoguery.

In this chapter, we explore what impact this decoupling has on democracy. We describe how political discussion in democracies has changed over time, as both communication technology and the number of people included in the demos have changed. We show that communication technology has previously increased the reach of political messages while also making such messages more public and less targeted towards particular individuals or groups. We then show how social media and big data combine to create echo chambers of political discourse that undermine the role that epistemic and cognitive diversity play in underpinning epistemic justifications of democracy.

Democracy and Demagoguery

Plato is infamous for his disdain of democracy. He held that decisions made by an unskilled and uninformed demos will always be inferior to those of philosopher-monarchs. Democratic policy will be determined by base desire rather than by reason. A state ruled by the people will inevitably succumb to the siren song of a persuasive orator whose lust for power and manipulation of the masses can only result in tyranny. To rule well, one must have expertise, knowledge and wisdom. It is obvious, then, that the decisions of an epistocracy will be superior to the decisions of a democracy. Two thousand years later, Sir Francis Galton harboured similar thoughts about decision making. He was surprised to discover, however, that after calculating the results of 787 bets on the estimated weight of an ox at a country fair, the median result of the *vox populi* was within 0.8 per cent of the actual weight (Galton 1907).

This unexpected result highlights the intriguing epistemic value of collective decision making involving disparate actors – that whenever people of diverse cognitive ability reason collectively in a setting that rewards truth-tracking, the collective judgement will be, probabilistically at least, superior to the judgement of any one individual. The superior epistemic value of collective reasoning is a theme found across a variety of disciplines, including economics (Hayek 1945) and science (Kitcher 1990)

Whilst Plato may have preferred an epistocracy, since the Enlighten-ment scholars have been illustrating democracy's epistemic power. Rous-seau thought that individuals stating their opinion on a matter by voting would elicit the general will of the people, a general opinion that would be superior to one's own (Rousseau 2012). Mill (1977: ch. II) argued that free expression in public debate allows us to exchange our errors for truth, while Dewey saw democracy as a way to share the rich store of accumulated wealth of human knowledge (Simon and Levine 1991).

These epistemic justifications of democracy have seen a resurgence in contemporary political theory in a range of accounts such as public reason (Rawls 2005), deliberative democracy (Habermas 1989; Goodin 2017), and procedural accounts (List and Goodin 2001; Estlund 2008). Despite their diversity in how they justify democratic legitimacy, epistemic accounts are united in their claim that democratic processes are better, on average at least, at tracking the truth on particular matters than any one individual is.

Plato's scepticism about democracy's epistemic value is justified, how-ever, when one considers the cognitive capacities and skills of its individual constituents. For over fifty years, political and social scientists have been documenting how poorly informed the voting behaviour of democratic citi-zens is (Converse 1964). News polls regularly show how widespread the public's lack of basic political knowledge and belief in untruths are. Two-thirds of American voters, for example, cannot correctly identify the three branches of government (Shenkman 2009: 4).

Yet even if citizens had the means and motivation to become adequately informed on all matters political, it is doubtful that they would even be capable of reasoning about policy rationally. Cognitive psychologists have documented an enormous range of biases and flaws in everyday human reasoning: the difference between how we should reason as rational beings, and how we actually reason. We accept things as true based not on their merits, but on how easy they are to believe or how good they make us feel (Frederick 2005). We form conclusions before we examine our premises (Tversky and Kahneman 1973). We make different decisions with the same information depending on the order in which it is presented (Hogarth and Einhorn 1992). We value avoiding losses far more than gaining the same amount (Tversky and Kahneman 1992). We seek out evidence likely to confirm our prior beliefs and avoid evidence likely to refute it (Nickerson 1998), and we believe things are true long after being shown they are false (Anderson, Lepper and Ross 1980).

Education and intelligence do not make us immune from reasoning irra-tionally about politics. When presented with empiric claims about cause and effect, increasing numeracy increases one's ability to reason correctly about scientific claims, but decreases one's ability to reason correctly about the same claims when presented as policy choices (Kahan et al. 2017). Our need to maintain congruence with our political identities trumps our desire to reason coherently about politics and these effects seem magnified by our reasoning skills.

Yet democratic decision processes, whether merely aggregative like voting, or transformative like deliberation, somehow manage to overcome these foibles of individual cognition and values to produce a collective epistemic virtue that is superior to that of any one individual. In a purely aggregative account of democracy such as Condorcet's Jury Theorem, voters need not interact beyond voting for majorities to deliver these superior epistemic outcomes. Condorcet's Jury Theorem is a mathematical proof that shows that as long as voters on average have a better than even chance of being correct on some issue, the likelihood of the majority vote being correct approaches certainty as the number of voters increases (Condorcet 1976).[1] To give the theorem some concrete context, if the average competence of the electorate is just 51 per cent (marginally better than a coin flip), then the majority vote of 101 voters has a 57 per cent chance of being correct, and that of 10,001 voters has a 99.99 per cent chance. Underpinning the superiority of collective over individual decision making in aggregative accounts like the Jury Theorem is the nature of randomness in our imperfect reasoning abilities. As we have seen, human cognition has many biases that lead to faulty and inconsistent reasoning. Yet if these random errors are normally distributed across large numbers of individuals, the errors will cancel each other out and an accurate approximation to the truth will be uncovered.

Transformative accounts like deliberative democracy take these epistemic claims further. Comprehensive and informed public discussion of political issues surfaces multiple points of view. Robust and substantive debate ensures that matters are decided on their merits. The public nature of the deliberation helps to identify flaws in one's own reasoning and position. While the requirements and epistemic claims of deliberative accounts may seem overly demanding or utopian to realist perspectives, the epistemic power of deliberative decision making has been demonstrated empirically in both experimental and field settings (Fishkin 1997; Luskin and Fishkin 1999; Neblo 2007). Yet this justification of democracy on epistemic grounds presupposes that the participants in this public discourse are seeking the truth, that they are voting and deliberating authentically, and not seeking to manipulate the outcome of the process for their own benefit. As history has shown, however, self-interest can lead to the subversion of democracy's truth-tracking capabilities for private ends.

Political manipulators corrupt democracy by employing demagoguery and sophistry. They do so by exploiting the psychological disconnect between what people do believe and what people should believe. Demagogues seek and maintain political power by exploiting prejudice and ignorance within the citizenry, and by portraying themselves as the only solution to society's real or imagined problems. Sophistry, on the other hand, uses argumentative and persuasive techniques to convince an audience of something even if it is inconsistent with the facts or the audience's own stated beliefs and commitments.

The Network and the Demos

The idea of democracy presupposes the notion of a demos – some determinate group of individuals who form a people. It is this people, and not some other, for whom democracy is the rule of, by and for. A stable democracy requires a shared identity and culture. Its people need to identify as one group if they are to hold sufficient solidarity necessary for collective rule. This shared identity need not be exclusive. An individual may identify with multiple overlapping peoples, but the individuals within a people must always identify as one.

A shared identity requires some means to share it. A demos requires some form of communication network for its culture, norms and political messages to be transmitted, understood and evaluated by its citizens. We define a political network, then, as the communication network between individuals who share some common political identity. The senders and receivers of political information – both explicit political messages as well as common norms and cultural information – are its citizens. The set of nodes and connections between them constitutes a given demos. The pattern of these connections is the network's topology which represents the political structure of the demos. In this light, democratic institutions can be conceptualised as mediated communication networks connecting private individuals (the citizens) with their collective identities (their citizenship). What demarcates one demos from another, then, is a function of the communication networks that connect the citizens of those demoi.

It is our contention that democratic societies require decentralised or peer-to-peer democratic topologies within their public spheres in order to realise the democratic demands of popular sovereignty and political equality. If citizens are to form a shared identity and engage in informed political discourse with each other, then they require a shared public forum in which to do so. Autocratic societies, by contrast, require only centralised topologies. They require only a means for the ruler to communicate with citizens and not for citizens to communicate with each other.

Yet these political topologies are themselves a function of the communicative medium. In the early democracies such as Athens, communication was limited to face-to-face discussion or parchment. The extent of political communication was limited by the range of one's voice or how far a letter could be carried. The scope of shared political identity was therefore limited to one's neighbours and the neighbour's neighbours.

In Athens, one could stand in the agora and shout to be heard by all (and so broadcast the message), or one could whisper to individuals in private (narrowcast the message). The scope for sophistry was greatest in private. When conversing with an individual, one could develop a rich understanding of their values, motivations, wants and needs. One could craft a message that was highly targeted to maximally exploit this understanding and exploit the other's cognitive biases for one's own ends.

When speaking to all in the agora, however, the scope for sophistry was more limited. The increased diversity of individual values made specific appeals to emotion and authority more difficult, as what might persuade some could dissuade others. Furthermore, because the agora was a forum of public debate, others were able to respond. Different perspectives could be offered and flaws in one's argument could be easily identified by others, while being called out as a sophist carried a reputational cost.

A technological trade-off that helped to keep democracy epistemically robust began to emerge. Because broadcasting in the agora was simplex, that only one thing could be said at any one time, political messages were most effective when they were targeted to appeal to the largest part of the demos.

Because the simplex nature of broadcast messages limits their ability to discriminate message content between audiences, there is additional incentive to engage in truthful public discourse if one's intent is to persuade. Without denying the role of ethos and pathos in rhetoric, logos is central to influencing public opinion. Truth, reason and logic are effective ways to shape policy in democratic settings and this served to provide democracy with a degree of epistemic robustness from those seeking to manipulate the truth.

As communication technology developed, so too did the scope of political rule and association. The invention of the printing press and rise of pamphlets and newspapers as modes of political communication allowed for political messages to reach larger geographical areas and audiences, increasing the possible scope of democratic association. Communication via print was no longer ephemeral like speech but persistent. Unlike face-to-face discussion, these new technologies were mediated by a publisher, giving them a degree of communicative privilege. Political identity was no longer an emergent property of a decentralised network. Print allowed political identity to be constructed (Somers 1994), and the shared identity necessary for larger demoi had arrived. Democracies began to emerge from revolution in France and the American colonies, and suffrage expanded in the United Kingdom.

Unlike communication by letter or parchment, pamphlets and newspapers were available to all (who could read). It was the public character of print media that helped to maintain democracy's epistemic robustness against sophistry by individuals seeking to subvert the truth-tracking characteristics of democratic procedures for their own gain. Attacks against the legitimacy of the political process, the media and political opponents are all tools through which demagogues can undermine democratic political networks and turn them into more autocratic ones (Levitsky and Ziblatt 2018: 23–4). Nonetheless, these attacks are visible to all if they are conveyed via broadcast messages. Political manipulation carries a reputational cost when publicly identified, and alert citizens of the demos can respond to these attacks and defend the democratic nature of their political network.

The emergence of privately operated printing presses also tempered somewhat the communicative privilege of publishers and print's more centralised topology. Private presses allowed a greater range of political messages to be produced and distributed, even if they were critical of the state (Benkler 2006: 186). Pamphlets served as public duplex communication, as individuals who disagreed could respond with political messages of their own in the same medium, much like the crowd of the agora yelling back. The cognitive diversity and value plurality so essential for democracy's epistemic virtue was maintained.

Yet print introduced a new characteristic that was previously absent from political discourse – anonymity. Printed messages allowed for the source of the message to be disguised, either by publishing them anonymously or by attributing them to a pseudonym. This anonymity could be used to enhance the truth-tracking features of public discourse or to undermine it. When we lack any means to judge an author's authority, we must rely instead on the content of their message. We are less likely to filter their message through some prior belief we have about them and their motivations.

While newspapers increased the reach of political messages, they also made political communication more unidirectional and simplex. While audience members could still respond in the same medium, it required finding a printer or newspaper willing to print their response. Duplex communication became a privilege as the costs of printing and distribution increased. The range and distribution of newspapers also began to change as industrialisation increased the economies of scale of newspaper printing (Benkler 2006: 187). Smaller, local newspapers found it more difficult to compete with cheaper, mass-produced newspapers with larger geographical audiences.

The developing asymmetry between active speakers and large, passive and geographically dispersed audiences was further intensified by the development of radio and television in the twentieth century. Mass media allowed messages to be broadcast across a geographical range unmatched by earlier technologies. It allowed governments to address their entire population instantly. These broadcast messages are accessible to all with the technology necessary to receive them. As a result, the message's audience is the entire population, rather than specific sections of it. The simplex communication of these mass-media networks from transmitters to passive receivers also makes them vulnerable to centralised control (Benkler 2006: 196). The operators of mass-media broadcast networks enjoy significant communicative privileges, as they decide what messages to transmit and whether they are presented favourably.

Yet the communicative privileges afforded to those who control mass-media comes at the cost of the ability of communicating directly to a specific group without the rest of the audience receiving the same message. Mass-media messages are expensive to produce, so speakers have strong motivations to make their messages acceptable to a broad audience. It becomes less cost-effective to tailor political messages towards a specific group within the broader audience. The accessibility of broadcast political messages imposes its own constraints on the kind of messages that are sent. Tailored messages that strongly resonate with specific groups may inspire greater resistance from other groups in the audience. Political speakers who utilise mass-media therefore must either accept that their message will only resonate with a specific group (and that their target audience is sufficiently large to overcome the political backlash from other groups), or present messages that are interpreted differently by different groups, so that the target group hears a message that resonates strongly with them without antagonising the broader audience (that is, 'dog-whistling') (Goodin and Saward 2005: 471).

The development of personal computers and the Internet created new possibilities for computer-mediated communication (CMC) between individuals, regardless of their geographical proximity. Unlike the passive reception of messages via mass-media, CMC is interactive (Ess 2004: 77). The arrival of the Internet was hailed as promising an 'electronic Agora', where all individuals could again have political discussions as equals (Rheingold 1994: 14).

Big Data and Democracy

The dream of access to a world of diverse perspectives and informed political discourse seems a long way from the experience of many Internet users
today. Yet the disconnect between the Internet's promise for democracy and
the reality of its threat to it is not the result of one thing but the confluence
of two – the rise of social networks and big data analytics.

The network dynamics of contemporary online social media are diverse,
so it will be useful to examine how these affect the epistemic virtue of
democracy. A social network is simply a form of computer-mediated communication designed to allow individuals to easily connect and interact
with others across the Internet, both publicly and privately. Individuals can
choose to follow accounts operated by individuals or groups that interest
them. This presents strengths and risks to democracy's epistemic claims to
truth-tracking. The freedom to follow other users in social media echoes
the early Internet's promise of decentralising political networks and reducing the communicative privilege of broadcasters. Diverse perspectives are
allowed to flourish and network connections based on social proximity or
shared interest help to identify relevant new sources of information.

However, the same factors also present new risks. Users of social media
networks also tend to associate with others who share the same interests
and characteristics, an effect called homophily (Tufekci 2017: 9). This can
lead to an 'echo chamber' where users find themselves interacting with others who share and reinforce their existing views, while also reducing the
visibility of other perspectives and evidence that contradicts their beliefs
(Vaidhyanathan 2018: 92).

Interactions in social media may be classified as open or closed. Open
interactions are public in that they are visible to other social network users.
Examples of open interactions are Twitter and Instagram posts as both the
followers of a particular account and other Twitter or Instagram users can
access a user's public posts from a URL. They are equivalent to broadcast
messages on mass-media or via traditional web pages in that they are accessible to all. Closed interactions are messages restricted to particular users,
such as those following a particular account.

One risk to the epistemic virtue of democracy is that closed social networks appropriate the public sphere and make it private. Once private and
shared only among similar individuals, political discourse loses some of
its epistemic robustness as ideas are no longer challenged by diverse perspectives. Errors in reasoning become more difficult to identify owing to
our biases that make objective evaluation of arguments congruent with our
beliefs difficult (Taber and Lodge 2006). Another risk is that the cost of

sophistry is reduced in private discourse. There is less chance that manipulative rhetorical techniques will be seen by those less sympathetic and who might be dissuaded by them.

Parallel to the rise of social networks was the rise of big data – the use of significant computation power to analyse large data sets to identify patterns that can be used to guide decision making (boyd and Crawford 2012: 663). By tracking an individual's behaviour across millions of separate interactions online, huge databases of user analytics can be generated. Online activity can be matched against an individual's offline behaviour from commercial datasets, purchasing history, cellular data and voter roles to aggregate hundreds or thousands of individual demographic, geographic and pyscho-graphic data points into a behavioural profile. Statistical techniques such as machine learning are then used to find correlations between user characteristics until a predictive model of individual personality is developed.[2] Importantly, big data analytics provides the holders of the data with high fidelity insight into the effectiveness of political communication. A/B testing of websites and advertising, the process of randomly assigning different versions of a webpage or advert to users and measuring click-through rates to evaluate relative performance, have been embraced by political parties. Where once the effect of a skilled orator's rhetoric had to be assessed by watching the reactions of the crowd, now web-based sophistry can be measured with statistical precision. And when sophistry becomes more effective, the truth-tracking propensity of democracy is placed at further risk.

It is the confluence of social media and big data analytics that now undermines the epistemic justifications of democracy. Social network operators use the interactions individuals have on their platform to refine the content presented to them in the future. This refinement tracks what content users interact with and displays more content similar to that in the future. The refinement is based on what individuals are likely to respond to, regardless of whether the content is accurate. The algorithms that determine what social media users see in the future are thus attention-tracking, rather than truth-tracking as we would desire from a credible news source.

The attention-tracking nature of social media is guided by the need to gain advertising revenue. Advertisers are motivated to target groups and individuals most likely to respond to their messages. The attention-tracking nature of social media is further illustrated by the emergence of hoax news sites that are concerned only with the amount of social media traffic they generate. While newspapers have long reported hoaxes to increase circulation (and hence advertising revenue),[3] such misinformation is broadcast so that sceptical audiences and other news sources can debunk it. However, if hoax news stories are agreeable to users' biases, they are likely to pass unchecked within groups that share similar views thanks to confirmation bias. Hoax news stories can therefore be narrowcast towards groups in the global audience that are likely to accept them.

This ability to tailor hoax stories to appeal to various groups without the stories being challenged by those outside the target audience risks undermining the democratic norm of mutual toleration (Levitsky and Ziblatt 2018: 102). By exaggerating or fabricating reports of the actions and beliefs of political opponents, those who receive news that reflects and builds upon their existing biases are less willing to see their opponents not just as rivals, but as malicious caricatures. This undermining of mutual toleration in turn damages the common identity of the demos as individuals within their separate echo chambers can no longer see each other as equals.

The capability of tailoring advertising to the interests of users also allows for tailored political messages to be directed towards those mostly likely to respond. Tailored advertising allows narrowcast political messages to be sent across communication networks of any size. This builds upon the duplex nature of communication via social media networks. Like a demagogue receptive to the verbal and non-verbal cues of face-to-face communication, those who send political messages across social media can quickly evaluate the effectiveness of their messages, and refine them accordingly. As the cost of sophistry has been reduced and its effectiveness improves, we are witnessing what has been dubbed computational propaganda – one of the most powerful new tools against democracy (Woolley and Howard 2017: 11).

These aspects of the combination of social media and big data analytics (the tendency towards homophily among users, the emergence of echo chambers, and the prominence of news items based on their ability to provoke responses) creates the new possibility for narrowcast political messages with a global reach. Narrowcast messages had previously been prohibitively difficult to transmit across communication networks with a considerable reach. The broadcast nature (and, hence, public visibility) of political messages to geographically dispersed audiences had served to constrain the type of claims that could be made without being held accountable for them. Open interactions on social media also maintain a degree of public accountability as they are broadcast messages. As such, political messages on social media that favour open interaction (such as Twitter) are perhaps less of a threat to the ability of citizens to understand each other, since they can see the same messages. It is the tailoring of messages to elicit responses from specific groups without the knowledge of the broader community that is troubling for the mutual toleration necessary for the demos to maintain a common identity, and for citizens to maintain the ability to fruitfully discuss political issues among themselves.

Conclusion

Democracy has surprising epistemic virtue when we consider the cognitive flaws of individuals who constitute the demos. Yet when we reason collectively in an environment that rewards truth-tracking, our social cognition is superior to that of any individual. The benefits of deliberation are at their strongest when diverse views are aired in public and we are given the opportunity to discuss issues with others. Even in the presence of sophists and demagogues who corrupt the truth for their own ends, the technological features of our communication networks, the trade-off between the reach of a message and the ability to discriminate its content within an audience, has historically provided democracy with a degree of epistemic robustness. Democracies have developed alongside communication technologies that allowed broadcast messages across large geographical areas and populations at the expense of limiting the speaker's ability to discriminate between different listeners.

While the Internet promised to reduce the communicative privilege of mass-media broadcasters and return the public sphere to a more decentralised and equal one, reality turned out differently. The confluence of social media and big data analytics has created new possibilities for political discourse which are global, multidirectional and highly targeted. Social media offers the perfect platform for political speakers to tailor their messages for separate audiences, rather than offer messages that must resonate with larger sections of the audience while also avoiding antagonising others. Citizens of the demos who receive political messages tailored to their interests, informed by news that reflects their biases, and reinforced by echo chambers filled with others of similar views, risk losing the mutual toleration of citizens with differing political views. This risks undermining the common identity necessary for a stable democracy to sustain itself. Only by recognising the risks these new technologies pose to how citizens are informed and may be influenced will the epistemic justifications for democratic societies continue to be compelling.

Notes

1. The Jury Theorem makes a number of assumptions about voter competence, voter independence and the objective correctness of some binary choice. Since Condorcet first published his theorem in 1785, many of these assumptions have

been generalised, strengthening the robustness of its claim to justify democracy on epistemic grounds (see Baker 1976; Owen, Grofman and Feld 1989; Berend and Paroush 1998; Kanazawa 1998; Fey 2003; and List and Goodin 2001).

2. Available at: https://www.youtube.com/watch?v=n8Dd5aVXLCc, last accessed 26 September 2019.

3. To give just one example, in 1835, the New York Sun printed reports of life on Mars (Wu 2017: 17–18).

References

Anderson, C. A., M. R. Lepper and L. Ross, 'Perseverance of Social Theories: the Role of Explanation in the Persistence of Discredited Information', *Journal of Personality and Social Psychology* 39(6) (1980): 1037.

Baker, K. M., *Condorcet: Selected Writings* (Indianapolis: Bobbs-Merrill, 1976).

Benkler, Y., *The Wealth of Networks* (New Haven, CT: Yale University Press, 2006).

Berend, D. and J. Paroush, 'When is Condorcet's Jury Theorem Valid?', *Social Choice and Welfare* 15(4) (1998): 481–8.

boyd, d. and K. Crawford, 'Critical Questions for Big Data: Provocations for a Cultural, Technological, and Scholarly Phenomenon', *Information, Communication & Society* 15(5) (2012): 662–79.

Condorcet, Marquis de, 'Essay on the Application of Mathematics to the Theory of Decision-Making', in Keith Michael Baker (ed.), *Condorcet: Selected Writings*, vol. 33 (Indianapolis: Bobbs-Merill, 1976).

Converse, P. E., 'The Nature of Belief Systems in Mass Publics', Critical Review 18(1/3) (1964): 1–74.

Ess, C., 'Computer-Mediated Communication and Human-Computer Interaction', in Luciano Floridi (ed.), *The Blackwell Guide to the Philosophy of Computing and Information* (Oxford: Blackwell, 2004), pp. 76–91.

Estlund, D. M., *Democratic Authority: a Philosophical Framework* (Princeton, NJ: Princeton University Press, 2008).

Fey, M., 'A Note on the Condorcet Jury Theorem with Supermajority Voting Rules', *Social Choice and Welfare* 20(1) (2003): 27–32.

Fishkin, J. S., *The Voice of the People: Public Opinion and Democracy* (New Haven, CT: Yale University Press, 1997).

Frederick, S., 'Cognitive Reflection and Decision Making', *Journal of Economic Perspectives* 19(4) (2005): 25–42.

Galton, F., 'Vox Populi (the Wisdom of Crowds)', *Nature* 75(7) (1907): 450–1.

Goodin, R. E., 'The Epistemic Benefits of Deliberative Democracy', *Policy Sciences* 50(3) (2017): 351–66.

Goodin, R. E. and M. Saward, 'Dog Whistles and Democratic Mandates', *Political Quarterly* 76(4) (2005): 471–6.

Habermas, J., *The Structural Transformation of the Public Sphere*, trans. Thomas Burger (London: Polity Press, 1989).

Hayek, F. A., 'The Use of Knowledge in Society', *American Economic Review* 35(4) (1945): 519–30.

Hogarth, R. M. and H. J. Einhorn, 'Order Effects in Belief Updating: the Belief-Adjustment Model', *Cognitive Psychology* 24(1) (1992): 1–55.

Kahan, D. M., E. Peters, E. Cantrell Dawson and P. Slovic, 'Motivated Numeracy and Enlightened Self-Government', *Behavioural Public Policy* 1(1) (2017): 54–86.

Kanazawa, S., 'A Brief Note on a Further Refinement of the Condorcet Jury Theorem for Heterogeneous Groups', *Mathematical Social Sciences* 35(1) (1998): 69–73.

Kitcher, P., 'The Division of Cognitive Labor', *Journal of Philosophy* 87(1) (1990): 5–22.

Levitsky, S. and D. Ziblatt, *How Democracies Die: What History Reveals about Our Future* (London: Viking, 2018).

List, C. and R. E. Goodin, 'Epistemic Democracy: Generalizing the Condorcet Jury Theorem', *Journal of Political Philosophy* 9(3) (2001): 277–306.

Luskin, R. C. and J. S. Fishkin, 'Bringing Deliberation to the Democratic Dialogue', *The Poll with a Human Face* (London: Routledge, 1999), pp. 13–48.

Mill, J. S., 'On Liberty', in *Essays on Politics and Society XVIII:213–310, The Collected Works of John Stuart Mill*, ed. J. M. Robson (Toronto: University of Toronto Press, 1977).

Neblo, M. A., 'Change for the Better? Linking the Mechanisms of Deliberative Opinion Change to Normative Theory', *Common Voices: the Problems and Promise of a Deliberative Democracy* (2007).

Nickerson, R. S., 'Confirmation Bias: a Ubiquitous Phenomenon in Many Guises', *Review of General Psychology* 2(2) (1998): 175.

Owen, G., B. Grofman and S. L. Feld, 'Proving a Distribution-Free Generalization of the Condorcet Jury Theorem', *Mathematical Social Sciences* 17(1) (1989): 1–16.

Plato, 'Sophist', in *Complete Works*, ed. J. M. Cooper and D. S. Hutchinson, trans. N. P. White (Indianapolis: Hackett, 1997), pp. 235–93.

Rawls, J., *Political Liberalism* (expanded) (New York: Columbia University Press, 2005).

Rheingold, H., The Virtual Community (London: Minerva, 1994).

Rousseau, J-J., 'Of the Social Contract', in Christopher Bertram (ed.) *Of the Social Contract and Other Political Writings*, trans. Quintin Hoare (London: Penguin, 2012), pp. 1–133.

Shenkman, R., Just How Stupid are We? Facing the Truth About the American Voter (New York: Basic Books, 2009).

Simon, H. F. and B. Levine, *The Collected Works of John Dewey, Index: 1882–1953. Vol. 18* (Carbondale, IL: SIU Press, 1991).

Somers, M. R., 'The Narrative Constitution of Identity: a Relational and Network Approach', *Theory and Society* 23(5) (1994): 605–49.

Taber, C. S. and M. Lodge, 'Motivated Skepticism in the Evaluation of Political Beliefs', *American Journal of Political Science* 50(3) (2006): 755–69.

Tufekci, Z., *Twitter and Tear Gas: the Power and Fragility of Networked Protest* (New Haven, CT: Yale University Press, 2017).

Tversky, A. and D. Kahneman, 'Availability: a Heuristic for Judging Frequency and Probability', *Cognitive Psychology* 5(2) (1973): 207–32.

Tversky, A. and D. Kahneman, 'Advances in Prospect Theory: Cumulative Representation of Uncertainty', *Journal of Risk and Uncertainty* 5(4) (1992): 297–323.

Vaidhyanathan, S., *Antisocial Media: How Facebook Disconnects Us and Undermines Democracy* (Oxford: Oxford University Press, 2018).

Woolley, S. C. and P. N. Howard, *Computational Propaganda Worldwide: Executive Summary* (Oxford: Oxford Internet Institute, University of Oxford, 2017).

Wu, T., *The Attention Merchants* (London: Atlantic Books, 2017).

Part Three

NINE

The Technics of a Gnostic World: an Ontogeny of Big Data

John MacWillie

In the physical world, parallel universes are being assembled out of digitally-encoded bits and bytes, part material, part immaterial, where we find signals and data being sourced from two billion personal computers, eight billion mobile devices, twenty billion non-mobile Internet-of-Things devices, and eighteen billion RFID tags. These devices account for the generation of trillions of bytes of data originating out of quotidian events, transactions, states, things, relations or combinations thereof (hyper-things) from financial, medical, administrative, transport, logistic, and personal and social media applications. But as enormous as this volume might be, it pales in comparison with yet more massive reservoirs of big data stored in hyperscale data centres (HDC), where years of such data is stored. While many are aware of the US National Security Agency's massive new data centre in Bluffdale, Utah, with its more than 1 million ft^2 of space for storing an estimated 5 Exabytes of data – a volume a hundred times greater than the contents of the Library of Congress – it has been dwarfed by China Telecom's Hohhot data centre in Inner Mongolia, which is ten times larger. It is in these HDC's that raw material is processed into information products for use by marketing executives and national intelligence analysts seeking to forensically discern our past and predict our future.

The market and political drivers behind this phenomenon derive from the promise and value of its access to as much data about target subjects that can be obtained, in as close to real-time as possible, and with sufficient detail to 'accurately' predict and affect a subject's behaviour – either for the purposes of seduction or interdiction. The owners and consumers of these colossal repositories have substantial resources to invest in these technologies, win a significant payoff if the solutions work, and suffer a significant cost if they do not.

Despite its market size and ubiquitous presence in our daily activities, we know very little about how big data works. What we do know is that big data is employed in many dimensions of our lives, often with disruptive consequences (Eubanks 2018; Ferguson 2017; Wachter-Boettcher 2017; O'Neil 2016; Schneier 2015). As a result, many critics argue that these products and the processes that underlie them are increasingly problematic for democratic societies. Concerned about the lack of prior consent by citizens whose behaviour is the source of these data, as well as enterprises offering little transparency into how these data are used, many critics conclude that the best remedial response is to give end-users greater control over the disposition of these data, as well as imposing more comprehensive government regulation.

Without disputing that these responses may be applicable under many circumstances, they are largely proposed in reaction to problems already exposed by the existence of big data in the first place. What about envisaging future challenges arising from the construction and use of big data based on what we already know? This chapter asserts that understanding the ontological modes and properties of big data will not only identify the trajectory of these issues but anticipate others as well. In this chapter I will:

- outline the principal ontological status of big data, as well as its modes and properties;
- focus on one property that is inherent to big data and has largely been ignored – complexity;
- expand my analysis by explaining how complexity arises from the instantiation of the technology stack utilised by nearly all big data projects; and
- conclude that among all these complexities, there should be a real concern about algorithms that mysteriously drive the extraction of value from the use of big data.

Big Data as an Ontological Thing

Ontology is the study of things, inclusive of all the things that comprise the world. Things may be large – the totality of the information system of the US Defense Department is a thing – and they may be very small – a capacitor is a thing even if it is also found in tandem with a resistor to create a high-pass signal filter, which is also a thing. In this sense, things are things in themselves and can be examined independently of whether they are part of some thing or something is a part of them. In other words, the kind of world we seek to examine is a flat ontology which comprises all the things in the world in which every thing is treated as equivalent. In the case of big data, we seek to understand it as an entity of its own kind.

An information industry analyst firm defines *big data* as 'high-volume, high-velocity and/or high-variety information assets that demand cost-effective, innovative forms of information processing that enable enhanced insight, decision making, and process automation' (Gartner 2018). Albeit an instrumental description, it is a starting point for grasping what constitutes big data.

Volume: In 1986, the world's storage capacity for data was 2.64 billion bytes (of which a mere 0.02 billion were digital). Sixteen years later, in what can best be described as a Gutenberg moment, the world began storing more digital than analogue data (Hilbert and Lopez 2011). Between 1986 and 2014, the compound annual growth rate (CAGR) for data storage increased by 31 per cent, while telecommunications capacity increased by 35 per cent (CAGR). Measured in terms of quantity of data storage capacity, this corresponds to an increase from 2.6 Exabytes to 4.6 Zettabytes (Hilbert 2015). These factors correspond to an estimate made a little over five years ago by IBM that the daily production of new data in the world was in the order of 2.5 quintillion bytes and that '90% of all the data in the world today has been created in the last two years' (Jacobson 2013).

Velocity: Big data exists because massive amounts of it can be moved around quickly. An early version of the Internet (late 1960s) transmitted data among computer nodes at a speed of 50 Kbits/second over copper telephone wires. In 1988, the first transoceanic fibre optic cable was deployed by AT&T, France Télécom and British Telecom (TAT-8) with a channel speed of 295 Mbits/second (Chafee 2012). By 2011, performance had increased to 273 Gbit/second (Hecht 2011). Today, 99 per cent of all global communications are carried by nearly 448 transoceanic fibre optic cables covering 720,000 miles (Starosielski 2015; Telegeography 2018). In the United States, there are 113,000 miles of long-haul fibre optic cable and another 3.5 million miles of short-distance fibre optic (Durairajan et al. 2015; Allen 2016). As a result, in 1992, there was a mere 100 GB of IP traffic per day. By 2016, the traffic had increased to 26.6 Tbits/second (Cisco 2017), and by 2021, that throughput is expected to double.

Variety: Amplifying the challenge of the high volume and velocity of data moving through systems is the extraordinary diversity in the types of data. Nearly 90 per cent of data moving across the Internet is unstructured, meaning that at any moment in time, the length and precise form of the contents of a data message are unpredictable. Examples of unstructured data include text data (word processing documents, email, SMS messages and tweets), multimedia (audio, video and graphic data), and mixed message types (social media posts, CAD/CAM designs and medical data images) such as the 500,000 comments, 293,000 status notifications and 136,000 photograph the 1.4 billion daily active users of Facebook post every minute (Noyes 2018).

What is absent from the industry definition of big data are two further, and I would argue, even more important properties: richness and complexity.

Richness: Because of the volume of data, the extraordinarily high transit rates and the unpredictable flow of data types, big data can be said to possess a property of richness. As every data element can be federated with any other data element, the permutation of these combinations generates whole new fields of semantic possibilities. This is an emergent property of big data.

Complexity: The property of complexity arises from this richness when large numbers of small parts of a whole interact with each other such that the behaviour of the whole is not predictable from the sum of its parts. In the case of big data, the virtual behaviour of data (signals, signs and markers) emerges from their manipulation and transformation into information. I refer to the assemblage that instantiates this process as the Big Data Technology Stack. Part of this Stack is visible – hardware, documentation, software schemas, data models and the presentation layer. An important part is not visible – particularly the algorithms employed to translate and analyse the data, automating the transformation of data into information. These algorithms computationally arrange relations, produce probabilistic interactions and generate effects, much of which is hidden not only from users, but from the technicians that construct the algorithms. It is this part of the Stack which I argue is a form of Gnostic knowledge which is not only hidden, but mysterious. The property of big data complexity, it turns out, is recursive and the starting point for analysis must begin with what is visible in the Big Data Technology Stack.

Complexity in Big Data

Complexity is the historical consequence of scaffolding pressures and opportunities. An ontology always has an ontogeny (the origin or development of a thing). To understand the property of complexity in big data, it is useful to understand the environment from which it arose.

Monolithic Machines

In the 1950s, the terminology and architecture of computers were adopted from the earlier industrial age. Computers were called computing machines, software was referred to as instructions, and a collection of data was known as files. Computer systems were complicated, but not complex. Housed in cavernous halls with their own life support systems, only the largest enterprises with the largest applications – accounting, reservations, insurance – owned these computers.

The strategic value of a computer is its ability to process data and its performance is measured in throughput and reliability. Data models are representations of the best way to store and retrieve data for a computer's given capabilities. As hardware costs and computer performance constraints drove data storage models, the earliest models were simple. Until the mid-1960s, computer data was primarily organised in flat files much like a card catalogue.

Data Models and Software

As the performance of computers began to improve, data architects began to reconsider how flat files might be reconstructed to achieve comparable increases in performance. In 1963, Charles Bachman invented a technology that enabled the integration of multiple data files into a single data management system while significantly improving performance. Corresponding to the success of these inventions was the emergence of a new class of data management professionals who organised themselves as the Data Actuating Technical Association – a crucial sign that the maturity of the technology was deemed worthy of an investment in building a career path (Yost 2017). Yet despite improved training, employee professionalisation, database architecture and faster computers, it was not long before users began demanding more intuitive and less time-demanding ways to access their data.

To meet these new requirements a series of preliminary innovations were required. First, databases are only valuable when the application software that utilises the data can be readily mapped to the business or technical problem at hand. Early methods of access were accomplished using low-level languages that were neither intuitive nor easy to use. With this objective in mind, the first successful high-level language, FORTRAN, was introduced in 1957. In short order, other such languages were created including LISP (1958), ALGOL (1958) and COBOL (1959). With these tools, programmers could build a layer of abstraction between machine logic and application problems. This was the first step in freeing data from the strictures of the machine.

The second significant achievement in this progression towards data independence entailed overcoming the slow mechanisms used for data storage and retrieval, including key punch cards and magnetic tape drives which stored and retrieved data serially. To overcome this limitation required randomly retrieving data independent of the order in which it was originally stored. IBM, in 1963, introduced an external hard disk drive with random access to 117 MB of data offering a dramatic improvement in performance.

The third innovation in the early 1960s was to modularise the hardware components of computers so that a firm only needed to acquire the components required to meet its specific business requirements. Not only would such a strategy bring the average price of a computer down, but it would make it possible for more enterprises to invest in computer systems. In 1964, the IBM 360 mainframe computer was introduced with just such modularity, creating an entire family of computers built upon common interfaces, giving enterprises the ability to scale computing power and cost to near-term business requirements.

Just as expanding a freeway to eliminate congestion often only encourages its use by more commuters leading to more congestion, so is the case with the history of database technology. The technical capacities these new technologies afforded enterprises only burdened the usability of existing databases. Responding to these challenges, in 1970, IBM engineer E. F. Codd proposed a new data model referred to as relational (RDBMS). It was based on a very simple first-order (predicate) logic and set theory. This approach to data modelling greatly eased the logic for accessing data. Shortly thereafter, two engineers at IBM Watson Lab developed a declarative language (SQL) for use with an RDBMS. No longer would programmers be required to write arcane code to access data. Now, in a somewhat intuitive way, users could simply type SELECT NAME, ADDRESS, LAST_ORDER FROM ACCOUNTS WHERE LAST_ORDER > 5000 to get a list of their most important customers. Data were in the process of being untethered from machines, computer centres and programmers.

Networks

With scalable computers, random access to data, a logical database model and a user-friendly data access language, the only remaining bond for data was geography. In the 1950s and 1960s, computers were connected to each other through point-to-point connections via telephone lines. The interface between computers was a modem that modulated and demodulated analogue and digital signals over telephone lines. To make these connections work, computers required protocols for how signals were to be transmitted and received, how errors were to be detected and corrected, and how blocks of signals were to be converted into data. Unfortunately, every computer manufacturer had its own proprietary set of protocols. This meant that computers and their attendant data tended to operate as islands, isolated from the processes and requirements of other business units located around the world.

Given its prominent role in producing computing solutions, IBM set out to solve these 'islands of Babel' with its 1974 introduction of Systems Network Architecture (SNA). This established a set of standards among IBM computers permitting remote terminals to access IBM computers, enabling computer-to-computer communication, and the development of end-user applications in which SNA capabilities were accessible via a common application interface. Data and users were further uncoupled from the underlying hardware wherever it may be located. While this product strategy was designed to consolidate IBM's dominant position in the marketplace, it inspired another vision by those working outside IBM of an entirely different model, decentred not only from the computer but from any proprietary constraints.

Miniaturisation, Modules and Distribution

While major improvements in database technology were being achieved, there was a similar revolution in hardware. Although the properties of semiconducting materials were first observed by Michael Faraday in 1833, it was more than 100 years before the development of the transistor at Bell Labs demonstrated the value of this property in the emerging field of electronics. Fairchild Semiconductors began mass production of miniaturised transistors in 1958, the same year that Jack Kilby produced a solid-state circuit using semiconductors. Using semiconductors to replace vacuum tubes reduced heat and electricity costs, significantly improved reliability, and, with improvements in manufacturing, allowed semiconductor circuits to become smaller and smaller. In 1971, Intel offered the first integrated computer on a semiconductor chip.

Personal Computing

Although IBM and other mainframe manufacturers extensively utilised integrated circuits, the rapidly falling cost of computer chips made them readily accessible to hobbyists. In 1975, the first microcomputer (MITS Altair 8800) was productised. A year later, Steve Jobs and Steve

Wozniak demonstrated their Apple I personal computer. While personal computers would morph into diverse forms (laptops, servers, workstations and, eventually, smart phones), the crucial thread for this story is that integrated circuits and the commercial success of personal computers drove down hardware costs and turned computer hardware into a commodity business. For the first time, software, including database systems, was now becoming increasingly more expensive than the hardware on which it ran. Over the following three decades, this cost inversion further commoditised hardware, altering the future architecture of data management.

The Internet

During this same period, research and development budgets for military technology were rapidly expanding. There were increased demands by Congress and the Pentagon for ways to improve technical collaboration on complex projects. In 1957, the US Defense Department created the Advanced Research Projects Agency (ARPA) to facilitate and accelerate innovation among universities, private laboratories and military research agencies. One of the most impactful innovations to emerge from ARPA was a proposal for a multi-node, interconnected computer network. This proposal saw fruition in 1969 in a network connecting four institutions on the west coast of the US. By 1975, fifty-seven connections had been established, and what was known as ARPANET would shortly evolve into the Internet.

Of the many inventions that lie behind the success of the Internet, two stand out as crucial. First, maintaining high reliability and performance meant that data had to move across the network without encountering queuing delays, congestion or connection failures. This problem was solved by breaking network messages into discrete packets and sending each on the fastest known routes without concern for whether all the packets took the same route. At the other end, packets would be reassembled into the intended message. This is known as packet switching.

The second challenge arose from connecting heterogeneous proprietary computers, operating systems and applications together seamlessly. This challenge was overcome by the development of a common interface, or protocol, comprised of layers of code that separately addressed the differences in hardware, software, type of network connection and application. Today, this protocol is known as TCP/IP and its ubiquitous adoption enabled transparent connectivity among tens of billions of data devices (Hafner and Lyon 1996).

Commodity hardware and transparent connectivity scaffolded another important discovery on the way to big data. In the early-1980s, two researchers observed that as computing problems became more complicated and data sets grew exponentially larger, traditional central processing architectures limited processing scalability. A proposed alternative employed a 'parallel, distributed' architecture in which hundreds or thousands of inexpensive, off-the-shelf processing nodes are connected to distribute capacity and demand. This architecture, they proposed, would prove to be more effective at solving 'really hard' computing problems, such as pattern recognition, at lower cost (Rumelhart and McClelland 1986). This architecture was endorsed by Sun Microsystems who promoted it with the tagline 'the network is the computer'.

On the Horizon of Big Data

The commoditisation of computer hardware focused attention on the relative importance of the second component of information systems: software and applications. Until the late 1970s, software was intimately bound to the hardware and operating system on which it ran. This meant that hardware, software and data were all hosted on a monolithic architecture, requiring proprietary and expensive applications. As hardware costs began to fall, it became increasingly obvious that application costs were not going to correspondingly fall unless the relationship between software and hardware was severed. Thus was born the vision of an operating system that ran on many vendors' systems. As a result, applications developed for the operating system Unix could be independent of proprietary systems – write once, run everywhere.

Client–Server Architecture

A corresponding initiative was undertaken for databases in which increasing amounts of application logic were embedded not in application software, but in databases with stored procedures. These developments resulted in a new information architecture called client–server in which personal computers hosted the presentation logic of an application, while much of the application and data access logic resided on an application server and the data itself on a data server. This division of capabilities was the beginning of the modularisation of applications. Just as hardware had begun to be modularised with the IBM 360, the client–server architecture contributed to breaking down software applications into software partitioned closer to where it could be utilised more efficiently.

World Wide Web

The creation of the World Wide Web (WWW) by Tim Berners Lee in 1989 significantly accelerated the trend begun with client–server architecture. In this next generation, the presentation of applications was managed by a browser at the end-user device; application servers became routing devices translating requests into network addresses; and data servers contained documents marked-up with hyper-text to control navigational flow. Perhaps most crucially, the architecture, much of its infrastructure and the protocols for using the WWW were designated open source and freed from any proprietary claims.

Search Engines

The most significant impact of the WWW is the democratisation of data sources in which every user becomes not only a consumer, but a producer of data as well. Between 1993 and 2007, the compounded annual growth rate in the total number of users of the Web increased by 59 per cent, while total data storage per capita increased by 21 per cent (CAGR). While access to many kinds of data became easier, the corresponding proliferation made searching for specific types of data increasingly difficult. In response, engineers at Digital Equipment Corporation invented AltaVista, a search engine that trawled the WWW identifying web sites, downloading documents from those sites and indexing the results.

Search engines are databases with a specific objective: find data as quickly as possible, prioritise the results into a meaningful order and present it to the user. Databases underlying search engines are unique in several ways. First, the kinds of data found in search engines are not like the data in traditional databases. Data in transactional databases are constantly updated or deleted, which requires that the integrity of data from multiple simultaneous alterations be preserved. By contrast, search engines are employed in applications in which data are rarely updated – new data are simply appended to older data. For search engines, the paramount criterion is speed of data retrieval. Secondly, search engine data are invariably being added at extraordinary rates and volumes. Thus, data storage needs to contract and expand, as well as be partitioned, dynamically. There is no time for the overhead management of traditional databases. This has led to an entire new layer in the Big Data Technology Stack which dynamically allocates storage and computing resources in order to minimise the response to real-time demand. Thirdly, while the data for transactional databases are usually input and managed by the same enterprise that owns the database, the sources for big data systems often come from repositories outside the big data enterprise which must integrate the heterogeneous sources into common formats, as well as normalising and scaling the data for consistency. This requirement incorporates yet another set of functionalities to the Stack referred to as 'Extract, Transform, and Load' (ETL) that is found in nearly all big data environments.

User Presentation

Electrons moving around silicon paths may correspond to logical representations, but they have little value as symbolic representations, the form most useful for human cognition. One of the earliest transformations of electronic representation into human-readable content entailed the application of vector graphics for the US Air Force's SAGE air defence system in the 1950s. In 1962, Douglas Engelbart proposed a research programme for 'augmenting human intellect' which integrated 'artefacts . . . for the manipulation of things or materials [and symbols]', 'language [given] the way in which the individual parcels out the picture of his world into the concepts that his mind uses to model that world', 'methodology . . . which an individual organizes his goal-centred (problem solving) activity', and training to realise the value of this augmentation (Engelbart 1962).

Engelbart's research programme is at the heart of continuing research into man–machine interfaces in which the boundaries between the two become less and less clear. The extraction of value from big data is entangled in the perceptions and manipulations of those data by the users of the data. One of the most advanced big data analytic applications in use today is Palantir Corporation's Gotham deployed in every major intelligence and defence agency in the US and the UK. As one senior executive put it, the goal for Palantir in meeting the future requirements of enterprises such as the National Security Agency is to identify 'how human beings would talk with data' (Greenberg 2013).

The Gnostic Condition of Big Data

The early data management systems of the 1950s were complicated and visibly clunky. The Big Data Technology Stack of today is complex and barely transparent. Many critics are quick to point out that what remains the most obscure, what may be said to constitute the Gnostic side of big data, are the algorithms that drive the initial transformation of data as well as the analytic and presentation layers of the Big Data Technology Stack. As complicated as the hardware, software and interconnectivity that underlie the possibilities of big data are, it is the algorithms that are the most problematic.

First, most algorithms are intentionally and prescriptively Gnostic. Algorithms developed by commercial enterprises are often deemed to be proprietary and protected by copyrights to ensure competitive advantages. Algorithms used in national security applications are usually deemed as classified and their status is embargoed by access controls and penalties for unauthorised disclosure. These prophylactics assure the owners of algorithms that, at least in the eyes of the law, the gaze of outsiders is restricted.

Secondly, algorithms are embedded in software that is often difficult to interpret. In the late 1950s and early 1960s, the development objective of most programming languages was to improve clarity and readability by requiring the use of procedural flows through discrete and structured blocks of related programmatic functionality. Unfortunately, these procedural languages often necessitated the production of redundant program code due to small but discrete differences in functionality. For this reason, a variety of object-oriented programming paradigms have been developed which allow functional details to be encapsulated (that is, hidden from a developer), provide a mechanism for the reuse of code through class inheritance and indexical redirection, and to require the instantiation of these classes through objects. This approach allows software to be used more like an appliance such as a toaster, where the details of how a machine operates are irrelevant to the operator. At the same time, this abstraction and encapsulation further obfuscates an accounting of precisely what effect algorithms have on the behaviour of data.

Thirdly, the latest developments in algorithmic computationalism have injected a fundamental philosophical shift in how we conceptualise the relationship between software applications and the data upon which they presumably work. Procedural and many object-oriented languages employ an imperative paradigm in which procedural rules are deductively applied (if . . . then . . . else) to manipulate the state of a program. More recently, the development of machine-learning systems, though they are developed using the same procedural languages, operate quite differently in that the logical mechanisms are inferential, relying not on rules, but on statistical patterns. Here the logic of the algorithm adapts not to the state of the software program, but to the fuzzy relations among the elements of the data. Depending on training and supervision, where outcomes can vary, accountability is reduced to heuristics.

Fourthly, the consequences and, thus the functionality of algorithms, are often inexplicable. Some engineers are quick to observe that they do not understand how some algorithms work in big data applications. In

2016, a senior engineer admitted that Google does not know why Google's ranking algorithm does what it does (Cimpanu 2016). In that same year, Microsoft unleashed Tay, an AI-based bot designed to learn from and engage with users of Twitter. It was not long before Tay adopted a racist, misogynistic vocabulary and had to be taken offline. Google's image classification technology has persistently misidentified African Americans as gorillas. Even after three years of working on the algorithm, Google engineers admit that they still do not understand why. To 'fix' the problem, Google simply prohibited the system from identifying gorillas (Vincent 2018). The evidence suggests that AI engineers are increasingly blaming the data being used for training algorithms as the primary culprit for these unintended consequences rather than algorithms or the developers themselves (Korolov 2018). There is, however, another possibility that lurks in these examples, namely, that the prejudices of the data redefine the processes of the algorithms.

In the case of machine learning, it is the task of the human analyst to select a model, set the initial conditions, construct the training set for the learning process, and await the results. How the machine computes the results is only known theoretically and rarely specified. As one critic puts it:

> These algorithms produce the process, the mediation, the gap-spanning implementation that unites their engineers' problems and solutions. And since they do this through the million-fold iteration of simulated neural networks, the computational constructs they spit out tend to be both effective and inscrutable. (Finn 2017: 183)

Returning my attention to Palantir's Gotham product, the mystery of this process is best captured by its own promotional literature. It all begins 'with data from multiple sources', which 'fuses the data into a human centric model', 'tag[s], secure[s], and track[s] all the data', and brings 'the data to life for human-driven analysis' (Palantir 2019). To achieve this resurrection, Gotham flattens the content of data giving users the tools to reconstruct entirely new semantic contexts. The real complexity of this organisation of data does not become apparent until the information constructed from the data is organised and presented as knowledge. This 'dysanalytic' process becomes even more distracting with its eye candy-like presentation features that turn information into either aestheticisms of meaning or simulated relationships of real-space. The aesthetics of representation (already three or four layers removed from the raw data) blind the analyst to their own prejudices about how the world works. These are, I argue, metaphors for the illusion of knowledge which lead to a presumption of understanding, known in military-intelligence jargon as actionable intelligence. It is this circle of reasoning that transforms 'raw' data into information, creating the possibilities of knowing the unknown, justifying a claim to real 'understanding' and the warrant to act.

What Palantir does not mention is that the organisation of the data (represented as entities, events and flows) is exclusively proprietary. That, as the New York City Police Department (NYPD) discovered in 2017, is not just a problem for outsiders seeking to understand Gotham, but is problematic even for Palantir's customers. The NYPD chose to stop using Palantir and move to an IBM product. When the NYPD asked Palantir for the output of analytic work done to date as well as a translation key to map this output to a new platform, Palantir replied that fulfilling this request would reveal trade secrets and it would not comply (Alden 2017). Thus, the contradiction between data being brought to life and not having access to knowing how that life comes to be in the first place underscores just how problematic the role of the algorithm is in public discourse.

Conclusion

This chapter asserts that big data constitutes a new kind of thing which can be examined ontologically. It is an assemblage of other things comprising what I refer to as a Big Data Technology Stack. Each of the components is revealed to be in a constant state of progressive alteration. Thus, ontologically big data should not be conceived of as a stable entity, but rather as constituting unstable configurations including hardware upgrades, software updates, continuous streams of new data, and an ever-changing augmentation of human capabilities. More importantly, what runs through the fabric of big data is a contiguous network of software code which, in turn, are the material expression of algorithms. I argue that far too many of these algorithms are largely opaque to public inspection and accountability, and that their obscuration corresponds to a mysterious and inaccessible representation of the world. The principal concern is that algorithms lacking transparency define and bind the parameters of what might constitute an interpretation not only of the data, but of the processes by which the data are conceptualised. There is an apprehension that many of these algorithms are nothing more than a prosthetic substitution for reason undermining the authority of public discourse. As such, big data is a metaphorical iceberg – partly visible and partly hidden – and whether it poses a risk to the good ship Titanic largely depends on how naive we are about its future course and the viability of our social institutions.

References

Alden, W., 'There's a Fight Brewing Between the NYPD and Silicon Valley's Palantir', *BuzzfeedNews*, 2017, available at: https://www.buzzfeed.com/williamalden/theres-a-fight-brewing-between-the-nypd-and-silicon-valley?utm_term=.cfxPrDmO#.klog875b, last accessed 25 September 2019.

Allen, T. B., 'The Future is Calling', *National Geographic* 20(6) (2001): 80, republished 2016.

Chafee, C. D., *The Rewiring of America: the Fiber Optics Revolution* (Orlando, FL: Academic Press, 2012).

Cimpanu, C., 'Google's Search AI is like Skynet, Engineers Don't Understand What It's Doing', *Softpedia News*, 2016, available at: https://news.softpedia.com/news/google-s-search-ai-is-like-skynet-engineers-don-t-understand-what-s-it-doing-501504.shtml, last accessed 28 December 2018.

Cisco, *The Zettabyte Era: Trends and Analysis*, 2017, available at: https://www.cisco.com/c/en/us/solutions/collateral/service-provider/visual-networking-index-vni/vni-hyperconnectivity-wp.html#_Toc484556821, last accessed 5 March 2018.

Durairajan, R., P. Barford, J. Summers and W. Willinger, 'InterTubes: A Study of the US Long-haul Fiber-optic Infrastructure', *Proceedings of SIGCOMM 2015* (London: ACM, 2015), available at: http://pages.cs.wisc.edu/~pb/tubes_final.pdf, last accessed 20 April 2018.

Engelbart, D., *Augmenting Human Intellect: a Conceptual Framework*, 1962, available at: http://dougengelbart.org/content/view/138, last accessed 17 June 2018.

Eubanks, V., *Automating Inequality: How High-Tech Tools Profile, Police, and Punish the Poor* (New York: St. Martin's Press, 2018).

Ferguson, A., *The Rise of Big Data Policing: Surveillance, Race, and the Future of Law Enforcement* (New York: New York University Press, 2017).

Finn, E., *What Algorithms Want: Imagination in the Age of Computing* (Cambridge, MA: MIT Press, 2017).

Gartner, 'Gartner IT Glossary > Big Data', *Gartner.com*, 2018, available at: https://www.gartner.com/it-glossary/big-data, last accessed 10 March 2018.

Greenberg, A., 'Agent of Intelligence: How a Deviant Philosopher Built Palintir, a CIA-funded Juggernaut', *Forbes*, 2013, available at: https://www.forbes.com/sites/andygreenberg/2013/08/14/agent-of-intelligence-how-a-deviant-philosopher-built-palantir-a-cia-funded-data-mining-juggernaut/2/#24b4eb6bab0f, last accessed 10 February 2018.

Hafner, K. and M. Lyon, *Where Wizards Stay Up Late* (New York: Simon & Schuster, 1996).

Hecht, J., 'Ultrafast Fibre Optics Set New Speed Record', *New Scientist*, 19 April 2011, available at: https://www.newscientist.com/article/mg21028095.500-ultrafast-fibre-optics-set-new-speed-record, last accessed 5 March 2018.

Hilbert, M., 'Quantifying the Data Deluge and the Data Drought', 2015, available at: https://papers.ssrn.com/sol3/papers.cfm?abstract_id=2984851, last accessed 4 March 2018.

Hilbert, M. and P. Lopez, 'The World's Technological Capacity to Store, Communicate, and Compute Information', *Science* 332 (2011): 60–5.

Jacobson, R., 'Industry Insights: 2.5 Quintillion Bytes of Data Created Everyday. How Does CPG and Retail Manage It', *IBM Consumer Product Industry Blog*, 24 April 2013, available at: https://www.ibm.com/blogs/insights-on-business/consumer-products/2-5-quintillion-bytes-of-data-created-every-day-how-does-cpg-retail-manage-it, last accessed 4 March 2018.

Korolov, M., 'AI's Biggest Risk Factor: AI Gone Wrong', *CIO*, 13 February 2018, available at: https://www.cio.com/article/3254693/ais-biggest-risk-factor-data-gone-wrong.html, last accessed 20 February 2018.

Noyes, D., 'The Top 20 Valuable Facebook Statistics – Updated February 2018', *Zephoria*, 2018, available at: https://zephoria.com/top-15-valuable-facebook-statistics, last accessed 4 March 2018.

O'Neil, C., *Weapons of Math Destruction: How Big Data Increases Inequality and Threatens Democracy* (New York: Crown, 2016).

Palantir, 2019, available at: https://www.palantir.com/palantir-gotham, last accessed 23 May 2019.

Rumelhart, D. and J. McClelland, *Parallel Distributed Computing*, 2 vols (Cambridge, MA: MIT Press, 1986).

Schneier, B., *Data and Goliath: the Hidden Battles to Collect your Data and Control Your World* (New York: W. W. Norton, 2015).

Starosielski, N., *The Undersea Network* (Durham, NC: Duke University Press, 2015).

Telegeography, *FAQ*, 2018, available at: https://www2.telegeography.com/submarine-cable-faqs-frequently-asked-questions, last accessed 7 May 2018.

Vincent, J., 'Google Fixed Its racist Algorithm by Removing Gorillas from Its Image-labelling Tech', *The Verge*, 12 January 2018, available at: https://www.theverge.com/2018/1/12/16882408/google-racist-gorillas-photo-recognition-algorithm-ai, last accessed 7 February 2019.

Wachter-Boettcher, S., *Technically Wrong: Sexist Apps, Biased Algorithms, and other Threats of Toxic Tech* (New York: W. W. Norton, 2017).

Yost, J., *Making IT Work: a History of the Computer Services Industry* (Cambridge, MA: MIT Press, 2017).

TEN

Trust and Algorithmic Opacity

Steve McKinlay

'I want to see you not through the machine,' said Kuno,
'I want to speak to you not through the wearisome machine.'

E. M. Forster (1909)

Introduction

For well over a century, scholars have forwarded cautionary tales of a dystopian age where supposedly super-intelligent machines control all aspects of our lives. E. M. Forster in his 1909 novella *The Machine Stops* imagines a post-apocalyptic world where people so reliant upon a machine for their existence begin to worship it as a living, moral agent in its own right. In the tension between technology and rationality the inhabitants of Forster's fictional world lose all connection with nature and, consequently, their morality, trusting the machine more than they do each other. In many senses Forster's machine-mediated horror story has become something of a reality. One reading of Forster might suggest that the effects of technology do more than just simplify or make our lives more convenient, but that the technology utterly infiltrates our worldview rather than merely augmenting it. For the inhabitants of Forster's world, the machine is self-validating, authoritative, in a sense omniscient, exhibiting an unnerving undercurrent of malevolence.

While the emerging reality today is not fully comparable to Forster's imagined world, many parallels can be drawn. We are increasingly witnessing the use of complex, artificially intelligent computer algorithms in decision-making processes across a wide variety of socio-technical environments. Such contexts include industry, universities, governmental agencies, law enforcement, non-profit sectors, insurance companies, medical providers, employers, amongst many others. Such systems are used to influence decision making in areas ranging from pre-trial risk assessment to sentencing and probation.

The use of these algorithms is globally widespread and contextually varied. Concerns about the proliferation of such specialised software are relatively new and have primarily been discussed from ethical perspectives. Recent and popular focus by mainstream media as well as academia has been situated around privacy issues. While privacy issues are important and deserve analysis, I argue here that there are other issues at stake. Further, I contend that these issues may have much deeper implications for individual autonomy within free democratic states. How do we guarantee that authorities tasked with making decisions that impact our daily lives ensure those decisions are transparent and equitable? It is unlikely that the normative and epistemic values built into such systems will be acceptable to everyone. Differences of moral opinion regarding how decisions in social housing, insurance, welfare and policing, for example, can result in fraught emotional debate at the best of times. To complicate matters further, many of the individuals affected by such decisions live at the fringes of society and, as such, issues related to social and distributive justice can be compounding. In many cases agreement regarding algorithmic decisions between those tasked with implementing the decision and the decision-subject will not be found. The question then arises, who should prevail in order that the ethical principles of universality and impartiality are upheld?

Some contend that these questions can be answered only with a detailed understanding of the internal process by which such algorithms operate. For the most part, however, for many, often including software developers themselves, just how machine-learning algorithms work is unclear or opaque. Opacity is most evident at the algorithmic level. While the output of such systems, usually in the form of a classification or statistical weighting, is readily understandable with regard to the question the algorithm is trying to answer, just how and why a particular output was produced from the input parameters is much harder to grasp. The question arises, is there anything we can know about why a decision was arrived at by a machine-learning algorithm. That is, does algorithmic opacity necessarily entail epistemic opacity? While the inner workings of an algorithm may be opaque to its users, it might not follow that some form of epistemic access to the underlying model exists. If this is the case, what might that tell us about decisions made by such algorithms, and will this be sufficient for acceptable levels of trust to obtain between users of such systems and the

decision-subjects impacted by those decisions? How are such systems altering our conception of trust? Is it possible to formulate a conception of trust
that might be applied to automated decision-making processes? Finally,
what implications do the proliferation of such intelligent systems have for
freedom, autonomy and ultimately democracy? This chapter will consider
these questions, and while it stops short of offering any kind of specific
policy advice, I examine several conceptions of trust that take into account
issues of automation, accountability and opacity, characteristics of twenty-
first-century machine learning algorithmic decision-making systems.

Bias and Opacity

The legal profession and regulatory bodies have been important guardians
of equity and fairness in the service of protecting basic rights such as liberty,
freedom and individual autonomy. The increasing practice of combining
large disparate sets of data in conjunction with deep-learning algorithms,
however, is typically unregulated and free from governing restrictions. The
use of these systems by private organisations and government agencies
are often justified in utilitarian terms. For example, if we can successfully
identify and prevent a significant percentage of offenders from reoffending
(in the case of predictive policing), or if we can identify a child at risk of
abuse, then some bias and the presence of false negatives in the system seem
to be tolerated. The individuals and families represented in the data sets of
such examples are usually those that have accessed welfare systems, or had
interactions with law enforcement, family law and other social services. The
over-representation of such groups within these systems tends to build bias
into the software, thus feeding back into future outputs and predictions.
To make matters worse, the moral imperative of the agencies and users of
these algorithms frequently focuses on active enforcement based upon the
predictions made. This tends to be at the expense of any concern for marginalised or minority groups that are regularly over-represented within such
data sets. To date there is little evidence of any fiduciary duty impinging on
developers or the employers of such systems upon their data-subjects as
there might be in other professions such as doctor–patient or lawyer–client
relationships.

From an ethical perspective the risk of not acting upon information that
suggests an individual might be predisposed to commit a heinous criminal
act, or that a child may be at risk of abuse needs to be carefully weighed
against concerns regarding the reliability of the output. It is also acknowledged that harms can also come from exclusively human-made decisions
as from algorithmically influenced ones. Sometimes those harms are

manifestly justifiable, such as keeping a criminal locked up, or removing a child from an abusive environment. The ethically interesting cases are those where black-box algorithms have been shown to produce errors (Price 2017) or bias (Zarsky 2016). Algorithms are only as good as the science they are based upon and potentially inherit the same value-laden biases of their human developers (Brey and Soraker 2009). Nissenbaum (2001) argued that machine-learning algorithms embody the values and norms of the developers, thereby potentially reproducing bias. Furthermore, algorithms trained on data that already exhibit bias or inequality in terms of race, gender or other attributes are likely to simply duplicate that inequality in their output. The input attributes and training methods are designed and configured by software developers with specific desired outcomes in mind and this has been shown on many occasions to privilege some outcomes over others (O'Neil 2016).

There are a number of important philosophical and ethical issues that arise with regard to the use of artificially intelligent learning algorithms and data within such contexts. Many of these issues are due to a lack of transparency in black-box algorithms, what many have called algorithmic opacity. What does this really mean? Burrell (2016) describes three forms of algorithmic opacity. The first is the deliberate attempt to hide the internal workings of an algorithm by the organisations or government agencies developing and utilising them. The second is 'technical illiteracy', simply being unable to understand the workings of an algorithm due to being insufficiently skilled in the technical domain. The third, and the one I shall focus on, is the inability to comprehend in any meaningful way the inner workings of an algorithm that has been developed using machine-learning techniques. Thus, while an interpretable model may be produced as a design mechanism by which the algorithm is developed, by the time the algorithm is trained to produce acceptable results its internal processes are largely uninterpretable. It is this form of opacity that I argue entails not only algorithmic but epistemic opacity.

While Burrell's first two forms of opacity represent algorithmic opacity the third entails something stronger. However, I argue that this form of opacity is still at least theoretically explainable. Burrell describes the third form of opacity in terms of algorithms that are largely or wholly uninterpretable not by virtue of the processes they either operate under or were developed by, but with regard to the volumes of data they are designed to analyse. This form is not only a function of the complexity of the algorithm itself, but the vast volume and dimensionality[1] of the data set in question. While exceedingly complex, it seems, at least theoretically, that algorithms in this category could still be explained in some conceptual way. There are, I argue, some factors, not addressed by Burrell, that potentially increase the complexity and opaqueness of machine-learning algorithms.

Artificially intelligent machine-learning algorithms are often developed as layered neural networks. Such systems have multiple layers of weighted nodes. The initial layers accept input parameters that correspond to an existing data set. These parameters would normally be readily understandable, they could be attributes of administrative or demographic data related to individuals within the context in which the algorithm is employed. Internal layers, however, are hidden. As the system is trained to produce desired outputs, nodes programmed to accept input within these internal hidden layers alter their weightings without human intervention. The internal decision logic of such algorithms thus is altered in subtle ways as the algorithm trains on historical data. As a result, it is virtually impossible, not only for an ordinary person but also for the developers of such systems, to explain precisely why a learning algorithm came to a particular outcome or decision. All we can often say is that the output is in some way correlated to previous similar cases in the historical data set to a level of accuracy similar to that of a human decision. The opacity in such cases is an inescapable side-effect of the development and training methodology of machine-learning algorithms.

The question to consider here is whether algorithmic opacity necessarily entails epistemic opacity. We can begin to understand the issue with reference to similar arguments in the philosophy of science. Philosophically and from a computer science perspective issues related to opacity are not new. Humphreys (2004), for example, describes computational processes as being epistemically opaque with regard to the relationship between the abstract model that defines the process, the model that ultimately underlies a simulation, and the output of that system. 'A process is essentially epistemically opaque to X if and only if it is impossible, given the nature of X, for X to know all of the epistemically relevant elements of the process' (Humphreys 2009).

An analogous issue in philosophy of science is whether the user of a scientific instrument needs to understand the processes between the inputs and outputs in order to ascertain the accuracy of the instruments' representation of reality (Humphreys 2009). Humphreys makes a distinction between an individualist epistemology, whereby a single scientist or computer coder might be able to verify or explain a procedure or proof, to a social epistemology, where work has been divided amongst teams of programmers or scientists such that no single person understands all of the processes that generate a particular outcome (ibid.).

Humphreys makes a related point that magnifies the issue of epistemic opacity. Referencing Bedau (1997), he argues that in some situations a computer simulation itself will result in novel macro-level features. Such 'features' are essentially unexpected emergent patterns, or what Bedau terms 'weak emergence'. A good example of such behaviour can be seen in the AlphaGo game case. The case involved a game of Go between one of the world's top players, Lee Sedol, and AlphaGo, an artificially intelligent computing system developed by Google researchers. The AlphaGo system was developed using a deep-learning neural network algorithm and trained by allowing the system to play itself hundreds of thousands of times. Eventually, it had trained itself well enough to consistently beat humans every time. In the match against Sedol, AlphaGo at the thirty-seventh move executed a move that no human Go player could understand. Another champion Go player watching commented 'that is not a human move, I've never seen a human play that move ever'. We might, at least conservatively, conclude at this point that machine-learning algorithmic reasoning is nothing much like human reasoning. Certainly, in almost all such cases of weak emergence it is unlikely that any human agent would have epistemic access to the inner workings of an algorithm exhibiting such behaviour. In these cases, it seems we have a strong argument for epistemic opacity. If it turns out that there are cases of truly epistemically opaque algorithms, should we trust the output of such systems? And what implications, if any, might our trust in such systems entail for society in general? I now turn to these matters.

Trust, Non-human Agents and Accountability

I have developed a picture of algorithmic opacity and its relationship with a stronger version of opaqueness, epistemic opacity. I now outline some typical conceptions of trust. While I initially acknowledge a distinction between more orthodox notions of interpersonal trust and what is often called e-trust or trust related to our interactions with and within informational environments, I will try to find tolerable reciprocity between the two conceptions. I intend the term 'informational environment' to include digital interactions between human actors across digital platforms, such as the Internet, as well as our exchanges with and between artificially intelligent agents. I argue that a distinction can be made between trust relationships that are merely digitally mediated interactions between human individuals and those where artificially intelligent agents interacting with large data sets are involved.

Just how we might interpret trust relationships between artificially intelligent decision-making algorithms and humans is an open problem.

To unpack the problem, we need to consider the relationship between orthodox notions of interpersonal trust and e-trust. I consider the issue of opacity, accountability, our right to having decisions made by machines explained to us, and how that impacts trust relationships between individuals, decision-making algorithms and the institutions using these systems. Finally, I consider what implications the increasingly use of such algorithms, particularly within authoritative contexts, might have for democracy and individual autonomy.

While there are some exceptions,[2] trust is essentially a relational concept between humans or individuals and groups. To trust an individual, a group or an institution, is to willingly relinquish some control to the trustee, that is, we trust commitments made by a trustee will be honoured. We trust the bank with our money, we trust doctors with our medical care and, of course, we hopefully trust our significant others to have our best interests at heart. These trust relationships are supported by epistemic, normative, empirical and sometimes less rational forms of evidence. Thus, as the trustor, we form beliefs that give us reason to rely upon the trustee to meet specific commitments. Nevertheless, trust involves a degree of risk that cannot be entirely eliminated.

While there are various philosophical construals of trust and there has been some work regarding trust in the digital world, what is sometimes termed e-trust (Weckert 2005; Ess 2010; Taddeo and Floridi 2011), most models of trust are interpersonal by nature. Our trust-based decisions may not always be rational on epistemic or practical grounds. However, we like to think our perceptions of trust are in some sense well-grounded. The structure of trustworthiness is built upon a foundation of sufficient evidence. If trust is warranted on such grounds, then risk factors are minimised. Pettit (2004: 109) argues that our acts of reliance serve to promote our own ends, according to our beliefs, thereby maximising our expected utility. If trust is warranted then most of us would likely agree that it is justified or well-grounded, minimally we might expect that it would be at least plausible.

Simpson (2017: 444) calls this evidence-constrained trust. Simpson's arguments deal primarily with trust related to digitally mediated communication amongst individuals. This will be different to conceptions of trust that might apply to our interactions with non-human algorithmic entities. However, it is informative to examine Simpson's approach such that we can highlight the distinction. Simpson argues that digitally mediated communications can support evidence-constrained trust. I argue that the opposite is the case regarding opaque algorithmic decision-making systems. For Simpson, online communications are just another kind of communication similar to everyday face-to-face communications between individuals.

Provided the technology affords an experience for the users approximating to that of offline communication, a case can be made that supports evidence-constrained trust.

There are cases where trust can be built outside evidence-constraints. Simpson claims that plenty of instances can be imagined where a trustor commits to being trusted in ways not supported by evidence or indeed the perceived trustworthiness of the trustee. In some cases, this points to a form of affective trust between individuals ('I trust my husband will not cheat on me') which sits outside most rational accounts. In other cases, trust points to cognitive (but falling short of epistemic) justification ('I believe you are an honourable person, therefore I trust you with this'). Given the evident plurality in our conceptions of trust we might contend that there will be some instances of trust that are appropriate only given full epistemic access to the evidence at hand. I argue this is the required standard requisite for trust relationships to hold between humans and algorithmic entities.

Our interactions, and our trust relationships (if such relationships can exist) with algorithms, in particular those kinds of algorithm that interact with large data sets and support decision making, are quite different to those between human individuals. The work now performed by artificially intelligent algorithms was in many cases specialised human work. For example, a social case worker might analyse a case file in order to come to a decision regarding the welfare of a child. A probation officer might perform a similar process with an offender's case file, ultimately making an evidence-based, informed decision as to whether a convicted offender ought to be released from jail. We may or may not trust the individuals in these roles to make just and appropriate decisions based upon the information available. In such cases we would reasonably expect them to be able to furnish adequate explanations with regard to decisions taken if and when required. Accountability here is tightly coupled with the individuals tasked with making and implementing the decisions.

Accountability in such contexts involves the rights of the decision-subject in expecting that a decision maker be able to provide acceptable justification as to why a particular decision was made. The question of accountability when intelligent algorithms provide decision-making output is largely unclear. The way in which an organisation operating the algorithm decides to justify such decisions may vary significantly. Justifications might refer to the data and training methods used to develop the algorithm, the scientific rigour behind the development of the system, the prior historical success of the system or justification may not be offered at all.

Binns (2017) raises the question of how we might deal with situations when conflicts arise between a decision maker and decision-subjects. In these cases, to what extent are decision makers justified in imposing algorithmic decisions that decision-subjects find objectionable? The hard question is how we might reconcile differences between epistemic, normative and moral standards when algorithmic decisions are taken (ibid.: 2). The appropriate attribution of accountability and how that might be enforced with regard to the use of opaque decision-making algorithms will be closely linked to public trust in the use of such systems. This may act as a check on algorithmic decision-making systems by forcing those that would use such systems to justify their output against acceptable epistemic and normative standards (Binns 2017). Such justifications ought at least to be compatible with the ethical principles of universality and impartiality, while acknowledging that there may be disagreements in individual cases.

Explanation and Predictive Algorithms: Towards a Trust Relation

Many of the kinds of opaque algorithms discussed above have a predictive function. Algorithms are used to predict whether a convicted criminal will re-offend, whether a child could be in an abusive family situation. Our ability to predict something, a particular event obtaining, a regularity or some specific phenomena typically goes hand-in-hand with an explanation. While, in some cases, an individual may be able to successfully predict an event or regularity occurring, the absence of an extant explanation renders the credibility of such predictions weak. It is the existence of an explanatory scientific story behind the prediction that lends credibility to the justifying factors. All valid and true explanations rely upon evidence for their support.

The outputs of decision-making algorithms in almost all the contexts discussed above are treated as evidence to support further actions. These actions have the potential to significantly impact the personal interests, welfare and autonomy of the decision-subjects involved. Given the influence such decisions have on our autonomy as individuals we might rightfully expect a minimal set of conditions that would apply to contexts where algorithmic decisions are taken as actionable evidence. If some form of e-trust relationship can indeed be formed between the decision-subject and the algorithmic entity making the decision, those minimal conditions will comprise a form of acceptable justification to the decision-subject and that justification ought to involve an explanation as to why the decision was taken. The argument here is that explanations are implicitly required for e-trust in socio-technical environments.

Roth-Berghofer and Cassens (2005) and Sørmo, Cassens and Aamodt (2005) suggest a set of 'explanation goals' that might be applied in knowledge-based systems. The focus will be on the first two goals suggested, the first being 'transparency'. In systems where the stakes are high, that is, where an individual's autonomy could be significantly impacted, it is entirely reasonable to suggest that the decision-subject be entitled to an explanation as to why and how the system came to a surprising or anomalous result. The transparency goal would allow users, or independent third-party auditors, to examine all parts of the system, including design models, to understand and be able to explain how a system came to a particular result. Unfortunately, transparency rarely exists in many of the contexts where decision-making algorithms are used for reasons discussed above.

The second explanation goal is 'justification'. The aim of this goal is to increase the level of confidence that the conclusion the system came to is supported on ethically sound, rational and scientific grounds. The public need to be assured that such systems are working in a way that embodies ethical principles, that the dignity and autonomy of the decision-subject is respected, and that principles of universality and impartiality are upheld. Roth-Berghofer and Cassens (2005) suggest that this form of explanation can potentially be de-coupled from the actual reasoning process itself. Thus, a much simpler explanation might be possible compared with the process the algorithm works through to come to a particular conclusion. Pieters (2011) argues justification is the most important explanation goal in AI. The primary question in such systems, Pieters argues, is 'why'. Why was the decision, diagnosis or advice given by the system? Note that answering the 'why' question is more nuanced than the 'how' question. System developers are well versed at explaining how a system works. However, explaining why also requires an intimate knowledge of the data associated with the decision process. It is likely that answering why questions will require a causal story to accompany the explanation.

Pieters (2011) makes a distinction between explanation-for-trust and explanation-for-confidence. An explanation, according to Pieters, can either aim at acquiring trust or, in a lesser case, confidence. While explanation-for-trust requires a precise explanation of how a system works, explanation-for-confidence merely aims at engendering confidence in a user or decision-subject that the system is operating within some set of agreed acceptable parameters. It may be, in the case of epistemically opaque algorithms, full explanations, explanations-for-trust, are not possible. It should be noted here that full explanations of many aspects of human behaviour are often not possible. However, we seem to find other forms of evidence to support trust relationships. Our relationships with AI algorithms are unlikely to be as nuanced.

The output of such algorithms can sometimes be explained only in terms of prior probabilities or as a statistical correlation with similar historical data patterns over large numbers of trails. How explanations may go some way towards Pieter's explanation-for-confidence, but are unlikely to satisfy the requirements for his explanation-for-trust. In certain situations, establishing trust relationships with epistemically opaque artificially intelligent entities qua machine-learning algorithms may simply not be feasible. Furthermore, it should be noted that outputs of such systems indicating very high statistical scores are no more explanatory than those indicating very low probabilities. For example, imagine a candidate scoring only 2 per cent on a system that has been developed to indicate the likelihood that that candidate will make a 'good employee' compared with a candidate that scores 85 per cent. An explanation-for-trust would require an explanation as to why the candidate scoring 85 per cent would make a good employee just as much the requirement that the 2 per cent score be fully explained. High probabilities are neither necessary nor sufficient for explanation. Both high and low probability scores require explanatory stories if any form of trust is to obtain.

Ethical Implications and Conclusions

If the foremost arguments as to why we should accept such systems end up being utilitarian ones, that is, the system produces acceptable results comparable with human operators, only more efficiently, then it seems we have reduced what once was a nuanced human activity to something akin to the operation of an automatic door or a thermostat. Rogue results from such systems do occur. We might be tempted to tolerate such results, false alarms and bias errors in favour of the utility these systems offer on the proviso that, not unlike automatic doors, instances of malfunction can be brought within acceptable tolerance levels. This will be cool comfort for those whose lives are adversely impacted by the use of such algorithms. What remedy is available to those who happen to have their life ruined by the output of an algorithm whose processes we are unable to explain? And what has happened to human culture when algorithmic efficiency is favoured over justice, liberty and autonomy? A world where machines regulate human behaviour, and where the output of such systems provides actionable evidence for corporates, government agencies and law enforcement. Yet this is precisely the danger we face, and in a fundamentally unregulated environment many policymakers are largely ill-equipped to grapple with the issues, relying instead upon 'technical experts', many with personal or economic agendas, to guide the development, implementation and ultimately provide justification for such systems.

Underlying effective democracy are the principles of accountability, transparency and separation of powers. Opaque artificially intelligent algorithms, whose decisions are either not self-explanatory or unable to be adequately explained by those developing and implementing them, undermine these principles. Their unfettered use not only raises significant moral questions, but may ultimately undermine the trust we have in the institutions that employ them. Fixing our most fundamental societal issues is unlikely to be achieved by machine-learning algorithms. Or, if they are, that may well come at a cost that proves to be appallingly unpalatable. Understanding many of the social mores AI algorithms are being increasingly tasked with analysing is very human and nuanced. It relies upon experiences and realities that are not easily measured or quantified but that are nonetheless intrinsically meaningful and essential. Reliance upon such software, particularly within the authoritative and regulatory contexts discussed above, is likely to have profound implications for the relationship between individuals, the state and ultimately democracy.

In 2015, Ted Striphas coined a term 'algorithmic culture'. Striphas was concerned about the way many technologies, including those discussed here, are shaping and influencing culture. The offloading of work to computers, databases and other technologies is requiring us to redefine our orthodox notions of evidence, trust and explanation. As humans, we are at times unable to fully explain our actions or decisions, and the same is true for some kinds of AI. Clune (2017) argues that it might just be something inherent about intelligence itself that only part of its nature is exposed to rational explanation, the rest perhaps is simply inscrutable or subconscious. Thus, it seems we are on the banks of the Rubicon with regard to AI. If we cross, that is, if we build and implement machines that either themselves or their creators are unable to explain, then we may be taking a blind leap of faith.

Unless adequately addressed these issues will have significant implications for society as a whole. While the implications are widespread, at particular risk are those such as the underprivileged, people living under nominal living conditions or at the fringes of society. The potential problems arising go right to the heart of freedom, privacy, autonomy, liberty and, therefore, democracy. Institutions and governments must ensure that structures and principles are implemented that put fundamental human rights at the forefront. In this way we might be reassured that decisions made are ultimately human decisions and the dignity, liberty and autonomy of individuals remains paramount.

Notes

1. Dimensionality in data analytics refers to the number of possible combinations between many (in some cases hundreds) of data attributes and vast quantities, often millions of rows, of data.
2. While we would not trust wild animals, we might trust our pet dogs and, of course, many people place their trust in some form of divine entity.

References

Bedau, M. A., 'Weak Emergence', *Noûs* 31 (S11) (1997): 375–99.

Binns, R., 'Algorithmic Accountability and Public Reason', *Philosophy and Technology*, 2017, https://doi.org/10.1007/s13347-017-0263-5, Springer.

Brey, P. and J. H. Soraker, *Philosophy of Computing and Information Technology* (Amsterdam: Elsevier, 2009).

Burrell, J., 'How the Machine "Thinks": Understanding Opacity in Machine Learning Algorithms', *Big Data and Society* (2016): 1–12.

Clune J., cited in W. Knight, 'The Dark Secret at the Heart of AI', *MIT Technology Review*, 2017, https://www.technologyreview.com/s/604087/the-dark-secret-at-the-heart-of-ai, last accessed 5 May 2018.

Ess, C. M., 'Trust and New Communication Technologies: Vicious Circles, Virtuous Circles, Possible Futures', *Knowledge, Technology & Policy* 23(3/4) (2010): 287–305.

Forster, E. M., *The Machine Stops* (Oxford: Oxford and Cambridge Review, 1909).

Humphreys, P., *Extending Ourselves: Computational Science, Empiricism, and Scientific Method* (New York: Oxford University Press, 2004).

Humphreys, P., 'The Philosophical Novelty of Computer Simulation Methods', *Synthese* 169(3) (2009): 615–26.

Nissenbaum, H., 'How Computer Systems Embody Values', *Computer* 34(3) (2001): 120–19.

O'Neil, C., *Weapons of Math Destruction: How Big Data Increases Inequality and Threatens Democracy* (New York: Crown, 2016).

Pettit, P., 'Trust, Reliance and the Internet', *Analyse und Kritik* 26 (2004): 108–21.

Pieters, W., 'Explanation and Trust: What to Tell the User in Security and AI?', *Ethics & Information Technology* 13(1) (2011): 53–64.

Price, W. N., 'Regulating Black Box Medicine', *Michigan Law Review*, 2017, SSRN: https://ssrn.com/abstract=2938391.

Roth-Berghofer, T. and J. Cassens, 'Mapping Goals and Kinds of Explanations to the Knowledge Containers of Case-based Reasoning Systems', in H. Munos Avila and F. Ricci (eds), *ICCBR 2005* (Berlin: Springer, 2005), vol. 3620 of LNCS, pp. 451–64.

Simpson, T. W., 'Telepresence and Trust: a Speech-Act Theory of Mediated Communication', *Philosophy of Technology* 30(4) (2017): 443–59.

Sørmo, F., J. Cassens and A. Aamodt, 'Explanation in Case-based Reasoning: Perspectives and Goals', *Artificial Intelligence Review* 24(2) (2005): 109–43.

Striphas, T., 'Algorithmic Culture', *European Journal of Cultural Studies* 18(4/5) (2015): 395–412.

Taddeo, M. and L. Floridi, 'The Case for E-Trust', *Ethics and Information Technology* 13(1) (2011).

Weckert, J., 'Trust in Cyberspace', in R. J. Cavalier (ed.), *The Impact of the Internet on Our Moral Lives* (Albany, NY: University of New York Press, 2005), pp. 95–120.

Zarsky, T., 'The Trouble with Algorithmic Decisions: An Analytic Road Map to Examine Efficiency and Fairness in Automated and Opaque Decision Making', *Science, Technology & Human Values* 41(1) (2016): 118–32.

ELEVEN

Opacity, Big Data, Artificial Intelligence and Machine Learning in Democratic Processes

Ramón Alvarado

The first decades of the twenty-first century saw an initial hubris regarding the prowess of computational methods such as big data, artificial intelligence and, more recently, machine learning. However, the opacity related to these computational methods – the inability to access, examine or even identify relevant aspects of their inner workings – is consequently at the front and centre of recent concerns. Understanding the different kinds of opacity and the ways in which they are present in these computational methods is a fundamental step towards understanding the challenges they present to democratic processes in general.

The general argument of this chapter is the following: epistemic opacity, and particularly its distinct forms, must be taken into account in order to accurately assess the profound challenges that computational analytic methods such as big data, artificial intelligence and machine learning pose to democratic processes. This is because it is important to understand that a significant aspect of the novel challenges brought about by these computational methods is of an epistemic nature. That is, knowing participants of democratic processes are being left behind as technologies used in the various facets of democratic processes continue to grow in complexity and size beyond what is humanly tractable. If we take a free and knowing agent as a fundamental player in the dynamics of democratic processes, the opacity of computational methods such as big data, machine learning and artificial intelligence are in fact a significant challenge to democratic processes as a whole.

Democratic Processes

A democratic process can be many things. It can be a parliamentary or con-gressional legislative procedure within a democratic country. It can also be the act of voting for members of such institutions by individual citizens. In between these two types of democratic process there are several other inter-actions that also count towards or against the aims of democratic processes. For example, the dissemination of information through electoral campaigns that are now often mediated through diverse computational methods and general digital infrastructures that – as I will show below – due to their complexity and scale push an informed citizenry further and further away from a thorough understanding of the core mechanisms by which these processes function. As we will see, the opacity inherent to computational methods is not always a direct result of malicious intent. In fact, in some cases opacity is generated simply by the inherent size and/or complexity of the technologies underlying such processes. However, the effects of the ever-growing epistemic distance between the processes that guide contem-porary democratic procedures and the agents that partake in such proce-dures are nevertheless detrimental to both the agent and the process itself.

While this chapter does not go into detail of any particular instance of opacity in real-life democratic processes, the conceptual discussion of epis-temic opacity has implications for a wide range of democratic processes. These processes encompass those which require the mediation of conven-tional computational infrastructure in general, as well as those processes which indirectly make use of computational analytic methodology such as big data, machine learning and artificial intelligence. The processes in the former category are those in which computers are directly deployed in tech-nology used to execute a relevant part of a democratic process, for example, voting machines. The latter category includes other aspects of the demo-cratic processes in which computational analytics have a direct or indirect effect on the democratic process and/or on those who take part in a demo-cratic process. Examples of these latter processes include the kind of analyt-ics used to evaluate constituency and district maps, but they also include the type of processes which disseminate electoral information through tar-geted campaigning.

Epistemic Opacity

In its simplest sense, a system is deemed to be opaque in some form if all or some of its parts are not immediately accessible to inspection. Here, I will refer to this overly broad sense of opacity as 'general opacity'. Paul

Humphreys, who contextualised the term in the literature of computer simulations, defines it as follows:

> General opacity: 'A process is epistemically opaque relative to a cognitive agent X at time t just in case X does not know at t all of the epistemically relevant elements of the process.' (Humphreys 2004; 2009)

Described this way, many things qualify as opaque to many different agents. To many of us, for example, whatever is under the hood of our cars will be opaque. Similarly, well-established democratic procedures, such as the way the Electoral College works in the United States, remain opaque to many of those that participate in them.

A common problem related to general opacity arises from the fact that software systems often require many components. Several people and often several distinct companies also make each of those components. In this sense 'many hands' are involved in the development of software systems. The motley and compartmentalised features inherent to software development (Winsberg 2010) bring about an analogous problem to what ethicists call the 'many hands problem' in responsibility ascription (Nissenbaum 1994). The 'many hands problem' stipulates that attributing responsibility in a setting in which there are many agents with varying degrees and kinds of involvement is extremely difficult. Corporate, military, manufacturing and other settings in which many agents are involved and in which the kind and degrees of responsibilities are distributed in unequal ways are problematic for responsibility ascription. When it comes to computational methods, however, the 'many hands problem' is not only about responsibility ascription, but also about which component is causally responsible for any relevant aspect of the system's behaviour. Hence, inspecting computational systems is a non-trivial epistemic challenge. If we consider that producing a single software product can take a whole research team, or a group of such teams, and that each of the individuals or groups may have varying and distributed responsibilities we can see that the 'many hands problem' has a uniquely serious effect on the way we ascribe responsibility, accountability and/or even causality in contexts where more sophisticated computational methods play a role.

General epistemic opacity as defined above is a relative kind of opacity. Given the example above of the 'many hands problem', someone, somewhere could access an existing spreadsheet with all the relevant information regarding the provenance of a given component and therefore alleviate the relative opacity vis-à-vis that particular agent. And while it may take a longer time and a large amount of resources, the same can be said about each and all of the components of an industrially produced piece of equipment. That is, in principle, the relevant details of the opaque system in question – in this case a large-scale industrial or military project or equipment – can be known. The fact that general epistemic opacity is a relative kind of opacity also makes it less of an epistemic challenge. If you do not know how something works, for example, you can ask someone that does or can be assured that someone, somewhere knows and rely on their expertise (Barberousse and Vorms 2014). This kind of opacity also captures instances in which the same system is opaque to an epistemic agent at one time and transparent to the same epistemic agent at another time. That is, if you do not know how a system works you can, in principle, learn how it does so. Because few of us are experts at anything, or because few of us can be experts at everything, many systems/processes will be generally opaque to most of us.

Identifying a system as opaque in the manner described above offers little information concerning the different sources of opacity or the features of the system that make it so. Too many systems qualify as opaque in this manner without much information about the different ways by which such opacity occurs. To counter this overly general sense of opacity in Humphreys' definition others have suggested that knowing the specific sources of opacity (Kaminski 2018), and dealing with them on a case-by-case basis is the only approach to appropriately address issues of opacity and trust in technology (Pitt 2010). Kaminski (2018), for instance, suggests that some instances of opacity in computer simulations will arise by virtue of the social aspects of a process such as the number of people or teams that participate in a scientific project – this is another version, focused on epistemic obstacles, of the 'many hands problem' I described above. This kind of epistemic opacity, which derives from social aspects of a system, also includes instances of opacity that are due to intentional corporate and/or state secrecy, as well as the kind that arises due to technical illiteracy (Burrell 2016). An interesting example of the kind of corporate secrecy that is of immediate social consequence are predictive algorithms deployed in a growing and diverse set of judicial procedures in the United States. These algorithms and the way they reach conclusions on things like the probability of criminal recidivism are kept opaque not only from the judges who use them for sentence or parole considerations, but also from the people whose life they affect and the lawyers navigating the judicial system on their behalf (O'Neil 2016). The use of these technologies offers the present discussion a way to elucidate an important aspect of the nature of the challenges posed by opaque systems to democratic processes. While the consequences of using opaque predictive algorithms in the judicial system has immediate social and ethical consequences in the lives of those directly affected, the broader challenge to democratic processes as a whole is that they are ultimately closed to epistemic recourse (Kitchin 2014): there is no way for those using them or affected by them to understand them, there is no way to navigate them and, importantly, there is no way to challenge their results. In this sense, these kinds of opaque systems represent a challenge to democratic processes insofar as an informed citizenry, a transparent bureaucracy and challengeable governance are considered essential to the flourishing of any democratic system. While the court procedures of city and state judicial systems may not be directly understood as democratic processes in themselves, this example helps to elucidate what makes the use of opaque data analytics and machine-learning systems in bureaucratic decision making something to be genuinely worried about in the context of democratic institutions.

A different source of opacity from those discussed above emerges from the different ways in which the mathematical elements of a computational process function or malfunction together. Mathematical error, for example, is inherent in computational components. Due to discretisation techniques and resource constraints, computational approximates of continuous equations rely on rounding results. Memory slots for individual digits in conventional computers, for example, are often less than the number needed for the full representation of particularly large calculations. When each of the multiple components and processes in a computer simulation round up or down mathematical results to accommodate for these kinds of constraints, the discrepancies between what should be and what the computer produces are non-trivial. Though there are important developments in the ways in which computer scientists are able to assess and correct for this kind of error, these developments are yet to be scaled up towards a general application in software development. Rather, these developments are the kind of resource-intensive proofing techniques that only high-precision coding benefits from. Knowing where and when the rounding error generates as well as the magnitude of it represents a significant epistemic challenge. Furthermore, the kind of challenge exemplified by mathematical opacity points towards a kind of epistemic opacity which may prove to be even more resistant – or in fact impervious – to inspection than the relative kind of epistemic opacity exemplified in the general definition above. This is particularly the case when a machine yields significantly different results when no changes in the conventional elements of a computational inquiry – components, code, architecture, data, parameters and so on – can be detected (Kaminski 2018).

Mathematical opacity also points to a kind of opacity whose origins are not rooted in limitations on the part of an agent, but rather on properties and features of the system under investigation.[1] Hence, mathematical opacity is already several steps removed from the kind of opacity due to technical illiteracy mentioned above. Regardless of an agent's mathematical and technical know-how, the details of a mathematically opaque system will remain hidden.

A difference noted by Humphreys (2009) provides a possible way to sort between the instances of opacity described above. While some of the generally opaque systems are relative to a specific time and to a specific agent (agent X at time t), a subset of opaque systems will not be opaque in this relative way. Some systems will be opaque to an agent at all times or to all similar agents all the time. This can be because the nature of the agent makes it impossible to access all the epistemically relevant aspects of such a system. Humphreys calls this kind of opacity essential epistemic opacity and defines it the following way:

> Essential opacity: arises 'if it is impossible, given the nature of X, for X to know all of the epistemically relevant elements of the process'. (Humphreys 2009)

Thus, we can differentiate between those systems that are generally and relatively opaque and those that are insurmountably opaque to agents like us.[2]

In order to better visualise the epistemic implications of a system's essential opacity, consider the following scenario. Imagine there is an error that has to be fixed in a computer such as the direct recording electronic (DRE) systems used in the United States to vote in federal and local elections (Norden and Famighetti 2015). Imagine an erroneous result, in a preliminary test or in an actual election, is known but the source and/or nature (hardware or software) of the error is not. When it comes to computational methods, as we briefly touched upon above, the many hands problem simply becomes more complex. The hands (teams/corporations/institutions) involved, the components necessary and the software are only some of the factors. A more troubling fact is that the inner workings of the components and algorithms in such systems are not always accessible to other agents, users or even those in charge of testing them (Parnas, Van Schouwen and Kwan 1990; Symons and Horner 2014; Burrell 2016). As I will show below, each of these components includes a large number of lines of code that make up its software, and this alone can make the difference between a system that is generally opaque and one that is essentially opaque. Although some would argue that there are ways to ensure that some of the code is accessible, most of the time the practices that ensure such transparency are not available or even viable, particularly if the code in question is legacy code – code that was written by others, often a long time ago – or if it is code written in a highly idiosyncratic manner. Further, as I will detail below, some efforts turn out not to be validly applicable in relevant cases. This is because computational methods have at least three very particular properties when it comes to error: the first is that, unlike any hardware technology, software is particularly sensitive to error (Corbató, 1990; Parnas, Van Schouwen and Kwan 1990: 638); secondly, unlike any hardware technology, the nature, source and distribution rate of its error cannot be assumed to be random (Parnas, Van Schouwen and Kwan 1990: 638); and, thirdly, testing software is notably difficult (Symons and Horner 2014; 2019).

Symons and Horner (2014) exemplify one kind of difficulty in testing software code by considering a trivially small software program consisting of 1,000 lines of code. On average 1 out of 10 of those 1,000 lines of code will be a command that has the form if/then/else and not just if/then. If we wanted to exhaustively check a similar size program that only had if/then commands it would be pretty straightforward. All that there is to do is to check each one of the 1,000 lines of code. However, when the code includes an if/then/else command it bifurcates the possible paths that the code can take and therefore increases the lines of code to check. A straight-forward program with 10 command lines has 10 lines to check. A 10-line program with one if/then/else command has 20 lines to check. A program with 1,000 lines of code and an average of 1/10 commands being an if/then/else command will have enough lines of code to check to make the task, even at the fastest possible computation speed, take several times the age of the universe (Symons and Horner 2014; Symons and Alvarado 2016). Software systems involved in computational methods such as those required for artificial intelligence, and even some smaller subcomponents of them, have software whose number of lines of code by far exceed the number used in the example. A thorough assessment of the proper execution of each line of code then is for all immediate intents and purposes not feasible. A task that would take anywhere near the age of the universe to be completed is a task that, as a process, is opaque to many more agents than just humans and our technologies. So, this process is in effect essentially epistemically opaque.

Someone may say as an objection that if we consider a breakthrough in computing processes, like quantum parallel computing, we could sig-nificantly increase the speed at which testing software could be done. If so, exhaustively testing an average software system would be in fact possible. While this is true, it is hard to see how decreasing the time of a task from several times the age of the universe to half or a quarter of that is genuine progress (Symons and Horner 2014). This task remains opaque. Still, it can be argued that exhaustive testing of code lines is only one way of assessing reliability in software systems. A more useful approach is to conduct tests on random samples of a system's code. By using conventional statistical inference theory, one can randomly select samples of code and test their execution. By inference, and with the assumption of random distribution of error in the system, a reliability assessment of the samples should give us an idea of the rate of error in the whole system. If 20 sample lines out of 100 fail to do what they are supposed to do, then we can say that the system as a whole has a 20 per cent failure rate.[3] However, there are two main issues with this approach. Even before software systems reached the size and complexity seen today, it was well established that the nature and distribution of error in software systems is not like that of other systems (Parnas, Van Schouwen and Kwan 1990: 638). This is because of two reasons. The first is that while in other engineering projects one can assume certain resilience to small errors, in software even a punctuation error can be catastrophic (ibid.: 637). Secondly, the kinds of error that can affect other engineering projects can be assessed by assuming that these errors are 'not highly correlated' (ibid.: 638). Because of the interconnectedness of software functioning and the fact that many errors are due to design (Floridi, Fresco and Primiero 2015), errors in software cannot be considered statistically independent (Parnas, Van Schouwen and Kwan 1990), nor can they be considered randomly distributed (Parnas, Van Schouwen and Kwan 1990; Horner and Symons 2014). Thus, deploying statistical inference techniques to test samples under the assumption that the errors found will be randomly distributed is an invalid approach when it comes to software (Horner and Symons 2019).

Further, even if this technique were valid consider the following. If the number of lines of code to be tested is of the order of magnitude postulated in the example above, what constitutes a significant sample set? Testing even 5 per cent of the lines of code of a system with 100,000 lines of code and an average path complexity of one if/then/else bifurcation per every 10 lines would put us in the same position as with the original example. It would take ages to do. If we managed to test 1 per cent of the lines it would be difficult to say that we now have a dependable assessment of the system's reliability. It is not clear that path complexity catastrophe applies directly to machine-learning techniques. But it does apply to most of the components underlying its implementation. Big data processes are equally affected by this problem (Symons and Alvarado 2016). Insofar as artificial intelligence algorithms are designed as symbol manipulation techniques with Boolean thresholds, they are similarly vulnerable. Similarly, if these systems rely heavily on machine-learning techniques such as convolutional neural networks, then the fact remains that the components used to implement them are opaque in the ways described above.

A crucial element of reliability assessment is to understand the source, the nature and the rate of error in a system. If our inquiry concerns the reliability of a system, as it would have been in the case of assessing computational methods deployed in the service of democratic processes, the source, nature and rate of error are relevant elements of the system. Not being able to assess the reliability of a system is enough to not trust it (Symons and Alvarado 2019). This is particularly the case if these systems are voting machines with which voting for national elections is being done. If, as stated at the beginning of this chapter, a manageable level of transparency is essential to democratic processes and political campaigns, as part of democratic processes are socially consequential settings, then any and all computational systems used as aids to policy-related issues ought to be amenable to reliability assessment. Without this, trust cannot be adequately justified (Symons and Alvarado 2019), and without trust democratic systems can be easily undermined.

Big Data, Machine Learning and Artificial Intelligence

Despite many overlapping features, artificial intelligence, big data and machine-learning techniques can be differentiated by examining the way in which each of them is deployed and what practitioners expect to get from them (Marr 2016). David Robinson, for example, suggests that 'data science produces insights; machine learning produces predictions; and artificial intelligence produces actions' (Robinson 2018). Questions in data science are often associated with explanatory and exploratory queries seeking to extract causal, inferential and sometimes even mechanistic insights from datasets (Leek 2015). In contrast, machine learning does not require and often cannot consider human capabilities and needs – such as explanations and/or causal orderings of a tractable size – in order to work (Burrell 2016; Alvarado and Humphreys 2017). There is a sense in which if machine-learning processes were designed to be accessible to limited representational abilities of humans they just would not work (Burrell 2016: 5). Unlike the processes involved in big data analytics, the techniques of machine learning are used to compute complex Bayesian probability models which focus on attaining predictions. These predictions can be about future probabilities concerning a state of affairs in a system. They can also be about the probabilities that a certain object and/or data set does or does not contain a feature identified through known or discovered properties. However, there is a sense in which all three computational methods are also often deployed simultaneously and/or are contained within one another. This is particularly the case in artificial intelligence techniques which could not be deployed without the use of big data analytics and which also often include the dynamic processes of learning algorithms in order to optimise their actionable results.

In this section I will treat all three methods as members of the same statistically-driven computational techniques in order to elucidate what sets them apart from the instances of opacity which emerge from the more conventional computational methods discussed above. When these methods are deployed in socially consequential contexts such as bureau-cratic procedures or democratic processes, their epistemic challenges are of a different order. This is because the opacity at play in this context takes on many dimensions. The kind of essential epistemic opacity discussed above – related to either path complexity in software testing or mathemati-cal opacity at the component level – is at play at the most basic level of computational systems: their code and algorithmic operation. In systems such as machine-learning software the issue is exacerbated by the fact that machine-learning algorithms run many iterations of the same models of analysis with slight difference in parameters. So not only are there many agents involved in the process, or many components, but also many pro-cesses. Hence, the obstacles to access the epistemically relevant features of a system are beyond their underlying algorithmic nature. In the case of arti-ficial intelligence systems, for example, sometimes thousands of substan-tially different models are run in order to arrive at the optimal solution for a given task. The 'many hands' problem thus becomes a 'many models' or 'many everything' problem, something that Domingos (2012) deems 'the curse of dimensionality' in machine learning.

When it comes to machine learning, the number of lines of code or the number of people involved in developing the system is not the only ele-ment that contributes to its opacity. Rather, the scale of data, the number and properties of salient features that will be picked up by the process, the alterations to the main code done by the learning aspect of the pro-cess all contribute to its complexity and opacity (Burrell 2016; Alvarado and Humphreys 2017). This in itself constitutes an important departure from the algorithmic opacity related to testing lines of code: the algorithm itself may prove to be intractable, but also the weights and properties used by the algorithm to optimise its output will be unknown. Furthermore, the hidden statistical structures – say, for example, spuriously related data items at the deeper analytical levels – will be unreachable for anyone trying to assess whether the results are valid. Alvarado and Humphreys (2017) call this 'representational opacity'. This sort of opacity occurs when a data-processing method finds a 'concealed statistical structure' (ibid. 2017) within a data set that cannot be interpreted by or represented to us. It arises not only from the size of the system or how complicated it is to follow, but rather from the required dynamics of its working. According to Jenna Burrell (2016) these complexities arise due to the scale at which machine learning is required to be deployed to work as intended. The many dimensions in which machine-learning methods work quickly become intractable. If they are coupled with the 'many hands' problem and the path complexity problem, we can see how the level of opacity at play in these technologies is unprecedented.

When it comes to socially consequential contexts, the validity of the results of a big data or machine-learning analysis is not the only aspect of concern. The fairness and desirability of the elements considered in the analysis is also something to worry about. In this sense, even the fact that the machine will be using a discovered relation between one item and another could be questionable in itself. Predictive algorithms that take into consideration implicit or explicit racial elements for judicial procedures – whether or not they indeed show a statistically significant relation to a relevant aspect of the inquiry – are something that most advocates of fair justice systems would find undesirable (O'Neil 2016). The main problem for the purpose of our discussion, however, is that both these kinds of deep analytic considerations and the operations necessary to discover their statistical relations will be essentially hidden from our sight.

Consider the following. When district maps are analysed through the use of highly sophisticated big data analysis in order to optimise the outcome for candidates of a specific party, there is reason to worry. The reason, however, is not merely the fact that those using these techniques are seeking an advantage through the politically questionable practice of parsing out districts in arbitrary ways. Rather, the worry is that they are using a technique that is often not amenable to inspection and/or challenge because of the many reasons listed above. Similarly, when people are being targeted through marketing campaigns designed to exploit their cognitive vulnerabilities in order to nudge their electoral behaviour (Zuboff 2019), there is an added insult to the social injury that is rooted in the use of opaque technologies. When big data analytics, machine-learning algorithms and the decisions of intelligent systems are deployed in these contexts, often neither those that use them nor those that are affected by their use fully understand the mechanisms by which they arrive at their results (O'Neil 2016). Often, the results associated with these technologies are used to parse individuals, or groups of individuals, into actionable categories. That is, these technologies are parsing people in ways in which something can be done to them without them knowing (Zuboff 2019). This in itself is a significant problem to a democratic society (Murray and Scime 2010; Cadwalladr 2017). And yet, consider that data analytics and predictive techniques are not only used within some democratically established systems, but sometimes even outside them to assess the probabilities of democratisation of seemingly undemocratic societies (Kimber 1991). These assessments in turn inform and possibly influence global interventions that seek, ironically, to nudge nations towards more democratic structures of government.

The common thread in the examples above, however, is that the computational methods that make such interventions possible are themselves opaque in a way that leaves the agents affected by their implications devoid of epistemic recourse. That is, given the broad discussion above of the different ways in which these technologies are opaque – inaccessible to agent understanding, inspection and/or challenge – these technologies diminish the likelihood of an informed citizenry at the helm of democratic processes. This is more reason to tread carefully in their deployment and to make sure that while they may be used for speculative and exploratory work, they are only cautiously attached to policy-making procedures. We have to come to terms with whether deploying a system whose reliability we cannot assess is something that we should do. In this sense, both what is reliable and what is trustworthy would have to be redefined in a way that omits appeals that are rooted in explicit explanatory criteria and assume the diminished – if perhaps pragmatic – epistemic stance that only predictive prowess matters when we are to justify why they are so. If this is the case, the role of the epistemic agent, us, at the core of democratic processes will be significantly reduced (Gorton, 2016).

Conclusion

This chapter does not address the many possible threats that arise when computational methods such as big data, machine learning and artificial intelligence do or do not work as intended and/or the repercussions either way.[4] Rather, this chapter focuses on the fact that if they do or do not work as intended, the reasons why they do or fail to do so will be beyond inspection or revision because of their opacity. This fact alone should suffice as a warning going forward. This is particularly the case if our ability to create a conscious, revisable democratic environment implies the need for free, deliberate and knowledgeable choice.

Understanding the different kinds of opacity present in these computational methods is a first step towards transparency. If the opacity in question is insurmountable, then understanding so provides at least a way to consciously allocate resources where they may make a difference. It will also provide a reason to think twice about the contexts and the ways in which we deploy and trust these technologies going forward.

Notes

1. This is in fact a very important distinction, albeit one for which I do not have space to elaborate in this particular chapter. Suffice it to say that in the context of explanations of epistemic opacity some will point towards the limitations on the part of the agent and some will point to features of a system. As it will become clear as we move forward, what both general and essential opacity have in common is that they are agent-based accounts of opacity. Both place the source of opacity within the agent. Furthermore, some other systems/processes will be opaque due to limitations that almost any other agent would have, even agents significantly superior to us. Inevitably, while the distinction between general and essential opacity will capture many instances, it will fail to capture instances of opacity that (a) do not respond to, or (b) do not emerge from the limitations or abilities of agents. I call these instances of opacity agent-neutral and agent-independent, respectively. Similarly, it would be incorrect to assert that the opacity in agent-neutral cases is due to the nature of X when X stands for an individual/specific kind of agent if the instance of opacity arises by virtue of a property shared by all finite epistemic agents.

2. In most cases, this can, of course, mean humans as a whole species of knowers. However, and depending on the system and the agent, it can also mean whatever finite cognitive agent with limited epistemic resources encounters such an opaque system. While this last point is a deeply philosophical one on the nature of cognitive agents and the kinds thereof in the universe, the point here is merely to illustrate that some systems may be opaque to any conceivable agent that is not older than the universe itself. So, for example, if finding something out can take two times the age of the universe, then in principle any agent that is younger than the universe itself and whose life will last less than the age of universe itself, will not have time to figure it out. In more practical terms, in the near future, this will apply to any finite machine or process that we take to be a knower too.

3. The probability assessments in actual software testing are a lot more sophisticated and intricate than the example shows, but for all intents and purposes, they function by the same statistical principles whose assumption is being challenged here.

4. For a thorough overview of these threats, see boyd and Crawford (2012); Amoore (2014); O'Neill (2016); and, more recently, Zuboff (2019).

References

Alvarado, R. and P. Humphreys, 'Big Data, Thick Mediation, and Representational Opacity', *New Literary History* 48(4) (2017): 729–49.

Amoore, L., 'Security and the Incalculable', *Security Dialogue* 45(5) (2014): 423–39.

Barberousse, A. and M. Vorms, 'About the Warrants of Computer-based Empirical Knowledge', *Synthese* 191(15) (2014): 3595–620.

boyd, d. and K. Crawford, 'Critical Questions for Big Data: Provocations for a Cultural, Technological, and Scholarly Phenomenon', *Information, Communication & Society* 15(5) (2012): 662–79.

Burrell, J., 'How the Machine "Thinks": Understanding Opacity in Machine Learning Algorithms', *Big Data & Society* 3(1) (2016): 1–12.

Cadwalladr, C., 'The Great British Brexit Robbery: How Our Democracy was Hijacked', *The Guardian*, 2017, available at: https://www.theguardian.com/technology/2017/may/07/the-great-british-brexit-robbery-hijacked-democracy, last accessed 10 January 2020.

Corbató, F. J., 'On Building Systems that Will Fail', in *ACM Turing Award Lectures: 1990*, ACM, 2007.

Domingos, P., 'A Few Useful Things to Know about Machine Learning', *Communications of the ACM* 55(10) (2012): 78–87.

Floridi, L., N. Fresco and G. Primiero, 'On Malfunctioning Software', *Synthese* 192(4) (2015): 1199–220.

Gorton, W. A., 'Manipulating Citizens: How Political Campaigns' Use of Behavioral Social Science Harms Democracy', *New Political Science* 38(1) (2016): 61–80.

Horner, J. and J. Symons, 'Reply to Angius and Primiero on Software Intensive Science', *Philosophy & Technology* 27(3) (2014): 491–4.

Horner, J. K. and J. Symons, 'Understanding Error Rates in Software Engineering: Conceptual, Empirical, and Experimental Approaches', *Philosophy & Technology* (2019): 1–16.

Humphreys, P., *Extending Ourselves: Computational Science, Empiricism, and Scientific Method* (Oxford: Oxford University Press, 2004).

Humphreys, P., 'The Philosophical Novelty of Computer Simulation Methods', *Synthese* 169(3) (2009): 615–26.

Kaminski, A., 'Der Erfolg der Modellierung und das Ende der Modelle. Epistemische Opazität in der Computersimulation', *Technik–Macht–Raum* Wiesbaden: Springer 2018), pp. 317–33.

Kimber, R., 'Artificial Intelligence and the Study of Democracy', *Social Science Computer Review* 9(3) (1991): 381–98.

Kitchin, R., *The Data Revolution: Big Data, Open Data, Data Infrastructures and Their Consequences* (New York: Sage, 2014).

Leek, J., *The Elements of Data Analytic Style*, Victoria, BC: Leanpub., 2015, available at: https://leanpub.com/datastyle.

Marr, B., 'What Is the Difference between Artificial Intelligence and Machine Learning', *Forbes*, 6 December 2016, available at: https://www.forbes.com/sites/bernardmarr/2016/12/06/what-is-the-difference-between-artificial-intelligence-and-machine-learning, last accessed 10 January 2020.

Murray, G. R. and A. Scime, 'Microtargeting and Electorate Segmentation: Data Mining the American National Election Studies', *Journal of Political Marketing* 9(3) (2010): 143–66.

Nissenbaum, H., 'Computing and Accountability', *Communications of the ACM* 37(1) (1994): 72–81.

Norden, L. D. and C. Famighetti, *America's Voting Machines at Risk* (New York: Brennan Center for Justice at New York University School of Law, 2015).

O'Neil, C., *Weapons of Math Destruction: How Big Data Increases Inequality and Threatens Democracy* (New York: Crown, 2016).

Parnas, D. L., A. J. Van Schouwen and S. P. Kwan, 'Evaluation of Safety-critical Software', *Communications of the ACM* 33(6) (1990): 636–48.

Pitt, J. C., 'It's not About Technology', *Knowledge, Technology & Policy* 23(3/4) (2010): 445–54.

Robinson, D., 'What's the Difference between Data Science, Machine Learning, and Artificial Intelligence?' Variance Explained, 9 January 2018, available at: http://varianceexplained.org/r/ds-ml-ai/, last accessed 29 January 2020.

Symons, J. and R. Alvarado, 'Can We Trust Big Data? Applying Philosophy of Science to Software', *Big Data & Society* 3(2) (2016).

Symons, J. and R. Alvarado, 'Epistemic Entitlements and the Practice of Computer Simulation', *Minds and Machines* 29(1) (2019): 37–60.

Symons, J. and J. Horner, 'Software Intensive Science', *Philosophy & Technology* 27(3) (2014): 461–77.

Symons J. F. and J. Horner, 'Software Error as a Limit to Inquiry for Finite Agents: Challenges for the Post-human Scientist', in T. Powers (ed.), *Philosophy and Computing: Essays in Epistemology, Philosophy of Mind, Logic, and Ethics* (Berlin: Springer, 2017).

Symons, J. and J. Horner, 'Why there is no General Solution to the Problem of Software Verification', *Foundations of Science* (2019): 1–17.

Winsberg, E., *Science in the Age of Computer Simulation* (Chicago: University of Chicago Press, 2010).

Zuboff, S., *The Age of Surveillance Capitalism: the Fight for a Human Future at the New Frontier of Power* (London: Profile Books, 2019).

TWELVE

The Big Data Paradox and Its Importance to Strategy and Military Systems Development

Tim McFarland, Jai Galliott and Massimiliano Cappuccio

Introduction

For militarily advanced countries, conflict is becoming increasingly infor-mation-centric. As a tool for supporting strategic and tactical decisions, designing weapons and increasingly as a weapon (or target) in itself, data and the infrastructure for gathering and processing it is critical to the success of military undertakings. Complex operational environments, large battlespaces and adversaries that follow unconventional strategies place heavy demands on commanders who must make, and justify, deci-sions which depend on huge numbers of variables. Accordingly, armed forces gather and process vast amounts of data from many sources, both military and civilian, to support those decisions. The task of gathering, storing and analysing that data increasingly falls within the scope of 'big data' projects.

Armed forces are aware of the stakes, as suggested by the vast resources allocated by American, Chinese and other armed forces to the develop-ment of big data technologies during the past ten years. Those technolo-gies offer unprecedentedly effective tools for systematically retrieving information and establishing correlations within extremely large, hetero-geneous and unstructured data sets. The unstructured data that are actively harvested and interpreted by mining technologies come not only from traditional data storage devices, but from virtually any online system. The advantage offered by the capillary presence and interoperability of these technologies enables an innovative concept of intelligently selective col-lection and analysis: much better than its precursors, big data technol-ogy identifies context-sensitive information, recognises and compares the occurrence of relevant patterns across many formats and media, reveals the presence of unobvious correlations among large numbers of variables, and generates predictions about their most likely effects.

Big data has great potential to support security through intelligence collection, in particular (Thuraisingham et al. 2017). Surveillance and reconnaissance operations benefit from big data's capability to scan very large environments, detecting specific individuals, facilities, weapons or other threats (Andrejevic and Gates 2014): pattern recognition routines are used to automate the analysis of footage recorded by UAVs patrolling seas to spot objects of interest (Costlow 2014). The Defense Advanced Research Projects Agency (DARPA) developed two data-mining programs to anticipate unapparent threats during the US-lead mission in Afghanistan. The first (Nexus 7) was 'to predict insurgent attacks', using the same kinds of predictive technologies developed by Amazon to infer customers' purchases (Weinberger 2017). The second (More Eyes), used a crowd-sourcing technique to collect data voluntarily shared by local communities in Afghan provinces, catalysing 'the local population to generate "white" data useful for assessing stability at multiple levels (regional, provincial, district and village)' (Weinberger 2017).

Big data also serves logistics by optimising the management of space and time, streamlining workflow and reducing the need for manpower, hence, increasing the efficiency of operations (Yang et al., 2016). Relevant programs here include the Conditioned-based Maintenance program (Zhai et al. 2018); the Joint Medical Asset Repository; the Person-Event Data Environment (Vie et al. 2015); and a 2014 DARPA program called 'Mining and Understanding Software Enclaves' (Costlow 2014; Lele 2018).

To summarise, big data technologies allow armed forces to extract actionable information from the data they collect, but also present new risks which must be carefully managed. Being a new field in which technology is surging ahead and new applications are appearing almost daily, the risks it presents are constantly changing and are not well understood, and frameworks for managing those risks are still developing (Finlay 2014; Gandomi and Haider 2015). This chapter aims to assist with that development effort.

Philosophers have questioned both the nature and the validity of the knowledge provided by data-mining techniques, raising various concerns of an epistemological nature. Ebach et al. (2016) point out that, while big data's potential to extract significant information is huge, it is also associated with exaggerated or misdirected expectations. Big data can effectively establish correlations based on statistical distribution, but its ability to generate authentic explanations is limited.

Big data analyses also tend to filter out models and contents that could challenge a user's biases. This tendency creates 'filter bubbles', a phenomenon made familiar to Internet users by the advent of personalised web content combined with data-based profiling (Pariser 2011). Such bubbles encourage evidence-denial and generate self-fulfilling prophecies because the system tends to target pre-selected information sources with pre-selected relevance criteria, and produces effects that selectively strengthen its own models.

Another problem pointed out by the critics of big data is the unjustified trust in its efficiency (Tenner 2018). The ability to scan and compare extremely large sets of documents, combined with the seemingly omniscient power of data mining, creates the illusion that automated systems are more reliable than their human counterparts, while they lack the common sense, creativity, and authentic innovation that are unique of the human critical mind.

In what follows, we focus on the idea of the three 'paradoxes' of big data that stem from these more general issues, as put forward by Neil M. Richards and Jonathan H. King: transparency, identity and power (Richards and King 2013). They are applied here in a military and security context to offer a simple framework that may assist in identifying risks that might threaten the success of big data operations in these fields of operation. The next three sections discuss each of the paradoxes in turn, and the final section offers some thoughts about addressing challenges that have been identified.

Transparency Paradox

The transparency paradox is the observation that '[b]ig data promises to use this data to make the world more transparent, but its collection is invisible, and its tools and techniques are opaque' (Richards and King 2013: 42). The issue of transparency is significant as it underlies most of the concerns about the collection and use of big data by government and corporations: privacy, consent and accountability. On the one hand, a lack of transparency can incite resistance from those whose data is collected and used, prompt restrictive responses from lawmakers and undermine efforts to apply big data techniques to problem areas in which they could yield real benefits. On the other hand, a degree of opacity is a practical requirement for some applications, and, on a technical level, is a natural quality of the complex systems and algorithms employed.

Broadly, four types of factors contribute to a lack of transparency in the workings of big data operations as they pertain to the military: commercial, legal, physical and technical. Commercial considerations often dominate because much research and development of big data systems is done by corporations. In many commercial fields, an ability to gain insights from big data analysis is widely seen as becoming critical to companies' chances of success, and governments' ability to effectively govern; consequently, the market for big data technologies is estimated to be worth tens of billions of dollars per year today, growing to hundreds of billions in the coming years (Columbus 2018). It is a commercial necessity for developers of big data technologies to closely guard their innovations.

Legal measures are similarly employed by big data vendors to prevent competitors and others from learning the details of their systems' operations. Private sector bodies generally protect their innovations as trade secrets and other forms of intellectual property, while public bodies may, depending on their role, be bound to secrecy by national security legislation.

Stringent physical security measures protect the data centres which house data collected by big data systems. Given that they frequently house valuable commercial and national security assets, physical access to data centres is generally tightly controlled and restricted to authorised personnel only. Outside the data centre, many of the devices used to collect and process data also enjoy a level of physical security, often by dint of being discreet and ubiquitous to the point that they do not attract attention.

Finally, the technical nature of big data systems tends to limit transparency. The inherent complexity of big data algorithms, and the broader systems used for gathering and processing the data, naturally impart a degree of opacity to the systems. Encryption is also widely employed in various ways to prevent unauthorised access to both gathered data and the systems which gather and process them.

In many applications, military organisations have a legitimate need for secrecy which would be well served by this tendency towards opaque operation. Intelligence gathering is perhaps the canonical example. However, secrecy must be managed carefully. Transparency in the handling of data is generally important to people subject to the outcomes of data-based decision making and, by extension, to organisations seeking to employ big data for their own purposes. Where legal, ethical, social or practical considerations require a degree of transparency, it is necessary for data-gathering organisations to provide it, without defeating the purpose they hope to achieve.

Transparency from Outside

Military big data systems potentially gather and process data, directly or indirectly, from and about a very wide range of entities:

> machine data is generated by the movement of ships, aircraft and vehicles, satellites in space, drones, Unmanned Aerial Vehicles (UAVs), reconnaissance aircraft, sensors and Battle Field Surveillance Radars (BFSR). Human generated data include data from social media sites like YouTube, Facebook, [Twitter], and so on. Business data is generated from all e-commerce transactions. (Haridas 2015: 72)

With some entities the military has a relationship which constrains its behaviour in relevant ways, often via moral or legal obligations. Galliott identifies one basis of such obligations in an 'implicit contract' according to which 'the military has an obligation to effectively and efficiently provide for the safety and security of the state and its people, while ensuring that it does not [act] against the people's broader interests' (Galliott, 2015: 50–1). An adequate level of transparency on the part of military organisations engaged in data collection and processing is arguably a practical necessity for, if not an intrinsic part of, such a contract. A state that bears protective obligations to its citizenry, and fulfils those obligations via military force, must have sufficient information about military activities which potentially affect the interests of its populace to fulfil its obligations.

Further, a degree of transparency is necessary to secure a reasonable level of support from service members and the general public; people are less likely to object to personal data being collected and used for military purposes if the fact and manner of collection and processing is understood. The US Army's Human Capital Big Data (HCBD) initiative recognises this and states, 'Individuals are entitled to understandable information about how the Army collects data on them, who has access to that data, and how that data will be used and secured' (Lester et al. 2018: 108).

The problem of how to manage unanticipated secondary uses of data sets has also motivated a large proportion of the legal and ethical discussion about big data. Much of the power of big data analysis comes from using previously collected data in new ways to produce new insights (Richards and King 2014: 421). Analytical tools designed to mine data sets for previously unidentified correlations often lead to unexpected and valuable inferences and predictions, to the extent that such activity is a major driver of the global market for big data sets.

Despite the potential value to be realised from secondary uses of data, some uses result in scandal, which creates public distrust and threatens the organisations which take part. A recent and prominent example is the furore over the use by data analysts Cambridge Analytica of data gathered from Facebook users. Cambridge Analytica 'offered tools that could identify the personalities of American voters and influence their behaviour' (Granville, 2018), powered by private data scraped from users' profiles, largely without their consent (Watkin, 2018). As discussed elsewhere in this volume, the political and public response has been very damaging to the firms involved and has arguably cast suspicion on other organisations engaging in big data analytics.

The power to find new correlations between apparently unrelated entities comes at the cost of transparency in how collected data is being used, in that neither the entities which supply data nor the entities to which the data collector is accountable can know of those secondary uses in advance. The resulting threats to privacy and accountability have already prompted regulatory responses in some jurisdictions. For example, European law recognises a principle of 'purpose limitation' by which data that is considered personal must be used only for 'specified, explicit and legitimate purposes and not further processed in a way incompatible with those purposes' (Forgó, Hänold and Schütze 2017: 17).

The rapid progress of data protection regimes around the world suggests that organisations collecting and processing data will be subjected to even tighter regulation in the future. They must carefully design transparency measures to satisfy all legal and other requirements, and ensure political support, without undermining the purpose for which data is being collected.

Transparency from Inside

It is a common observation that useful big data analytical results have been achieved at the expense of greater complexity in the software that is used to analyse data (de Laat 2018: 536–9). In some cases, algorithms have become so complex that the interpretability or explainability of decisions based on analysis of big data sets has suffered in the search for accuracy; the decision maker knows what the analysis recommends, but does not know why.

If the results of data analysis are to be used in making a decision, but those results cannot be adequately explained by the entity responsible for making the decision, the usefulness of the analysis is curtailed. Decisions for which a rationale cannot be provided are likely to be seen as arbitrary and unreasonable, and will often incite resistance in those affected by the decision (Galliott 2016, 2017, 2018; Galliott and Scholz 2018; Wyatt and Galliott 2018).

As discussed, armed forces personnel are accountable to the state to which they belong. Implicit in that is the ability to explain decisions and actions made in the course of their duties. In an armed conflict, legal obligations require that parties responsible for tasks such as selecting targets and authorising the use of force be able to account for their decisions (Pilloud and Pictet, 1987: 680). That required level of certainty demands a high degree of transparency from any data analysis which contributes to targeting decisions.

Identity Paradox

The identity paradox concerns data about people. It is based on the observation that '[b]ig data seeks to identify, but it also threatens identity' (Richards and King 2013: 43). Many governmental and corporate big data operations aim to compile information about people, building profiles by which an analytical process can identify important characteristics of those people. The paradoxical aspect is that decisions based on a person's profile may influence, or even alter, the identity of the person on which it is based. Richards and King (2013) cite examples of audience data collection by Google and Netflix, and how that information might shape the search results and viewing recommendations they deliver, and in turn shape the views of the audience who consumes that content (ibid.: 44). Much of the concern expressed about big data in academia and the media relates to the possibility that it will be used (or abused) to interfere with the lives of profiled individuals.

There is a corollary to the identity paradox, not explicitly mentioned by Richards and King: that the way a data gatherer interacts with a data subject is based on the assembled profile of that person, an abstraction that is certainly incomplete and may contain errors. Decisions which require a decision maker to accurately account for the individual characteristics of a data-subject risk being based on a poor understanding of that person. Systemic errors in large sets of profiles may distort the results of analysis performed on those profiles. Actions based solely on incomplete profiles risk being inappropriate, unjustifiable or arbitrary.

Shaping

Big data analysis is a powerful means of shaping behaviour. The most obvious example is the huge growth of the online advertising market fuelled by technologies which track Internet users across websites, record their purchases and other online activities, and link those details to other data, including their contacts and perhaps their real name and address. More broadly, governments and corporations have for some years been engaging in a practice known as 'nudging': that is, guiding behaviour through subtle, non-coercive measures based on insights into behavioural psychology, increasingly backed by profiles assembled in big data operations (Thaler and Sunstein 2008).

Less dramatically, software which is used to make judgements on the basis of gathered data may be perceived as biased, leading to public controversy. Such controversies harm the image of the organisations involved. That is so regardless of their intentions, and, to an extent, regardless of whether there is substance to the damaging claims. Any organisation that gathers and uses big data, including armed forces, must avoid being perceived as using that data in biased or manipulative ways.

There is also regulatory risk associated with claims of manipulation or bias. Governments, which have an interest in protecting the rights of their populace and reining in exploitative practices, have begun to react strongly to abuses of data-derived knowledge by organisations. Following the revelations about Cambridge Analytica's activities, various governments conducted investigations and several legal complaints were filed (Solon and Graham-Harrison 2018). Some legislatures have passed laws protecting the interests of people whose data may be utilised for commercial or governmental purposes (European Commission 2018).

Analysis of social media data can also be very useful for intelligence organisations. For example, 'During the first two weeks of the 2011 Egyptian revolution, "over 32,000 new groups and 14,000 new pages were created on Facebook in Egypt"' (Van Puyvelde, Coulthart and Hossain 2017: 1411). Any restrictions on access to social media data, or risk of bad publicity or legal repercussions stemming from such access, are therefore a concern. Armed forces wishing to realise the benefits of access to such information must carefully manage both their conduct and the public perception of their activities so as to avoid scandal.

Errors

Regardless of the purposes for which personal profiles are intended or how they are compiled, the data on which those profiles are based will not be perfectly accurate, whether due to sampling biases, errors or omissions in individual profiles, or other flaws. The problem of dealing with bias which might affect inferences drawn about the population from which a sample is taken, is common to all studies relying on statistics, and has been widely analysed (Kaplan, Chambers and Glasgow 2014).

A problem that is perhaps more characteristic of emerging applications of big data is the possibility of flaws in the data or software used in automated decision-making systems, which result in incorrect decisions being made about individuals. This problem is not unique to big data operations, having existed for as long as organisations have been using gathered data about people as an aid in decision-making. It becomes particularly important, though, where there is an effort to delegate more decision-making to machines, with less direct human involvement, especially in the deployment of lethal force.

The possible consequences of errors in automated decision-making are as diverse as its applications. Where the data and decisions relate to an armed force's own service members, the core consideration is perhaps trust, which carries 'an amplified importance in the military because life and death outcomes as well as national security are at stake' (Schneider, Lyle and Murphy, 2015: 17). Sharing personally identifiable data, or data which may be used for purposes which affect one's interests, necessarily means trusting the entity collecting that data to protect the interests at stake, both in terms of keeping the data confidential and adopting responsible practices in making decisions based on those data.

In combat situations, the consequences of poor automated decision-making practices might be much more dire. Consider the developing role of data analysis in targeting decisions. There has been some controversy about revelations that the NSA has used metadata from 55 million Pakistani mobile phone users to generate intelligence designed to support drone strikes (National Security Agency 2012). Dubbed the SKYNET program, the system aimed to identify people who might be couriers carrying messages to and from Al Qaida members, based on data such as which towers their phones connected to at what times, call patterns and so on.

Power Paradox

The power paradox is based on the idea that power will be concentrated in those organisations which are able to gain new insights from data analysis at the expense of other organisations and people whose data is collected and analysed. This is because insights yielded by data analysis will often have security, strategic or commercial value, enhancing the power of entities that possess them over those that do not.

This is partly an issue of civil–military relations, but also an issue within and amongst the units of armed forces and alliances. It is not simply a matter of transferring power from one group to another, though. The resulting power imbalance, and the lack of clarity about its limits and how they will be regulated, creates risks for organisations engaged in big data analysis: 'Not knowing the appropriate legal or technical boundaries, each side is left guessing. Individuals succumb to denial while governments and corporations get away with what they can by default, until they are left reeling from scandal after shock of disclosure' (Richards and King 2013: 45). That is the paradoxical aspect: by gaining power in the form of the insights yielded by data analysis, an organisation also takes on risk in two forms: first, due to rapidly evolving and poorly defined legal limits on the acquisition and use of that power; and, secondly, due to the possibility of data breaches by adversaries, criminals or insider threats.

Concentrating Power

It is common for development of a new technology to concentrate power in the hands of parties which operate it. Big data is no exception, and big data systems possess two characteristics which indicate that some concentration of power is inevitable.

First, a consequence of the transparency paradox is that the sharing of information is only in one direction, from data-subjects to analysts. This is particularly true in a military context where collection may not be public knowledge, even amongst soldiers and military units. If analysis of that data reveals some pattern or insight which yields an advantage to the analyst then, in a real sense, 'information is power'.

Secondly, big data capabilities are heavily reliant on infrastructure (Andrejevic and Gates 2014: 188). Beyond the advanced hardware and software needed to effectively store and analyse huge quantities of data, an organisation must have access to equipment and networks to gather the data, as well as specialist staff to build and maintain that infrastructure and analyse the gathered data. Those needs represent significant technical and financial barriers to entry for individuals and small organisations that may otherwise yield military advantage.

Unsettled Rules

Existing laws and organisational policies regulating the acquisition and use of data are not always appropriate for the applications and capabilities unlocked by big data analysis. The rules and policies most at issue are those relating to the privacy of people whose data is gathered and processed. For military operational purposes, privacy is less likely to give rise to significant legal risk; commanders must be as certain as circumstances allow about important decisions, such as selecting targets, but have considerable latitude in the sources of information they draw on to achieve that certainty. The risks of controversy and negative public perception remain, though.

The degree of risk borne by armed forces relying on big data analysis is also likely to depend heavily on the level of human control over each decision: is it a human-made decision backed up by data analytics, or a machine-made decision followed by humans? If the former, then it is less likely to raise novel concerns. If the latter, then the degree of human 'ownership' is at issue: what degree of human oversight or direct human involvement in decision-making is required?

Practices adopted by some governmental and corporate entities have already raised significant concern among regulators and the public; consequently, new uses of big data are increasingly viewed with caution and scepticism (which may be unrelated to their potential value) (Mawad et al. 2018). Perceived abuses are likely to provoke a backlash, including restrictive regulatory measures. Those practices have developed in part due to the absence of clear regulatory limits on the gathering and use of data. Consequently, regulators around the world are responding with laws which place increasingly stringent requirements on organisations accessing potentially sensitive information about people. That regulatory environment is rapidly changing, and so presents a risk to organisations seeking to make long-term investments in big data, including the military.

Data Breaches

While accumulating data allows an organisation to gain power, it also makes the organisation an attractive target for parties seeking to obtain the data for their own purposes. This risk is inherent in the possession of data. Given the sensitivity of the data that is typically stored for military purposes, the threat of attempted breaches is high.

Successful breaches may be disastrous for affected organisations and for individuals whose data is compromised. Breached organisations suffer, at least, scandal and loss of trust. Individuals whose data is stolen may become victims of identity theft or other attacks. Of course, many more serious threats may follow from an adversary or criminal gaining access to information with strategic or security value.

Responding to the Challenges

The big data paradoxes are based on the idea that certain types of risk are inherent in big data systems and operations: the opacity necessary to protect and exploit sensitive data tends to limit accountability and public support; decisions about people based on data-derived profiles risk being intrusive and manipulative, and are only as accurate as the data on which they are based; insights derived from big data analysis entrench and extend existing power imbalances and may force organisations into uncharted ethical and legal territory.

Consideration of the three paradoxes in relation to a specific application of data analysis yields a basic taxonomy of the types of risk to be managed. Managing those risks is then an exercise in data governance, a field that faces a raft of new challenges from the growth of big data. New applications, new methods of gathering and analysing data, the expanding scope of data-driven activities and their reach into people's lives, and higher levels of reliance on analytical outcomes by governments and corporations are all testing the limits of established data governance practices.

Part of the challenge for organisations attempting to establish new data governance regimes is that early exploitation of big data by government and private industry has triggered changes in societal attitudes which have not yet settled, but which must be reflected in governance procedures. Attitudes to privacy are perhaps the prime example. The extensive monitoring of individuals which has led beyond the 'surveillance state' to the emergence of the concepts of the 'surveillance economy' and 'surveillance capitalism' has raised widespread concerns about protecting individual privacy and has prompted responses from companies and regulators (Hirst 2013; Zuboff, 2015).

More fundamentally, some scholars have proposed that the idea of privacy needs to be re-examined in the light of the new challenges and promises offered by big data. These proposals would move away from viewing privacy as secrecy of information, and instead focus on confidentiality of shared information (Richards and King 2014; Soria-Comas and Domingo-Ferrer 2016) and accountability of those entities with which information is shared (Mayer-Schönberger and Cukier 2013: 173).

Currently, though, the boundaries of what is legally permissible and socially acceptable are a moving target for organisations developing data governance regimes, military and non-military. As such, there is no comprehensive guidance for adapting organisational policies for big data management. It will require new expertise and perhaps new institutions.

For the foreseeable future, those changes are likely to be made piecemeal, but one theme emerging in the literature is the idea of using a trusted third party to monitor or audit big data collection and analysis (Mayer-Schönberger and Cukier 2013: 178–82; Richards and King 2014: 429–30). While review boards, auditing committees and similar bodies are a common means of overseeing organisational activities, their role in managing big data operations is still the subject of discussion. The role of a third party would be to help an organisation manage the risks inherent in big data operations without threatening the ability to achieve the aims of the operation. With respect to the transparency paradox, such a body would represent the interests of the state and individuals whose data may be in use, ensuring that their rights are protected, while also protecting sensitive operational information from being accessed by hostile parties. With respect to the identity paradox, it may act as a quality-control body, helping to ensure that errors in personal data profiles do not undermine the validity of decisions based on those profiles. The power paradox arises largely from a lack of clarity at a societal level about the rules which should govern use of data, and so is likely to persist until that broad clarity is achieved. However, a trusted review body could assist with the problem of reliance on third-party software if empowered to audit software for vulnerabilities and consistency with organisational requirements.

A significant amount of associated work will be required to support such an endeavour. An organisation, or a society as a whole, must first decide upon the principles and rules which an oversight body is to protect. Software standards must be developed in terms of auditability and transparency of operation. Professionals must be trained with the required analytical or auditing skills. In the meantime, the three paradoxes defined by Richards and King and applied here to the military may provide a useful framework for organisations putting in place their own governance solutions.

Conclusions

Applications of big data in military operations are not essentially different from civilian applications in areas such as finance, sociology and medicine. However, military applications are often unique insofar as they involve national security considerations and high levels of secrecy that reflect security concerns. As they are expected to comply with strict security and ethical protocols, military personnel using data-mining applications must undergo specific professional preparation to comprehend their obligations and entitlements and learn how to assess and counter possible threats. These include the paradoxes discussed in our chapter.

The military is accountable for the use of sensitive information about citizens and groups, as it is entrusted by society with a mandate to use potentially destructive technologies financed through public sources. However, in certain circumstances, the military might claim the right to decline any request to disclose whether it has collected sensitive information as part of a mission that made it indispensable. Whenever it claims such right, the military has to face the paradox of transparency.

Defence forces are accountable for the use of data-mining technologies that automate the process of profiling individuals, whether they target military or civilian populations. Further work is necessary to define the responsibilities and challenges, and to determine whether specific restrictions must be enforced. This work will need to account for the paradox of identity.

Finally, national or supranational institutions inquire about whether the armed forces have collected, stored or shared with third parties sensitive information in their own country or in allied countries. The military has the responsibility to balance privacy and security, protecting them both as much as is feasible. The use of big data to monitor and make decisions about people involves issues of legitimacy and justification, and as such it involves the paradox of power.

References

Andrejevic, M. and K, Gates, 'Big Data Surveillance: Introduction', *Surveillance & Society* 12(2) (2014): 185–96.

Columbus, L., '10 Charts That Will Change Your Perspective Of Big Data's Growth', *Forbes*, 2018, available at: https://www.forbes.com/sites/louiscolumbus/2018/05/23/10-charts-that-will-change-your-perspective-of-big-datas-growth/#1cabf9da2926, last accessed 28 September 2019.

Costlow, T., 'How Big Data is Paying Off for DOD', *Defense Systems*, 2014, available at: https://defensesystems.com/articles/2014/10/24/feature-big-data-for-defense.aspx, last accessed 28 September 2019.

de Laat, P., 'Algorithmic Decision-making Based on Machine Learning from Big Data: Can Transparency Restore Accountability?' *Philosophy & Technology* 31 (2018): 525–41.

Ebach, M. C., M. S. Michael, W. S. Shaw, J. Goff, D. J. Murphy and S. Matthews, 'Big Data and the Historical Sciences: a Critique', *Geoforum* 71 (2016): 1–4.

European Commission, *2018 Reform of EU Data Protection Rules*, available at: https://ec.europa.eu/commission/priorities/justice-and-fundamental-rights/data-protection/2018-reform-eu-data-protection-rules_en, last accessed 28 September 2019.

Finlay, S., *Predictive Analytics, Data Mining and Big Data: Myths, Misconceptions and Methods* (Berlin: Springer, 2014).

Forgó, N., S. Hänold and B. Schütze, 'The Principle of Purpose Limitation and Big Data', in M. Corrales, M. Fenwick and N. Forgó (eds), *New Technology, Big Data and the Law* (Singapore: Springer, 2017), pp. 17–42.

Galliott, J., *Military Robots: Mapping the Moral Landscape* (Farnham: Ashgate, 2015).

Galliott J., 'Defending Australia in the Digital Age: Toward Full Spectrum Defence', *Defence Studies* 16 (2016): 157–75.

Galliott J., 'The Limits of Robotic Solutions to Human Challenges in the Land Domain', *Defence Studies* 17 (2017): 327–45.

Galliott J., 'The Soldier's Tolerance for Autonomous Systems', *Paladyn* 9 (2018): 124–36.

Galliott J. and J. Scholz, 'Artificial Intelligence in Weapons: the Moral Imperative for Minimally-Just Autonomy'', *US Air Force Journal of Indo-Pacific Affairs* 1 (2018): 57–67.

Gandomi, A. and M. Haider, 'Beyond the Hype: Big Data Concepts, Methods, and Analytics', *International Journal of Information Management* 35(2) (2015): 137–44.

Granville, K., 'Facebook and Cambridge Analytica: What You Need to Know as Fall-out Widens', *New York Times*, 19 March 2018 available at: https://www.nytimes.com/2018/03/19/technology/facebook-cambridge-analytica-explained.html, last accessed 28 September 2019.

Haridas, M., 'Redefining Military Intelligence Using Big Data Analytics', *Scholar Warrior*, 2015, available at: http://www.claws.in/images/journals_doc/1511401708_RedefiningMilitaryIntelligenceUsingBigDataAnalytics.pdf, last accessed 28 September 2019.

Hirst, M., 'Someone's Looking at You: Welcome to the Surveillance Economy', *The Conversation*, 2013, available at: https://theconversation.com/someones-looking-at-you-welcome-to-the-surveillance-economy-16357, last accessed 28 September 2019.

Kaplan, R. M., D. A. Chambers and R. E. Glasgow, 'Big Data and Large Sample Size: a Cautionary Note on the Potential for Bias', *Clinical and Translational Science* 7(4) (2014): 342–6.

Lele, A., *Disruptive Technologies for the Militaries and Security* (Berlin: Springer, 2018).

Lester, P., P. Wolf, C. Nannini, D. Jensen and D. Davis, 'Continuing the Big Data Ethics Debate: Enabling Senior Leader Decisionmaking', *Joint Force Quarterly* 89 (2018): 106–13.

Mawad, M., H. Fouquet, N. Grant and D. Li, 'Scared by Facebook? Wait till Millennials are Selling their Data', *Bloomberg*, 2018, available at: https://www.bloomberg.com/news/articles/2018-06-08/scared-by-facebook-wait-till-millennials-are-selling-their-data, last accessed 28 September 2019.

Mayer-Schönberger, V. and K. Cukier, K., *Big Data: a Revolution that Will Transform How We Live, Work, and Think* (New York: Houghton Mifflin Harcourt, 2013).

National Security Agency, 'SKYNET: Courier Detection via Machine Learning', *The Intercept*, 2012, available at: https://theintercept.com/document/2015/05/08/skynet-courier, last accessed 28 September 2019.

Pariser, E., *The Filter Bubble: How the New Personalized Web is Changing What We Read and How We Think* (London: Penguin, 2011).

Pilloud, C. and J. Pictet, 'Protocol I – Article 57 – Precautions in Attack', in Y. Sandoz, C. Swinarski and B. Zimmermann (eds), *Commentary on the Additional Protocols of 8 June 1977 to the Geneva Conventions of 12 August 1949* (Geneva: Martinus Nijhoff, 1987).

Richards, N. and J. King, 'Three Paradoxes of Big Data', *Stanford Law Review Online* 66 (2013): 41–6.

Richards, N. and J. King, 'Big Data Ethics', *Wake Forest Law Review* 49 (2014): 393–432.

Schneider, K. F., D. S. Lyle and F. X. Murphy, 'Framing the Big Data Ethics Debate for the Military', *Joint Force Quarterly* 77 (2015): 16–23.

Solon, O. and E. Graham-Harrison, 'The Six Weeks that Brought Cambridge Analytica Down', *The Guardian*, 3 May 2018, available at: https://www.theguardian.com/uk-news/2018/may/03/cambridge-analytica-closing-what-happened-trump-brexit, last accessed 28 September 2019.

Soria-Comas, J. and J. Domingo-Ferrer, 'Big Data Privacy: Challenges to Privacy Principles and Models', *Data Science and Engineering* 1(1) (2016): 21–8.

Tenner, E., *The Efficiency Paradox: What Big Data Can't Do* (New York: Vintage, 2018).

Thaler, R. H. and C. Sunstein, *Nudge: Improving Decisions about Health, Wealth, and Happiness* (New Haven, CT: Yale University Press, 2008).

Thuraisingham, B., M. M. Masud, P. Parveen and L. Khan, 'Data Mining for Security Applications', *Big Data Analytics with Applications in Insider Threat Detection*, 2017, doi: 10.1201/9781315119458.

Van Puyvelde, D., S. Coulthart and M. S. Hossain, 'Beyond the Buzzword: Big Data and National Security Decision-making', *International Affairs* 93(6) (2017): 1397–416.

Vie, L. L., L. M. Scheier, P. B. Lester, T. E. Ho, D. R. Labarthe and M. E. P. Seligman, 'The US Army Person-Event Data Environment: a Military–Civilian Big Data Enterprise', *Big Data* 3(2) (2015): 67–79.

Watkin, W. D., 'Cambridge Analytica Used Our Secrets For Profit – the Same Data Could be Used for Public Good', *The Conversation*, 2018, available at: https://theconversation.com/cambridge-analytica-used-our-secrets-for-profit-the-same-data-could-be-used-for-public-good-98745, last accessed 28 September 2019.

Weinberger, S., 'The Graveyard of Empires and Big Data', *Foreign Policy*, 15 March 2017, available at: https://foreignpolicy.com/2017/03/15/the-graveyard-of-empires-and-big-data, last accessed 28 September 2019.

Wyatt A. and J. Galliott, 'Closing the Capability Gap: ASEAN Military Modernization during the Dawn of Autonomous Weapon Systems', *Asian Security* (2018); 1–20.

Yang, S., M. Yang, S. Wang and K. Huang, 'Adaptive Immune Genetic Algorithm for Weapon System Portfolio Optimization in Military Big Data Environment', *Cluster Computing* 19(3) (2016): 1359–72.

Zhai, C-G., X-B. Jiang, Y-X. Zhang and N. Liu, 'Research on the Optimization of Military Supplies under Big Data Background', *2018 International Conference on Big Data and Artificial Intelligence (BDAI)*, 2018, doi: 10.1109/bdai.2018.8546629.

Zuboff, S., 'Big Other: Surveillance Capitalism and the Prospects of an Information Civilization', *Journal of Information Technology* 30(1) (2015): 75–89.

Part Four

THIRTEEN

Beyond the Concept of Anonymity: What is Really at Stake?

Björn Lundgren

The aim of this chapter is to discuss anonymity and the threats against it – in the form of de-anonymisation technologies. The question in the title above is approached by conceptual analysis: I ask what kind of concept we need and how it ought to be conceptualised given what is really at stake. By what is at stake I mean the values that are threatened by various de-anonymisation technologies. It will be argued that while previous conceptualisations of anonymity may be reasonable – given a standard lexical, or common-sense, understanding of the term – the concept of *anonymity* is not sufficient given what is really at stake. I will argue that what is at stake is *our ability to be anonymous*, which I will broadly characterise as *a reasonable control over what we communicate*.

The concept of anonymity has not – unlike the closely related concept of privacy – been given much attention by philosophers. The word 'anonymous' comes from the Greek *anōnumos*, which originally meant 'without name' or 'nameless'.[1] However, as Kathleen A. Wallace notes, this is not the only sense of anonymity, neither is it the most interesting one (Wallace 1999: 23). According to Wallace a person P is anonymous, in a given respect, when others cannot coordinate traits so that P can be identified (ibid.: 25). Thus, we can conclude that on Wallace's view anonymity is *non-identifiability* or, technically, *'noncoordinatability of traits in a given respect(s)'* (ibid.: 25). While Wallace thinks of her definition as conceptual or metaphysical, her aim is also that it should enable us to analyse what is at stake (ibid.: 34).

Before Wallace, Helen Nissenbaum (1999) argued for a narrower conception of anonymity. According to Nissenbaum, what is at stake is non-reachability, that is, what matters is not whether you can identify me, but whether you (after identification) can reach me. On the one hand, Nissenbaum's narrower conception makes sense if we think of, for example, criminals, who occasionally may care less that we know they commit a crime, as long as they can avoid punishment. On the other hand, it is also reasonable to argue that it is too narrow, given that the task of avoiding reachability may incur harm because one is identified.

Finally, Steve Matthews (2010), while discussing anonymity in relation to the social self, argues for another conception. According to Matthews, anonymity is non-trackability. What matters is neither only not being identified nor only not being reachable, but not being trackable over our social contexts. Matthews illustrates his point using examples discussed by Laud Humphrey about male-to-male encounters in public bathrooms. Matthews points out that these men were both partly identified and reachable and that what mattered to them was not avoiding identification or reachability in the context of their encounters, but that they could not be tracked from one social context to another. Matthews thinks of non-trackability both in the physical sense of not being tracked down and in the more abstract sense that people cannot link a piece of information to a more complete account of who that person is (2010: 354ff.), which corresponds to both Wallace's and Nissenbaum's conceptions of anonymity.

The aim in this chapter is not to question the above conceptualisations of anonymity, nor to argue which is superior. They all give a fair account of a common-sense conception of anonymity. What I will question is instead whether they give a fair account of what is really at stake. By what is at stake I mean the values that are threatened by various de-anonymisation technologies. In order to fulfil this aim, I will simplify the above accounts and focus on some fundamental features they all share.

First, on these views, anonymity is a bivalent concept (that is, a person either is or is not identifiable, reachable or trackable). In the next section, I will show that anonymisation technology is probabilistic. However, this alone does not imply that there is anything wrong with focusing on a conception of the state of anonymity. Indeed, previous accounts do recognise that de-anonymisation is probabilistic (for example, the non-coordinability of traits on Wallace's view). Thus, in the upcoming sections I will also show that the risk to anonymity matters, not only because it increases the likelihood of de-anonymisation (or author re-identification), but because it affects our ability to be anonymous and because it can cause harm beyond de-anonymisation.

Secondly, on these views, anonymity is a relation between some information (which I take to include actions, since actions can be expressed in the form of information) and a person, that is, what is at stake is revealing that some information is linked to some person (henceforth I will simply speak of 'revealing linkages' as 'linkages'). Conversely, I will argue that a person can be harmed when information about that person is linked to other information about that person, without it being linked to that person. We can distinguish these two linkages by referring to the former as 'information-to-person linkage' and the latter as 'information-to-information linkage'.

I will summarise the above theses in an account that I will call *the common view* (since it seems to correspond with the common-sense idea of anonymity):

The common view: a person is anonymous relative to some information only if that person cannot be singled out as *the one* linked to that information.

Before I turn to show that this is not the concept we need, two further things need to be noted.

First, the common view uses 'information' in a broader and more inclusive sense than what follows from a close reading of the three considered accounts. Secondly, although there are various senses of anonymity, it should be clear from the discussion above that the common view corresponds to the colloquial language notion of anonymity as relating to some *particular* information (that is, one is anonymous relative to some particular information, as compared with being a person about which very little is known).

The remainder of this chapter is structured as follows. In the next section, I will introduce some basic information about de-anonymisation technologies and an elementary challenge from Paul Ohm (2010). At the end of that section, I will have introduced reasons to doubt whether focusing on anonymity is enough. However, the choice of what concepts that we need will still be open. Thus, in the third section I argue that the common view cannot make sense of future risks of de-anonymisation and, more importantly, that harm goes beyond de-anonymisation, concluding that what we need is a concept of *our ability to be anonymous*. In the fourth section, I will aim to explicate this ability. Last, in the fifth section, while the previous discussions will have focused on individual harms, I aim to briefly broaden the discussion to show that the concept can be applied to collectives as well as to situations when de-anonymisation is all-things-considered desirable. Finally, I will end the chapter by a brief summation.

De-anonymisation and Information Aggregation

We can speak of a person being de-anonymised in line with the common view as follows:

> *The common view of de-anonymisation:* a person that was previously anony-mous relative to some information is de-anonymised if that person can be singled out as *the one* linked to that information.

In this sense de-anonymisation is achieved by linking information that allows for the identification of a singular person. For example, if you know the ZIP code, sex and date of birth of a someone living in the US, then there is at least 61 per cent chance that the person can be identified (see Ohm 2010: 1705, fn. 4, which also includes relevant references).

The aim of this section is to clarify a few relevant technical aspects of de-anonymisation technologies. First, I will discuss the granularity of the information that can be used to de-anonymise someone. Secondly, I will discuss the aggregating power of de-anonymisation technologies and set the basis for my critique of the common view.

In the previous section I noted that Wallace's conception of anonymity as *non-coordinatability of traits*, indicated a narrower scope than the common view. Wallace explains that traits should be understood as similar to that of a definitive description (Wallace 1999: 25). Furthermore, she thinks that 'a person *is* each of her traits (mother, novelist, English speaker, professor of mathematics, licensed driver, social security contributor, and so on)' (ibid.: 26).

Thus, conceptualising anonymity in terms of traits seems to imply that only information that is fairly substantial in itself (that is, information that is constitutive of who we are) can be used to de-anonymise someone. This is problematic since de-anonymisation can be performed using information of extremely varying granularity. It is misleading to think that only information that is constitutive of who we are can threaten our anonymity.

Indeed, de-anonymisation technology shows that information that is seemingly insignificant can be combined to de-anonymise us. For example, Johansson, Kaati and Shrestha (2015) have shown how de-anonymisation can be achieved by analysing *when* a user posts information. By analysing individual posting times, they create a 'timeprint' that can be used to reveal who the author is. With machine learning the success rate of author identification was 90 per cent for a sample of 1,000 users (ibid.: 10). They also show how to improve the identification by adding a stylometric analysis (that is, an analysis of how we write).

Although we can have a meaningful discussion about whether one's writing style constitutes a trait, it is clear that a singular time when one posts on the Internet does not constitute a trait in the sense Wallace conceptualises it (although a timeprint might). Despite this, it is the singular posting times that are coordinated into a timeprint, which allows for de-anonymisation.

Thus, we need to keep in mind that virtually *any* information, irrespective of its granularity, can be used to de-anonymise us. Therefore, to protect anonymity, we cannot only protect information that is sensitive in itself, since seemingly insignificant information can – if combined – become significant. This must be properly considered when conceptually analysing anonymity, which is why I have defined the common view in terms of information (and not in terms of, for example, traits).

Seemingly insignificant information can also be used to reveal further information about identified persons. An illustrative example is that of Facebook 'likes' (Facebook 'likes' is a function that allows users on Facebook to react to postings – including links – on Facebook by giving a thumbs-up; in 2016, Facebook complemented the function with a wider set of reactions). Kosinski, Stillwell and Graepel (2013) built a model that could analyse binary sorted personal traits on the basis of what people had 'liked' on Facebook. The success rate was between 60 and 95 per cent and included (in order of correlation – from weakest to strongest): parents together/separated before age of 21; drug use; single/in a relationship; alcohol use; smoker; lesbian; Christian/Muslim; Democrat/Republican; gay; gender (Kosinski et al.: 5803, fig. 2). They also tested correlation to various personal traits (ibid.: 5804, fig. 3).

This example illustrates that the kind of technologies that are used to de-anonymise some anonymous information about a person can also be used to reveal further information about that person, which is not part of any anonymous set of information. That is, what is at stake here is not merely retaining anonymity of some *particular* information, because these technologies can be used to generally reveal information about a person. The best way to conceptualise this harm is arguably to say that the problem is that the Kosinski et al. model in conjunction with the Facebook 'likes' affects a person's *ability to be anonymous*, because it diminishes a person's ability to control what is known about that person. However, this does not mean that the disvalue of having more information about oneself available *cannot* be explained on the common view. For example, one could view this as a de-anonymisation of a large set of information. However, on the one hand, the model neither identifies nor makes a person reachable (providing a potential counter-example to Wallace's and Nissenbaum's conceptions). But, on the other hand, it could be argued that it makes a person more trackable over social contexts. The current question, then, is whether it is more reasonable to think of this as affecting our ability to be anonymous or our anonymity.

The above examples also relate to what Paul Ohm calls the 'accretion problem'. The accretion problem is that successful de-anonymisation functions as a key to further success. By linking 'anonymised' information with other 'anonymised' information one can de-anonymise (or re-identify, which is the concept that Ohm uses) further 'anonymised' information. Generally, success increases the chance of further success (Ohm 2010: 1746). In a nutshell, the information gained by de-anonymising someone's information in one situation can be further used to unlock other information to further de-anonymise someone's information in other situations.

As Ohm notes, the accretion problem neatly illustrates why successful de-anonymisation of insignificant information matters: it matters because it can be used to de-anonymise significant information and cause future harm (Ohm 2010). It also illustrates why the risk of de-anonymisation is important. That an ethical analysis must take risks into consideration, rather than only focusing on idealised cases, has been pointed out before (see, for example, Hansson 2003).

As previously noted, on the common view anonymity is a binary concept, but that does not necessarily make de-anonymisation non-probabilistic.

On the one hand, it could be argued that the relevant concept is a measurement of the risk of de-anonymisation, not whether someone is anonymous or not. For example, Ohm argues that we should apply a concept of informational entropy (corresponding to some conceptions of information and informativity; see Adriaans 2013, for an overview). Entropy functions as a measurement of possibilities, fewer possibilities imply a lower entropy, which implies a greater risk of successful de-anonymisation. When more information is linked, the possible links (to a person or other information) become fewer and, therefore, de-anonymisation becomes more probable.

On the other hand, a proponent of the common view may respond that what matters is anonymity and that the risk of anonymity matters only insofar as it affects our anonymity. Thus, the risk of de-anonymisation is only a disvalue insofar as it is actually realised. Proponents of the common view can then use Ohm's entropy-measurement (or something similar) to measure that risk.

However, harm does not stop with the *risk of de-anonymisation*. In the next section, I will argue that what is at stake here goes beyond the *risk of de-anonymisation*. First, we need a concept that also takes *future risks due to de-anonymisation* into consideration. Secondly, what is at stake goes beyond de-anonymisation as such, because there can be harm from de-anonymisation technologies without de-anonymisation.

The Risk of Future De-anonymisation and Harm Without De-anonymisation

In the previous section, I relied on insights from Ohm – and others – that showed how insignificant linkages can be instrumental for the de-anonymisation of more sensitive information. In this section, I will first show that Ohm's suggestion to use entropy is insufficient given future threats to our ability to be anonymous. Next, I will more broadly attack the common view presumption that what is at stake is only information-to-person linkage.

As previously noted, Ohm suggested is that the risk of de-anonymisation can be measured by the concept of entropy:

> . . . entropy measures how close an adversary is to connecting a given fact to a given individual. It describes the length of the interference chains heading in opposite directions, quantifying the remaining uncertainty. (Ohm 2010: 1749)

However, the problem is that while this gives us a measurement of the risk of de-anonymisation for a *given fact*, it cannot be used to measure future risks, given future *possible facts* (that is, something that would be a fact if a certain possibility is actualised in the future). Information-to-information linkage does not only affect the person's *current* ability to be anonymous, but also their *future* ability to be anonymous.

Here is an example: Jane has previously made a list of her favourite films available. While the list is clearly linked to Jane, there is no further anonymised information about Jane to which it could possibly be linked. Thus, on the common view, the potential harm of making her list known is limited to the harm of her list being known. On the view I defend, the existence of her list is also harmful because it affects her ability to be anonymous. The reason for this is simple: although it cannot currently be linked to any further information, it could be linked to future possible information (making Jane de-anonymised given her future actions). For example, consider that Jane creates an account on an online site that allows her to grade and rank movies (for example, the Internet Movie Database (IMDb)). Furthermore, suppose that her top-list (perhaps in conjunction with other previously available information) makes her IMDb account linkable to her. The example can be expanded, for example, by linkage from grading of all her films to making all her view-patterns available.

Suppose, for example, that she starts using an online streaming service such as Netflix. Further suppose that Netflix makes all their user data publicly available in an anonymised form (as they previously have, see Ohm 2010: 1720ff. for an over-view and a list of relevant references). If so, her currently available information would make it impossible for her, in the future, to keep her Netflix usage anonymous. As a result of that all of her viewing patterns would be available, which could be linked to reveal further information, etc. While de-anonymisation of her IMDb account may be an insignificant harm, in itself, her complete viewing-pattern (including both what she sees and when she sees it) would be possibly significant. Also, keep in mind that this further decreases her ability to be anonymous (via the accretion problem), both in the current situation as well as future possible situations.

On the common view, the information-to-person linkage between Jane and her IMDb account, via her top-list, would be the harm. On my view, that conclusion misses the fact that it was the previous release of her top-list that made the de-anonymisation and information-to-person linkage possible. On my view, we should reasonably consider *any linkage* harmful because it decreases our ability to be anonymous not only in the current situation, but in future possible situations. This is reasonably part of what is at stake. Conversely, a proponent of the common view would likely respond and argue that the harm here is future de-anonymisation of future possible facts, and that while we should recognise that information-to-information linkages was necessary for that harm, the information-to-information linkages was not harmful in itself, it was *only* instrumental for the de-anonymisation of information-to-person linkage. However, there can be harm from de-anonymisation technologies *without* de-anonymisation.

Consider the following example: suppose that a large set of sensitive information about Joe is linked so that it is knowable that it is about the same person, but not yet knowable whom it is about. Let us further presume that if Joe makes various kinds of communications, then these communications can be used to completely de-anonymise the sensitive information. Further, suppose that Joe knows this. This means that Joe would have to choose whether to communicate freely and, as a consequence, have a third party know that this information is about him, or whether to censor himself in order to keep it secret that the information is about him. (A similar example is discussed by Ohm 2010: 1748, however, Ohm's discussion is in line with the common view – that the de-anonymisation is the harm.)

In such a situation Joe is harmed, even if the information is never de-anonymised. Although this particular example may strike some as a rare situation, it reveals that what matters goes beyond avoiding de-anonymi-sation as such. Furthermore, the example can be modified to generalise to situations most of us encounter in our daily lives. For example, choosing whether to create a Facebook account, use the services of Google, use some smartphone apps, or use many other services that come without a monetary cost, but include paying with your information. Many people do deal with such trade-offs. The problems are several, such as the non-transparent usage of (personal) information, which the example of Facebook 'likes' illustrates (see Hull, Lipford and Latulipe 2011 for a broad discussion, although partly outdated, about privacy concerns relating to Facebook). Furthermore, avoiding social networks such as Facebook may, at least in some social circles, include a certain amount of social isolation. While it is reasonable to think that many are unaware of the exact consequences for their personal information, most are not completely unwitting. There are plausibly a fair amount of people making trade-offs similar to that of Joe.

However, it is, of course, rare that a person knows of the *specific* risks of being de-anonymised. Thus, suppose, conversely, that Joe without knowing revealed all this sensitive information about himself (that is, he accidentally de-anonymised himself in relation to this information and, thus, revealed a large set of sensitive information about himself). While the common view can sensibly explain why the de-anonymisation matters in a situation in which Joe unwittingly reveals all that sensitive information, the core of the problem is not necessarily captured by the common view, but in control over our communications. Paraphrasing on Matthews' examples, suppose that the information is a detailed account of Joe's sexual activities. Suppose further that while the information may be sensitive (in the sense that it is not something that Joe wants to share), it does not reveal anything about his social position or role, which was not previously known. For example, Joe may have accidentally revealed details to friends about one of his sexual encounters (which he did not want to share), although it is perfectly well-known what *kind* of sexual encounters that Joe engages in. Thus, the information can be harmful, although it does not affect Joe's social position. Neither would it contribute to him being reachable in a sense that matters, which he previously was not. Nor would it make him identified (by revealing any of his traits), since he is already identified as person that does x-like things. Thus, the common view (or, specifically, the three discussed conceptions of anonymity) does not capture what is really at stake in these examples. In the next section, I will turn to explicate *our ability to be anonymous* and to show that it captures what is at stake.

Explicating Our Ability to be Anonymous

What the above examples show is that the values of anonymity go beyond the common view (that is, beyond information-to-person linkage). Harm can result simply from information-to-information linkage. Why? Because it decreases our ability to be anonymous. In this section, I aim to explicate the concept of our ability to be anonymous (in line with previous examples). I will also aim to show how it differs from the closely related concepts of privacy and the right to privacy.

The simple suggestion is that our ability to be anonymous should be defined in terms of *a reasonable control over what we communicate*. What I mean by control is actually absence of others' control over what we communicate, since control is not necessarily mutually exclusive (that is, that a person has control of x does not imply that other people do not also have control over x). Furthermore, by communicating I do not merely mean communication by speaking or writing. Rather, communication is much broader: what I have in mind is communicative actions, by which I mean actions that lead to information being transferred. For example, this can be speech acts, written messages, bodily movements (for example, how a person reacts in a situation or that a certain person goes from one place to another), or basically any usage of Internet services (just by clicking on websites we communicate, although such communication should in most cases ideally be private). Thus, what I broadly mean by a *control over what we communicate* is that when communicating some information, I, to a person, P, one has control to the extent that only I is communicated to only P. Relative to this, harm mainly relates to two main types of risk (which, as the previous examples show, need not be actualised – since risk can be part of a trade-off with another value): (1) harm can result because the information intended for P is also at risk of being spread to Q; and (2) harm can result from the risk of others' ability to conclude that I implies J. However, since most communications actually have such a deductive, inductive or abductive; the *reasonability* condition is quite central. If I ask you to pass me the dessert, you can perhaps presume that I like cake. This is, on most occasions, unproblematic. However, the currently available techniques make it possible to perform information linkage that goes well beyond such ordinary everyday conversational conclusions. The same holds for communications intended for P, but (at risk of being) spread to Q. This is, standardly, something that P has control over. But we can maintain a reasonable control if P respects that we should maintain this control.

If we re-examine the previous examples we can see that this ability indeed captures what was at stake. First, Jane's ability to control her future communication was limited by unimportant information being linked to her. Because of information she was previously fine with communicating, it became impossible for her to keep other (more sensitive information) anonymous, which decreased her ability to be anonymous. Secondly, Joe had to choose between self-censorship and control over what was known about him (*mutatis mutandis* for the remaining variations), meaning that Joe was harmed, even without de-anonymisation, because his ability to be anonymous was seriously diminished.

Now, given that I talk about control over communications of (sensitive) information, it is easy to think that I am conflating our ability to be anonymous with privacy or the right to privacy. For example, according to Andrei Marmor, 'there is a general right to privacy grounded in people's interest in having a reasonable measure of control over the ways in which they can present themselves (and what is theirs) to others' (Marmor 2015: 3f.), and according to William A. Parent, '[p]rivacy is the condition of not having undocumented personal knowledge about one possessed by others' (Parent 1983: 269). However, if the overlap between these accounts of (the right to) privacy and our ability to be anonymous is, in fact, a conflation, then it is, arguably, these accounts – not mine – that are too broad. I have three things to say in defence of my conceptualisation: first, it is easy to conceive of an example that diminishes a person's control over what they communicate while having nothing to do with privacy. Suppose, for example, that Joe's sensitive information was his previously unknown business plans. Suppose further that although the business plans are sensitive they contain no privacy-sensitive information. Yet, by making it available, it affects his control over the ways in which he can present his business plan to others (that is, exactly the kind of control that Marmor discusses).[2] Thus, I would argue that it is control accounts of privacy (or the right to privacy) that are confused and in fact include too much (*mutatis mutandis* for Parent's account of possession of personal information). Secondly, the ability to be anonymous is reasonably also narrower than (the right to) privacy. Generally, there are situations which can diminish someone's privacy (or infringe upon the right) without affecting the control over our communications. For example, being seen in the nude by a former intimate partner standardly diminishes one's privacy (*mutatis mutandis* for the right), but given that it does not give the ex-partner access to any new information one's ability to be anonymous is not affected, since one's control over this information was already previously shared. Thirdly, that two concepts partly overlap is not necessarily a problem; it just means that our ability to be anonymous indeed has a lot to do with preserving privacy. Thus, while our ability to be anonymous is not conflated with privacy, privacy is amongst one of many values that the ability can help protect (see Matthews 2010: 355).

That completes the main aim of the chapter, which was to argue for – and explicate – a conception of the concept we need in order to analyse and address possible harms from de-anonymisation technologies. However, the harms I have focused on so far have been limited to individuals' harm from de-anonymisation technologies. In the next section, I will aim to show that the concept of *our ability to be anonymous* applies more broadly, by addressing good and bad usage of de-anonymisation technologies.

Dual Usage of De-anonymisation Technologies

In this penultimate section, I will briefly contextualise the challenges we are facing, to show how the concept of our ability to be anonymous works as an umbrella concept that addresses a complex and multifaceted debate. While the examples previously discussed – in relation to the aim of chapter – have focus on situations when de-anonymisation technologies cause harm for individuals, these technologies are actually so-called dual-use technologies (that is, they can be used for good, bad and neutral purposes).

On the one hand, the ability to be anonymous broadly protects against any potential harm due to others' control of information about us. For individuals, this relates to fundamental questions about autonomy and liberty, because the ability not only protects privacy but also offers protection against undue influence and manipulation. Focusing on the latter, not previously discussed issues, there is a whole industry that depends on aggregation of individuals' online behaviour in order to adapt commercials to fit with individual preferences or to manipulate individual preferences to fit the product. What is worse is that if applied on an aggregated level, information aggregation can be used for gerrymandering, or targeted manipulations can used to affect the political process (for example, by misleading people in order to make them vote for candidates they otherwise would not have supported). Although the dust is not yet settled on the 2016 US presidential election, some of the discussions concerning that election can serve as a good example of worst-case scenarios – when elections, indeed, are won by manipulating a large part of the electors. What I have in mind, amongst other things, is the scandal involving Cambridge Analytica, which 'harvested private information from the Facebook profiles of more than 50 million users without their permission' (Rosenberg, Confessore and Cadwalladr 2018).

On the other hand, the ability to be anonymous can be used for undesirable purposes. Indeed, sometimes de-anonymisation is desirable. For example, we standardly want to de-anonymise criminals. De-anonymisation techniques can also be used to help determine who the author of an ancient text is (for example, whether *Alcibiades II* was written by Plato or not). Also, information aggregation of people's communications can also broadly be used to gain useful statistical information, such as of the spread of influenza (see, for example, Ginsberg et al. 2009). More importantly, the ability to be anonymous can be used to achieve a false identity, for example, to engage in disinformation campaigns. Here again, the US presidential election can be used as an example (see, for example, Mueller 2019). However, as previously implied, a successful disinformation campaign also, to some degree, depends on having sufficient knowledge about your target.

While the concept clearly applies to the above examples, one may worry that the concept is not analytically helpful when addressing trade-offs between good and bad uses of the ability. One way to view the challenges we are facing is as a binary choice between good and bad usage of the ability to be anonymous and de-anonymisation technologies (that is, similar to the debate between privacy and security). On the basis of this supposition, one cannot protect ordinary individuals' ability to be anonymous without protecting criminals' ability to be anonymous. Lastly, I will argue that this supposition is false.

Consider, for example, Onion Routing (used, for example, by the Tor browser). Onion Routing protects against a digital Peeping Tom by providing protection against an outsider's access to both the content of communications and the communicators (see, for example, Goldschlag, Reed and Syverson 1999). Techniques such as Onion Routing can be used to protect against eavesdroppers for both good purposes (for example, protecting a whistle-blower against an oppressive regime) and bad purposes (for example, protecting terrorists plotting an attack).

While Onion Routing can be used for both good and bad purposes, it cannot give any protection against the traces the ordinary Internet user leaves by their online behaviour, such as using services that require you to log-in, contributing to online information, or because services log metadata (such as access time). This is because the distinct difference between aggregation of available information (making it possible to conclude that I implies J) and eavesdropping of private conversations.

Arguably the challenges to our ability to be anonymous are complex and multifaceted. But given that the activities of an ordinary person differ from those of a criminal, it is not unreasonable to think that it is possible to have a society that better protects some aspects of our ability to be anonymous, without leading to increased protection of criminal activity. The development of the Internet of Things – which will equip ordinary everyday electronics with smart sensors – will put everyone's ability to be anonymous at risk. However, while it is not logically impossible that, for example, a smart fridge could collect information that is helpful in the solution of a crime, it is not very likely. Thus, although there are arguably trade-offs to each option (for example, there are obvious individual benefits of aggregated analysis of a person's 'communications'), the trade-offs are not necessarily between bad and good uses of people's ability to be anonymous. Reasonably, successful criminals know better than ordinary citizens how to protect their ability to be anonymous (making use of techniques that few ordinary people apply). This does not only put ordinary individuals at a disadvantage, but – as the example with the fridge aims to illustrate – we can protect ordinary people's ability to be anonymous in ordinary situations without necessarily protecting the ability to be anonymous for more nefarious purposes.

Either way, the account of the concept of our ability to be anonymous, rather than anonymity, is indeed the most helpful concept to analytically disentangle and evaluate these issues.

Summation and Final Comments

In this text, I have defended two intertwined ideas. First, given the power of the available de-anonymisation techniques the challenges we are facing are best conceptualised by an *ability to be anonymous*, rather than by a concept of *anonymity*. Secondly, our *ability to be anonymous* can be conceptualised in terms of having *reasonable control over what we communicate.*

De-anonymisation and information aggregation can be used to analyse our communications and behaviour in a way that allows others to infer more information than what is intended or available analytically in the communication as such. On the one hand, this can infringe upon our (right to) privacy, force us into lose-to-lose trade-offs and be abused to manipulate us, something which puts the whole democratic society at risk. On the other hand, it can be used to de-anonymise criminals, to gain valuable aggregated information (such as the spread of influenza), and to uncover the source of disinformation campaigns.

While the techniques are both beneficial and disadvantageous, it is reasonable to presume that it is possible to protect individuals against harm, while retaining various benefits.

Last, I have avoided saying what we should do, but given the current technological development it is not unreasonable to think that we are at a crossroads. We either choose to act in way that protects our ability to be anonymous or we might move towards a society where the private sphere and our individual control of it, and possibly – as an extension – our autonomy, will be limited. Either way, what we need to analyse is not the concept of *anonymity*, but the concept of *our ability to be anonymous*.

Notes

1. See, for example, at: https://www.lexico.com/en/definition/anonymous.
2. It is important to point out that Marmor actually talks of the right to privacy as being *grounded* in an interest in a certain form of control, rather than being identical to that certain form of control. Thus, it is possible that Marmor would define the right to privacy in a different way. Hence, what is said above should not – without further qualification – be read as a criticism of Marmor's paper.

References

Adriaans, P., 'Information', *The Stanford Encyclopedia of Philosophy*, Fall 2013 edn.

Ginsberg, J., M. H. Mohebbi, R. S. Patel, L. Brammer, M. S. Smolinski and L. Brilliant, 'Detecting Influenza Epidemics Using Search Engine Query Data', *Nature*, 457 (2009): 1012–14.

Goldschlag, D., M. Reed and P. Syverson, 'Onion Routing for Anonymous and Private Internet Connections', *Communication of the ACM* 42(2) (1999): 39–41.

Hansson, S. O., 'Ethical Criteria of Risk Acceptance', *Erkenntnis* 59(3) (2003): 291–309.

Hull G., H. R. Lipford and C. Latulipe, 'Contextual Gaps: Privacy Issues on Facebook', *Ethics & Information Technology* 13 (2011): 289–302.

Johansson, F., L. Kaati and A. Shrestha, 'Timeprints for Identifying Social Media Users with Multiple Aliases', *Security Informatics* 4(7) (2015).

Kosinski, M., D. Stillwell and T. Graepel, 'Private Traits and Attributes are Predictable from Digital Records of Human Behavior', *PNAS* 110(15) (2013): 5802–5.

Matthews, S., 'Anonymity and the Social Self', *American Philosophical Quarterly* 47(4) (2010): 351–63.

Marmor, A., 'What Is the Right to Privacy?' *Philosophy & Public Affairs* 43 (2015): 3–26.

Mueller, R. S., 'Report on the Investigation into Russian Interference in the 2016 Presidential Election. Volume I', *US Department of Justice*, 2019, available at: https://upload.wikimedia.org/wikipedia/commons/e/e4/Report_On_The_Investigation_Into_Russian_Interference_In_The_2016_Presidential_Election.pdf, last accessed 28 September 2019.

Nissenbaum, H., 'The Meaning of Anonymity in an Information Age', *The Information Society* 15(2) (1999): 141–4.

Ohm, P., 'Broken Promises of Privacy: Responding to the Surprising Failure of Anonymization', *UCLA Law Review* 57 (2010): 1701–77.

Parent, W. A., 'Privacy, Morality, and the Law', *Philosophy & Public Affairs* 12 (1983): 269–88.

Rosenberg, M., N. Confessore and C. Cadwalladr, 'How Trump Consultants Exploited the Facebook Data of Millions', *New York Times*, 17 March 2018, available at: https://www.nytimes.com/2018/03/17/us/politics/cambridge-analytica-trump-campaign.html, last accessed 28 September 2019.

Wallace, K. A., 'Anonymity', *Ethics and Information Technology* 1 (1999): 23–35.

FOURTEEN

Big Data Analytics and the Accessibility of Public Inquiries

Philip Garnett and Sarah M. Hughes

Introduction

There is an increasing tendency for reasonably large heterogeneous data sets to be released digitally online as part of public inquiries or court cases. These data sets may be composed of PDF files, images and scanned handwritten documents; some voluntarily and intentionally released, others released only after requests or via leaks. The release of these data sets is often justified as necessary to improve the transparency of a process or the operations of an organisation. When the data is released willingly, the intention may be that the released evidence would support the conclusions of the investigation or inquiry, thereby reinforcing the legitimacy of the process. Where the release of documents is only in response to successful external requests for evidence, such as via a state's Freedom of Information process (FOI), the release is often part of an attempt to make the decision-making process more transparent to the public by third parties (such as researchers or journalists). When data is leaked, it is the leaker or whistle-blower who might be attempting to inform the public about a process or practice that they believe should be known. In many of these situations questions remain as to how useful the released data actually is, the politics of how accessible it is, and what the politics are behind its relative accessibility?

This chapter looks at two case studies to highlight some aspects of these issues. It argues that the tools normally associated with the analysis of much larger big data sets can be successfully applied to improve the accessibility of inquiries and similar processes. The two cases that we draw on are the court-martial of Private Chelsea Manning in the US (Burgess 2012), and the Leveson Inquiry into the Culture, Practice and Ethics of the Press (Leveson

Report) in the UK (Inquiry et al. 2012). We briefly also touch upon the materials that Manning leaked from US Army databases to WikiLeaks that lead to her court-martial.

The Manning trial of 2013 provides an example of a process whereby the supporting evidence, in the form of court exhibits and records, was released largely via a systematic process of FOI requests filed by a small number of individuals. The intention was to provide public access to a judicial process that otherwise would have been substantially more opaque. In comparison, the Leveson Inquiry, a public inquiry in 2012 in the United Kingdom, released some of the evidence and testimony that formed the bases of the findings to the public during the inquiry, by the inquiry. These two cases have been chosen because they share some common characteristics, most notably the nature, format and style of the data released. Where they differ significantly is in the process by which the data was released and made 'accessible' to the public. This chapter considers the immediate accessibility of the data, its long-term storage and accessibility, and how the techniques used in the analysis of big data could be applied to improve the accessibility of these data sets.

Data sets such as those from the Manning and Leveson cases are important because they often underpin decision-making processes; decisions that could have a profound effect on society. For the bases of these decision-making processes to be truly transparent (and fair) it is argued that it must at least be possible for interested parties to cross-reference the data with the outcome of the process. Understanding what data was collected, why it was collected, and how it fits together is therefore important contextual information, together with who released the data, and for what purpose. The format of the released data is significant for similar reasons, as controlling the accessibility (both in terms of ability to read or process the data and physically gain access to it) can exert control on how the process itself is viewed and the legitimacy of the decisions made.

Access to the data can be obstructed or obfuscated in multiple ways (Belcher and Martin 2013; Garnett and Hughes 2019). Barriers to downloading documents can be put into place, websites can be made difficult to navigate, or the data may be removed after an unspecified period of time. These features of data releases may be deliberate, subtle attempts by the state to obstruct access, designed to put off all but the most persistent researcher. Or they may be a consequence of time and budget restrictions, publicly available data being a low priority compared with the main focus of the inquiry or process. The data itself can also be of limited accessibility and use due to the file type or method used to prepare the document, together with being extensively redacted.

We argue that the public has a right to access information about what is done in their name, and the material upon which decisions are made. It has even been proposed that FOI should be a fundamental human right (Birkinshaw 2006). However, frequently when access is granted to this information (which is not guaranteed) the data is released in the form of large complex data sets that would be a challenge to navigate even for those involved in generating them. It can also be the case that the access granted is not straightforward, and denials or deferrals of access may not be forthcoming (Belcher and Martin 2013).

This chapter investigates the two above case studies where access to supporting evidence has been controlled or limited in some way, and the where resulting data sets present their own challenges of accessibility. We raise questions as to the potential impact of the nature of the data on this process, and its accessibility to the public. We argue that if it is assumed that societally significant insights might come from the analysis of these large data sets, then there is a need for tools to usefully extract valuable information. However, tools that are straightforward in use and freely accessible to the public do not yet exist, despite increasing interest from government, researchers, companies and other organisations in extracting value from such data. We end this chapter by presenting some examples of tools and technologies that could be applied in order to improve the accessibility of released documents.

The Cases: the Manning Court-Martial and the Leveson Inquiry

The court-martial of Private Chelsea Manning (2013) and the Leveson Inquiry (2012) are both examples of the release of documentary evidence in modern democratic states. In both cases the evidence was presented in a similar form: large quantities of PDF documents, unlinked, often unsearchable and with little meaningful metadata. This combination makes the data difficult to analyse, read and navigate productively. Consequently, the possibility for important pieces of information to go unnoticed is high, be it a singular fact or an interpretation based on an understanding or interpretation of connected facts. In the following, we provide background to Manning's court-martial, the data released by Manning that led to the trial and then the Leveson Inquiry.

The Manning Court-Martial

On 24 May 2010, Private Chelsea E. Manning was arrested by the US government on suspicion of leaking classified military material to WikiLeaks. At the time Manning was an intelligence analyst within the US Army, and in

2009 had been deployed to Iraq where she had access to the CIDNE-I and CIDNE-A military databases (termed for activity in Iraq and Afghanistan, respectively); these classified databases 'contained millions of vetted and finalized directories including operational intelligence reporting' (Manning 2013a). Manning found herself increasingly disenchanted with the actions of the US military and in January 2010 she began to download classified files from both CIDNE-I and CIDNE-A. Manning passed the files to WikiLeaks, after attempts to give them to the *Washington Post* and the *New York Times* failed when the newspapers did not respond. Manning returned to Iraq in February 2010 (Manning 2013b); between March and May 2010 she downloaded further documents and sent them to WikiLeaks. Her identity as the leaker was revealed to the authorities after Manning confided some of the details of her activity in an Internet chatroom, which resulted in her arrest while in Iraq.

In 2013, Manning was convicted at court-martial of multiple offences, including violation of the 1917 Espionage Act and stealing government property. As Manning was tried under military law, the details of her trial are not held in the public realm; the judge and prosecution decide what information is made public. Manning was sentenced to serve a thirty-five-year prison sentence in Fort Leavenworth, Kansas. However, in one of his final acts as president, President Barack Obama commuted Manning's sentence to nearly seven years of confinement, dating back to her arrest on 27 May 2010, and she was released on 17 May 2017. On 8 March 2019, Manning was held in contempt of court for refusing to testify before a federal grand jury investigating WikiLeaks, and she has since (with a brief release between 9 and 16 May 2019) been held in Alexandria City Jail, Virginia.

The Data Leaked by Chelsea Manning

For the purpose of this chapter, we are interested in the aspects of Manning's court-martial that were intended to be of benefit to the public: processes that can therefore be considered accountable to the public in some way. Therefore, the nature of the leaked data is interesting and useful contextual information. The Manning leaks took a variety of forms; however, the most well-known are the large document caches, including the Iraqi and Afghan war logs, and the US Diplomatic Cables that were downloaded from military databases. These document caches contain hundreds of thousands of documents revealing the inner workings of the US State Department and military, varying in classification status. Furthermore, the released material also contained a video recording of those in command of the US Army

Apache helicopter gunships killing a number of Iraqi civilians and two Reuters' journalists, and seriously injuring children that came to their aid.

Further classified documents, including State Department cables, provided details of the officially sanctioned cover up of rape and sexual torture (including of children) by military contractors. This material, despite now being in the public domain, has never been officially declassified.

The Leveson Inquiry

The Leveson Inquiry (July 2011–November 2012) examined the culture, practices and ethics of the UK press (Inquiry et al. 2012). The purpose of the inquiry was to investigate behaviours of the press subsequent to a number of scandals, which centred on illegal and unethical practices such as phone hacking. The most high-profile case of these was the hacking of murdered schoolgirl Milly Dowler's mobile phone by *News of the World* journalists, reported in July 2011. The journalists hacked into the voicemail of Milly Dowler's mobile phone looking for newsworthy information, leading her parents and the police to believe that she could still be alive (Davies, Francis and Greer 2007: 20–6). This action caused significant distress to the parents and changed the nature of the ongoing police investigation. The public outrage around this case led the government at the time to hold a public inquiry. This inquiry was to be conducted in two parts, the first, an investigation into the culture, ethics and practices of the press.

The second part, which was initially delayed in order to allow active criminal investigations into the employees of the *News of the World* to run their course, was intended to look in more detail at the specifics of potential criminal behaviour by News International (the owners of the *News of the World*) and other media outlets. This part was at first delayed and then cancelled by the government.

The Inquiry findings were published in a multi-volume report of approximately 2,000 pages, which can be freely downloaded or purchased for a fee (Inquiry et al. 2012; Leveson 2012: vols 1–4). During the inquiry, the evidence collected and provided by witnesses was released on a website. These releases often took the form of scanned images of documents contained in PDF files; these documents were not machine-readable and therefore could not be searched (some were handwritten). Following the end of the inquiry process the website was taken down and the URL forwarded to an archived version of the site held by the British Library. This version of the site lacks some of the functionality of the original due to the archiving process, however, it is still possible to retrieve the majority of the evidence (Anon 2011a).

The Process of Data Release

The process by which the data sets were released differs significantly between the Manning and Leveson cases, both in how the releases were triggered and what information was released and by whom. They also took place in different democratic nation-states, with contrasting legal frameworks. The Manning court-martial data was largely released due to a significant amount of work by a small number of dedicated investigative journalists. In normal courts-martial trials it is the judge and the prosecution that decide what information is released to the public.

The process by which Manning leaked the data, although not the focus of this chapter, is still worth briefly mentioning. Manning was able to download data from the US Army computer systems by copying onto a writable CD-Rom drive marked 'Lady Gaga', before smuggling it out inside a portable CD player and finally returning to the US on leave (Leigh 2010). This demonstrates, if nothing else, a degree of lack of internal security protecting the data and the systems which could access it. Interestingly, Manning was one of approximately 1.4 million military personnel with 'Top Secret' clearance, all of whom could potentially access the documents. The total security-cleared population in the United States was 4.8 million in 2012 (Aftergood 2012).

The Leveson Inquiry was a very different process, as it was intended to be a public inquiry from the start. Therefore, evidence was routinely released by the Inquiry on its own website as the proceedings progressed. Videos of some of the evidence were also recorded and made available. The Inquiry itself was protected from the Freedom of Information Act 2000, and therefore would only guarantee that 'as much information as possible will be provided on [the] website'. This indicates that perhaps not all of the material would be made public, and also that 'Lord Justice Leveson [had] discretion to allow witnesses to give evidence anonymously or in private'. Evidence could therefore be redacted, or otherwise censored, before uploading onto the website – or withheld from the public altogether.

This means that whilst the public could expect a degree of transparency in the release of the evidence of the Leveson Inquiry material, this was at the discretion of those running the Inquiry. It is also worth noting that the website for the Inquiry was shut down shortly after it reported. However, a limited version of the website has been stored by the National Archives and most of the evidence is therefore still accessible and available for download.

The Released Data

In the UK, it is common for public inquiries and the data from success-ful FOI requests to be released in the form of PDF files that often contain images of documents, some of which may be handwritten. These files are not always machine-readable and rarely have informative metadata (where metadata is data associated with a document or file that describes what it is, such as title, data, publishers, author and so on).

The difficulty of turning what was once a machine-readable document into a series of images embedded into a PDF file is likely to be due in part to the process of removal of metadata, and a method that makes any redaction process easier. One method, for example, will turn the individual pages of a PDF into image files, which can then be redacted and have any metadata removed if desired. These images are then turned back into a multipage PDF that is really only a container for the images. This is more secure than releasing an editable document which might contain information about the author(s) of the document, and perhaps even have the capacity to allow redactions to be removed if any were made. This practice makes it less likely that the content of the documents will be indexed by Internet search engines or other search systems, making the data set significantly more difficult to navigate but protecting the anonymity of the authors.

In the case of public inquiries, these documents are then uploaded onto a website, which may have limited information about the content of the document in the form of metadata. These websites may implement a basic search system that would allow the metadata to be searched. For example, on the Leveson website the search functionality was very limited; the evi-dence was presented via an alphabetical index that required the researcher to know something about what they were looking for to find a document. The other option was to scroll through the entire database. As such, the ability for researchers, or interested parties, to exploratively search for information was therefore not catered for. This could be due to a lack of resources to pro-vide a useful search system or a lack of desire to allow such search activity to take place – or indeed a combination of the two. Either way, it demonstrates that providing easy access to external actors is not a priority.

The Manning court-martial material provides an interesting compari-son here. As with the Leveson Inquiry, the documents were released to the public in the form of large PDF documents that have all the same problems detailed above. However, in addition to this one could suggest that it is possible to detect some of the potential reluctance on the part of the US government to release this data, as it was released only due to FOI requests by journalists who attended the trial. Further, the form and format of the released court-martial data indicates a similar reluctance. We have previously published on (Garnett and Hughes 2019; Hughes and Garnett 2019) how FOI requests are published via the US Army online FOI reading room, which has particular features that limit the access and use of this data. At the time of writing, this includes expired security certificates that the researcher needs to navigate around in order to reach the data, and which also make the web pages invisible to most search engines.

Big Data Analytics for Accessibility

Due to the problems described above, the use of released data is likely limited to all but the most dedicated researchers. It does not invite the public to engage with the process and data. We argue that this is not an excuse to exempt future inquiries or court cases from releasing data. Rather it is an invitation for the development of technologies and tools that can make the data more accessible, and enable more effective exploratory analysis.

Examples of Analytical Methods

The analytics tools associated with big data analytics provide potential solutions to these problems of analysis and accessibility (at the point where the data has been released in some form). The automated building of network databases mapping the relationships between documents is an area of active development, and one in which we are interested. Here various machine-learning tools can be deployed to characterise the documents in different ways, normally based their content. By way of example, name–entity detection can be used to extract information from the documents that might constitute a meaningful relationship (for example, it might be of use to be able to see all the documents that mention a particular place or person). Documents could also be classified based on the topics contained within using latent dirichlet allocation (LDA) or latent semantic analysis (LSA) (Hofmann 1999; Hofmann 2001; Blei, Ng and Jordan 2003). More advanced machine-learning technologies and deep-learning systems, such as Tensorflow or IBM's Watson, could also be applied to documents (High 2012; Abadi et al. 2016; Goldsborough 2016). Furthermore, if there are images contained within a release, image recognition could also be used to detect features or individuals. The consequences of this are, that if applied, along with basic optical character recognition to improve searching and indexing of documents, these machine-learning technologies could vastly improve the public's ability to navigate and access information released as part of processes like the Leveson Inquiry and the Manning court-martial.

Preliminary Results

Our own preliminary work has focused upon the processing of the Manning trial documents; we present here an outline of the methodology and some of our preliminary findings. Part of the philosophy behind this project was to develop tools that would improve the accessibility of the documents with minimal manual intervention. A lot of time can be spent processing documents to improve their machine-readability. Therefore, with the Manning trial data we focused more on developing algorithms to process the data as outlined below.

If all the court exhibit data released by FOI with reference to Manning is downloaded, it constitutes ~2,200 individual PDF files of varying page lengths. These files were processed out of large ZIP archives into individual folders, and the Tesseract OCR program was used to extract the text out of the files, which was then stored in the same folder (Smith 2007). A system of algorithms was then built using software packages, including both deep-learning and natural-language processing tools (in this case both Tensorflow and IBM Watson analytics) and other machine-learning libraries (implemented in Java).

This system of algorithms was then used to process the documents first into a document (MongoDB) database (High 2012; Anon 2016; Goldsborough 2016) where each entry consists of the binary PDF file, the raw extracted contents of the file (unprocessed), and then metadata which consists of various processed information from the raw extracted text. For example, a list of names extracted from the raw content would be stored as an array within the associated document metadata in the MongoDB database. It is here where the interventions in processing this data are made, if a change to produce metadata is required then the algorithms are changed automatically. This is more attuned with the philosophy of big data analytics where it is assumed that there is too much data to consider manual interventions, therefore machines are best placed to process the data.

The next phase in the processing of this data was to produce a complex network of the relationships between the documents based on the extracted metadata. For this phase we used algorithms to take the content of the MongoDB database and process it into a Neo4J network database (Neo4J 2014). Network databases store data in the form of nodes (objects with attributes) and edges (relationships between nodes, which can also have attributes).

Here each document forms a node in the database and the edges of the network are delineated by the different relationships between the nodes. These relationships are determined by the metadata in the MongoDB database. For example, an array of names of individuals or places could be mapped to an edge between two documents labelled with the person's name.

The resulting network database can then be used as a navigational aid for the researcher. If one finds a document of interest one can explore the other documents that the algorithms have linked it to. However, the network can also be analysed to find clusters of documents that could be about the same topics, or share similar content in other ways. Network community detection algorithms can then visualise and extract these clusters of associated documents.

Both predefined analytics and the ability to produce custom analytics could be provided for the investigation of inquiry data. As many data sets have similar characteristics, such as the style of the documents (which is the case for both the Manning and the Leveson data), there could be a number of standard tools that produce a network for enhanced search and navigation of the data. For example, pre-build algorithms for content analysis and templates for search queries and network analysis. However, the processed data could also be analysed using the database search languages (such as Cypher for Neo4J (Panzarino 2014)), and the capacity for different content processing provided by the use of plugin code.

Such analysis of networks of relationships developed from document databases has had an impact already in other domains. For example, the Enron email database, which was released as part of the criminal investigation into the Enron fraud, can be analysed to show the key individuals and their relationships from a network analysis of the frequency of their email communications (Diesner, Frantz and Carley 2005; McCallum, Wang and Corrada-Emmanuel 2007). The International Consortium of Investigative Journalists (ICIJ) has also used similar methods in their analysis of the leaked Panama and Paradise Papers (Cabra 2016). The ICIJ has released some of the leaked data in the form of a Neo4J database showing the relationships between some of the individuals and organisations in the papers in the form of an interactive, searchable, network database.

Conclusion

This chapter arose from the provocation that there has been increase in the release of large-scale digitalised datasets into the public realm through hacking, whistle-blowers, FOI requests and public inquiries. We discussed the implications of the form, content and accessibility of this data for big data analytics. This is important in liberal democracies, for public access to state processes and procedures – particularly in the context of public inquiries – is an integral part of holding systems of government accountable to the public. What our research unpacks, however, is that applying the tools of big data analytics is made harder for the researcher by a series of state practices (for example, lack of metadata, images embedded into PDFs and poorly indexed files). This chapter moved to address this, making suggestions for how researchers can use big data analytics to navigate this complex and politically charged field.

To this end, we drew upon two high-profile cases, the court-martial of US Army whistle-blower Chelsea Manning and the Leveson Inquiry into Press Standards in the UK. These diverse releases of datasets (including leaked data, FOI requests, redacted images stored in PDFs and 'public' inquiry data that are subject to the FOI) exemplified many of the challenges and possibilities of big data analytics faced by many researchers in this area. In the case of Chelsea Manning, we showcased this using the Tesseract OCR program to extract large data out of large ZIP files, downloaded from the US Army's FOI website. Following this, we used a series of algorithms, to process these documents into a MongoDB database, we then built a complex network of relationships from the extracted metadata. We demonstrated how this can be used to compile a network database that can be used to find clusters of documents around the same topic.

We argued that if the most value is to be extracted from datasets that are released, it is important that tools are developed to effectively engage with them. There is a need to avoid situations where data is released only to give a veneer of a transparent democratic process, when in reality the data is too large and/or incomprehensible to be accessible to the majority of the public. Another risk to be avoided is that a lack of public engagement with released information is used in the future as a justification for avoiding the commitment of resources to the release of information at all. Indeed, it could be argued that, for example, the Leveson Inquiry and its recommendations may have had profound consequences for the freedom of the press in the United Kingdom. Therefore, in a democratic state, the bases for those recommendations and the decisions made should be as transparent as possible.

The types of data discussed, trial documents, inquiry evidence and leaked data, all present challenges to archivists or the process of creating and maintaining archives of such events that have significance within cyberspace. The Leveson Inquiry website was not maintained very long beyond the length of the Inquiry. The final report and summary can be archived in libraries for future generations, but the evidence and the website itself presents more of a challenge. The UK National Archive is providing longer-term archiving, however, the problems of long-term digital storage remain (Hedstrom 1997).

In the case of the Manning trial documents, the long-term storage is provided by the US Army FOI reading room. It would be reasonable to assume that this is a relatively stable archive. However, the current state of the reading room reflects a degree of neglect (to the point where at the time of writing it is inaccessible to some browsers) that may or may not be benign (Garnett and Hughes 2019). This highlights the potential conflict of interest in a government being responsible for hosting data which is often critical of its own behaviour. The final case of how to archive important data that has been leaked but remains classified perhaps the most difficult challenge to archivists.

Both the Leveson Inquiry and the court-martial of Chelsea Manning raise wider questions of when, and to what extent, it is right to release evidence of actions done in the name (or defence) of a democratic society, to the members of that society. Access to the full outcome of the Manning trial and the evidential bases of the outcome of the Leveson Inquiry, are therefore essential to the debate. This is of further importance in the context of the long history in both the US and the UK of leaks and whistle-blowers, whose actions in hindsight have often been thought to have benefited society more widely. Therefore, we argue that it is essential that the wider public is able to understand the nature of what was done and the reasoning behind this. The judicial processes of a democracy should be as transparent as possible and the analytical tools being developed to process big data can make an important contribution to improving the utility and accessibility of any associated releases of evidence and other data.

References

Abadi, M. et al., 'TensorFlow: a System for Large-Scale Machine Learning', *12th USENIX Symposium on Operating Systems Design and Implementation (OSDI '16)* (2016): 265–83.

Aftergood, S., 'Security*Federation of American* 2012, available at: https://fas.org/blogs/secrecy/2012/07/cleared_population, last accessed 31 May 2018.

Anon, *The Leveson Inquiry*, 2011, available at: http://webarchive.nationalarchives. gov.uk/20140122144906/http://www.levesoninquiry.org.uk, last accessed 31 May 2018.

Anon, *MongoDB*, 2016, available at: https://www.mongodb.com, last accessed 26 September 2019.

Beckett, C., 'Wikitribune: Can Crowd-sourced Journalism Solve the Crisis of Trust in News?' *POLIS: Journalism and Society at the LSE*, 2017, available at: http://eprints.lse.ac.uk/76543, last accessed 30 May 2018.

Belcher, O. and L. L. Martin, Ethnographies of Closed Doors: Conceptualising Openness and Closure in US*Area* 45(4) (2013): 403–10.

Birkinshaw, P., 'Freedom of Information and Openness: Fundamental Human Rights*Administrative Law Review* 58 (2006): 177.

Blei, D. M., A. Y. Ng and M. I. Jordan, 'Latent Dirichlet Allocation', *Journal of Machine Learning* 3 (2003): 993–1022.

Burgess, E. B., 'Private: Badley Manning, WikiLeaks, and the Biggest Exposure of Official Secrets in American History', *Library Journal* 137(12) (2012): 94.

Cabra, M., 'How the ICIJ used Neo4j to Unravel the Panama Papers', *Neo4j Blog*, May 2016.

Davies, P., P. Francis and C. Greer, *Victims, Crime and Society* (Los Angeles: SAGE, 2007).

Diesner, J., T. L. Frantz and K. M. Carley, 'Communication Networks from the Enron Email Corpus "It's Always About the People. Enron is no Different"', *Computational & Mathematical Organization Theory* 11(3) (2005): 201–28.

Garnett, P. and S. M. Hughes, 'Obfuscated Democracy? Chelsea Manning and the Politics of Knowledge Curation', *Political Geography* 68 (2019): 23–33.

Goldsborough, P., 'A Tour of TensorFlow', *arXiv [cs.LG]*, 2016, available at: http://arxiv.org/abs/1610.01178, last accessed 26 September 2019.

Hedstrom, M., 'Digital Preservation: a Time Bomb for Digital Libraries', *Computers & the Humanities* 31(3) (1997): 189.

High, R., 'The Era of Cognitive Systems: An Inside Look at IBM*IBM Corporation, Redbooks*, 2012, available at: http://johncreid.com/wp-content/uploads/2014/12/The-Era-of-Cognitive-Systems-An-Inside-Look-at-IBM-Watson-and-How-it-Works_.pdf, last accessed 26 September 2019.

Hofmann, T., 'Probabilistic Latent Semantic Analysis', *Proceedings of the Fifteenth Conference on Uncertainty in Artificial Intelligence* (San Francisco: Morgan Kaufmann, 1999), pp. 289–96.

Hofmann, T., 'Unsupervised Learning by Probabilistic Latent Semantic Analysis', *Machine Learning* 42(1) (2001): 177–96.

Hughes, S. M. and P. Garnett, 'Researching the Emergent Technologies of State Control: the Court-martial of Chelsea Manning', in M. de Goede, E. Bosma and P. Pallister-Wilkins (eds), *Secrecy and Methods in Security Research: a Guide to Qualitative Fieldwork* (London: Routledge, 2019).

Inquiry, L., B. H. Leveson *An Inquiry Into the Culture, Practices and Ethics of the Press: Executive Summary and Recommendations* (Leveson Report) (London: The Stationery Office, 2012).

Leigh, D., 'How 250,000 US *The Guardian*, 28 November 2010, available at: http://www.theguardian.com/world/2010/nov/28/how-us-embassy-cables-leaked, last accessed 31 May 2018.

Leveson, Lord, *Ruling on Core Participants*, Leveson Inquiry, 2011.

Leveson, B., An Inquiry into the Culture, Practices and Ethics of the Press, Vol. 3', *The Leveson Inquiry*, 2012, available at: http://www.official-documents.gov. uk/document/hc1213/hc07/0780/0780.asp, last accessed 26 September 2019.

Manning *The Guardian*, 1 March 2013 (2013a), available at: http://www.theguard-ian.com/world/2013/mar/01/bradley-manning-wikileaks-statement-full-text, last accessed 31 May 2018.

Manning, C., 'Transcript US v Pfc. Manning, Pfc. Manning's Statement for the Providence Inquiry, 2/28/13', *Alexaobrien.com*, 2013b, available at: https://alexaobrien. com/archives/985, last accessed 31 May 2018.

McCallum, A., X. Wang and A. Corrada-Emmanuel, 'Topic and Role Discovery in Social Networks with Experiments on Enron and Academic Email', *Journal of Artificial Intelligence Research* 30 (2007): 249–72.

Neo4J, *The World's Leading Graph Database*, 2014, available at: www.neo4j.org, last accessed 25 September 2019.

Panzarino, O., *Learning Cypher* (Birmingham: Packt Publishing, 2014).

Smith, R., 'An Overview of the Tesseract OCR Engine', *Ninth International Conference on Document Analysis and Recognition (ICDAR 2007)* (2007): 629–33.

WikiLeaks.org, 'Collateral Murder', *WikiLeaks*, 2010, https://collateralmurder. wikileaks.org, last accessed 31 May 2018.

FIFTEEN

Developing an Ethical Compass for Big Data

Harald Stelzer and Hristina Veljanova

Introduction

The Internet and information and communication technologies (ICTs) have become an inseparable part of our everyday lives. Millions of Europeans make use of ICT products and services on a daily basis for carrying out various activities. The uptake of ICT in the last few decades has enabled the generation and aggregation of vast amounts of data sets, also known as big data. There are numerous attempts in the literature to define big data. For instance, one common framework defines big data as consisting of three dimensions: volume, velocity and variety.[1] Volume stands for the huge amount of data generated and collected through these technologies. Velocity relates to the increasing speed at which data are generated and processed, which is also expected to further accelerate. Variety encompasses the various types of generated data, including unstructured, semi-structured and structured data (Lee 2017: 294). In order to derive the greatest value of big data, a whole range of processes is needed that go under the name of big data analytics. Big data analytics enables the analysis of these large data sets with the aim of uncovering patterns, correlations, trends and to create knowledge that can be used in a variety of ways, such as making policy or business decisions.

Big data means big opportunities for multiple actors such as businesses, the research community, governments and consumers/users of ICT. However, it also comes with considerable high risks of misuse and a decrease of trust in ICT. These data can be used to influence and manipulate democratic decisions and steer consumer behaviour. In the light of the increased generation, collection and use of big data, as well as the opportunities and perils that go along with it, there is a strong need to establish an ethical framework that can guide decision-making about big data. The aim of such a framework would be to set the direction towards responsible and democratic employment of big data. In the following, we will start to develop such an ethical compass for big data by identifying core values, looking for potential value conflicts, and developing a set of ethical criteria and indicators for the evaluation of the morally permissible use of big data.

Identification of Core Values and Ethical Impacts

From an ethical perspective, we first have to ask which values are at stake when it comes to big data. There are many values out there that are relevant in the context of big data.[2] In our approach, we take as a starting point the fundamental European values, including human dignity, freedom, democracy, equality, anti-discrimination, the rule of law, respect for human rights, pluralism, tolerance, justice, solidarity and protection of EU citizens. It should be noted though that these values differ in their relevance and applicability for questions on big data. For instance, some of the values like human dignity are hard to grasp as they are very abstract. Others are considered instrumental. There are also values that do not seem to be directly influenced by big data, or whose influence is ambiguous and is determined by how data are handled and what frameworks are put in place. As we will argue, ethical issues and concerns revolve around six central values: privacy, autonomy, transparency, anti-discrimination, responsibility and security. We do not consider this list exhaustive, but rather a sufficient first step in the development of an ethical guidance for big data. The list is based on our underlying assumption of the role and relation of different values and their importance for ethical impacts of big data and ICT.

Big data can comprise both personal and non-personal data. Since personal data are the main subject of regulation and the law, it is this aspect of big data that will be the focus of our analysis.

Privacy

Privacy is undoubtedly the central notion in the big data discourse. When discussing privacy, an important distinction ought to be made between the contexts in which data are generated and used. Nissenbaum (2004) talks about privacy as contextual integrity. She argues that each context or sphere of life is characterised by a distinct set of norms that determine key aspects such as roles, expectations, behaviour and limits. This implies that practices of gathering and disseminating information should be appropriate to the specific context in which they occur, and should abide by the norms that govern the distribution of information in that particular context (Nissenbaum 2004: 136–43).

In her analysis on privacy, Spiekermann focuses on the purpose of personal data collection as the main assessment point as to whether the collection itself is to be considered ethical or not (Spiekermann 2016: 49). In that sense, when personal data are collected and used for legitimate purposes, this should not be considered ethically problematic. Ethically problematic are cases where the collected data are used beyond the initial context and purpose, which may result in harmful and discriminatory classifications and categorisations (Rössler 2005: 126; Spiekermann 2016: 49). This closely relates to two ethically problematic practices: data mining and cross-correlative data mining. Collecting and cross-correlating data from various databases (bank, health, shopping data) by companies or law enforcement agencies may reveal information and insights about individuals that would not have been discovered otherwise (EGE 2012: 64). Possible answers to such unethical consumer or government surveillance practices are purpose and collection limitation. Namely, the amount of collected data and the contexts in which they are used should correspond to a previously defined legitimate purpose as well as to the legitimate expectations of individuals.

Autonomy

Autonomy can be understood as the ability of the individual to make decisions regarding her or his life based on motives, reasons, preferences and desires that are intrinsically theirs. A common ethical concern regarding autonomy includes cases where individuals and their personal data are used as a means to advance some economic or political goals. Dean, Payne and Landry (2016: 489–90) have argued that data-mining activities should not only treat all those acted upon equally and in like manner, but also that the persons acted upon should be regarded as inherently valuable and not just as a tool. A further problem is the lack of awareness how these techniques may inhibit individuals' ability to make informed decisions (Brey 2007). Additionally, personalisation features and algorithms that tailor information may lead to the creation of 'filter bubbles'. This impacts on individual's autonomy since an algorithm decides what an individual gets to see, not what the individual him- or herself thinks they need to see (Pariser 2011). This limits the possibility of self-determination and impedes the flow of information that is essential for building one's views and, above all, for one's participation in a democratic society.

One possible way to safeguard autonomy is through informed consent. In the context of big data, informed consent stands for the possibility of the individual acting as a user to make an informed decision regarding activities with her or his personal data in an environment free of coercion and on the basis of complete and clearly provided information. Stelzer and Veljanova (2017: 19) analyse informed consent as constituting two acts: the act of being informed and the act of consenting. The first emphasises how information should be provided to the user, namely, it should be clear, unambiguous, relevant and easily accessible. The second stipulates the conditions under which the consent should be given, which implies the possibility of voluntarily opting in/out and withdrawing consent.

One tool for enforcing autonomy and informed consent are privacy policies. However, privacy policies are often considered to be too long, complex and time-consuming, and therefore fail to serve their purpose in many cases (Balboni and Dragan 2017: 10–11). To add to their effectiveness, privacy policies should be made more user-friendly and easily understandable. Additionally, they should also inform users about the rights they have in relation to their data, such as to access, modify, delete data or to oppose any (further) data processing.

Transparency

The possibility for informed choices also depends on the level of transparency as this can help to provide answers to questions as what is being done, how it is being done and by whom it is done (EGE 2014: 75). In the context of ICT, transparency can relate to several aspects, such as activities with users' data (collection, storage, use, dissemination), the products and services themselves (in terms of functionality and quality), and also the level of security and the security infrastructure where data are being stored and transferred. So, transparency is about providing information so that others can more easily predict and understand the actions that have been or may be performed, the manner in which they have been performed, as well as to locate those who can be held accountable and responsible if a setback of interests or an infringement of rights occurs. In that way, transparency encourages open communication, it instils a feeling of assurance and eventually it ensures more accountability. With that being said, transparency can be seen as a promotor of ethical behaviour, a culture of trust and democracy.

The need for transparency is further fortified due to the opaque and complex character of data collection. The informational asymmetry that exists between users and businesses, but also between citizens and the state, has substantially widened due to people's greater Internet presence and dependence on ICT. This has turned them into transparent subjects living under conditions of extraordinary transparency where the line between the public and the private sphere is blurring (Reidenberg 2015: 448–9). Therefore, by demanding more transparency and openness, users are given a valuable tool that could enable them to exercise more control over their own data (EGE 2012: 47). Providing transparency is a necessary condition for an ethical employment of big data. However, it is not sufficient since being transparent about one's practices does not justify the practices or the underlying decisions per se.

Responsibility

Questions on moral responsibility focus on three aspects: (1) who can be considered a moral agent; (b) what is someone responsible for (backward-looking responsibility in the sense of assessing the morality of someone's actions); and (c) what ought someone to do (forward-looking responsibility/responsibility as a duty)? When dealing with big data, we would need to provide answers to these questions. For instance, the inclusion of forms of artificial intelligence and in particular (self-learning) algorithms raises an important challenge as to whether technology can also be held morally responsible. Furthermore, we would also need to clearly establish what are the duties of those who collect, process and use big data. This brings to the fore one moral gap in the distribution of responsibility known as the 'problem of many hands' (see also Alvarado in this volume).[3] At the core of this problem lies the difficulty of identifying the person responsible for a particular outcome within a collective setting where the actions of many people have together led to causing that outcome. This would imply that usually a myriad of people like designers, engineers, programmers, researchers, managers, business companies, governments as well as users/consumers contribute to the collection, processing and use of data in one way or another. For Nissenbaum (1996) attributing moral responsibility to individuals seems to be a much more common tendency than attributing moral responsibility to collectives. In order to overcome such individualistic thinking, she suggests using the concept of accountability and consequently making it possible for groups or even organisations to be held accountable. Being accountable equates to being answerable for one's own decisions and actions. For Nissenbaum, accountability is a powerful tool that can motivate better practices and eventually lead to more reliable and trustworthy systems.

Anti-discrimination

The question of who is to be held responsible also relates to issues of justice based on what we owe to other people. One aspect of justice, which is especially important in the context of big data, refers to cases where people are discriminated against or treated differently for unjust reasons. Bearing in mind the capacity to collect, store, manipulate, transmit digital data, the main issues concerning justice relate to how data are being used, how people are treated based on their data and what are the implications thereof. Discrimination based on data occurs when collected data are analysed and categorised using certain parameters such as ethnicity, religious affiliation, gender, social status, educational background or income. Profiling with certain parameters could in some cases result in targeting individuals or groups that are already disadvantaged and may be further harmed by public hostility, subordination or exclusion. It could also lead to unjustifiably and unfairly excluding particular individuals or groups from certain benefits or opportunities. Given that the processing of data is usually carried out by applying various techniques or statistical methods, there is also the risk of data misinterpretation (Donahue, Whittemore and Heerman n.d.). If such 'faulty' data are ascribed to an individual, this may turn him or her into a 'false positive' and thus have negative implications on his or her life (EGE 2014: 75). For that reason, the accuracy, consistency and completeness of data are aspects that must be carefully considered (Spiekermann 2016: 56–7).

Decision-making based on algorithms is a further area where justice issues may arise, especially as a result of an increased tendency for the automation of decision-making processes. In spite of a widely accepted assumption that algorithms operate with less or no bias, many experts argue that the design and functionality of algorithms is far from value-neutral since the algorithm always reflects the values of the designer of the algorithm (Mittelstadt et al. 2016: 7).[4] This speaks volumes for including ethical evaluation as part of the design of technology as well.

Security

In the context of big data, we understand security as the freedom and protection from information-based harms which may come in various forms such as theft, identity fraud, unauthorised access, unauthorised data alteration and disclosure. Security issues concerning data can be more easily analysed when framed in categories, each pertaining to particular kinds of threat and vulnerabilities which can lead to particular harms. One way of categorising security issues is by distinguishing between system security, network security and data security. System security has its focus on the protection of system resources against viruses and any malicious programs. Network security is about protecting and securing network infrastructure. Data security has as its focus the protection and preservation of data against unauthorised access. This has in its scope not only data that (1) reside in computer storage devices, but also (2) data that are transmitted between computer systems since the process of transferring information between parties comes with high security risks (Tavani 2011: 175–8).

This brief overview of the most important security aspects points at the vital role security plays in the realisation of the other values already elaborated. If the confidentiality, integrity and availability[5] of data are not guaranteed, then this has implications not only on the privacy of data owners but also on their autonomy and beyond that.

Value Conflicts

So far we have identified six core values that are at stake when considering big data. We have not yet given a scale of importance of ethical impacts or tried to rank the moral values according to their importance. We have also not assessed the risks of occurrence of the violation of these values or the expected strength and scope of the violation, if it is to occur. Doing so would need an interdisciplinary impact assessment that we are not able to provide. We can, however, evaluate the values themselves that are at stake when considering these ethical impacts. Here we can focus on the relationships between these values, which can be done by identifying possible value conflicts and searching for ways to overcome them. It should be noted that conflicts may occur between some of the six moral values we have identified, but also between these moral values and other competing non-moral values such as efficiency, usability, convenience or profit. The latter are of particular relevance since experience shows that they appear to be one of the greatest rivals of the six moral values. Even though at first sight one may be inclined to favour moral values, practice shows that this is not always a black-and-white situation.

Value conflicts are natural as ICTs hardly ever influence one value while being neutral to all others. Also, attempts to mitigate the violation of one value may have negative effects on others (Reijers, Brey and Jansen 2016: 42).

Moreover, due to value conflicts as well as particular circumstances, we are often not able to fulfil all values, not even to a certain degree. One possibility of dealing with value conflicts are trade-offs. They not only emerge when considering different goals that are valuable from the same perspective, but there are further trade-offs or conflicts when the interests of one party are set against those of a different party. This is even more complex in the case of ICT and big data, where multiple stakeholders are involved, such as (a) developers: individuals or enterprises that take part in the design, creation and production of ICT; (b) providers: enterprises/businesses that offer and sell ICT to users; (c) end-users: individuals who interact with ICT for non-enterprise purposes; as well as (d) state institutions; and (e) the research community.

To gain a better understanding of cases of value conflicts let us start with a common everyday situation. For users the full enjoyment of the advantages offered by the Internet and many web-based services such as online shopping, social media or instant information reach very often comes at the cost of (parts of) their privacy. Users therefore often find themselves in a two-choice situation: do they abandon their interests in those other goods and the benefits they derive from them for the sake of the privacy and security of their data? Or do these other goods trump users' privacy and security concerns? Even though there are situations where it is possible for them to 'abstain' from giving away their personal data, in most cases participating in any online activity is a no-choice situation, it is simply a precondition for being part of society.

Users are not the only ones confronted with situations of value conflicts. Companies, when offering their products and services to consumers, very often seem to find themselves caught in between pursuing their interests (profit increase) and acting ethically for the purpose of preserving consumers' trust and loyalty. New technologies have enabled the cost-effective collection, storage and usage of immense amounts of data. Companies have recognised that potential and are trying to make the most use of it to support their businesses (OECD 2015: 144–5). However, if conducted unethically, these data activities could have negative implications on consumers' data privacy and security, and in the long-term on the company itself.

A further well-known value conflict is between users' data privacy/security and usability. Applying privacy-enhancing measures to ICT products and services may reduce the degree of user-friendliness and usability of a website or service. The same applies to security. Taking security countermeasures in cyberspace can reduce vulnerabilities and possible threats, but at the same time it may affect the degree of user-friendliness. Moreover, taken from a business perspective, companies investing in strict security measures may unintentionally divert their consumers from using their services because of a loss in user-friendliness, convenience and flexibility. Some research findings show that most users put usability before security, especially concerning graphical passwords (Dhillon et al. 2016). This makes the privacy/security vs usability trade-off a matter which should be carefully dealt with.

Another example of conflicting situations of values includes users' privacy and data-driven innovation. Data have great potential because they generate new knowledge, encourage innovation, create new opportunities and foster the emergence of new products, services, processes (OECD 2015: 21). However, data collection and processing may directly or indirectly diminish users' privacy if carried out unethically. This points at the need to consider how the potential of data-driven innovation can be used without jeopardising values such as privacy.

The last example of conflicting values includes transparency and security. Transparency would mean demanding more information regarding how secure users' data are and what security measures companies take. The question of interest here is: what is the level of transparency needed to narrow down the information asymmetry between companies and consumers, which at the same time does not come at the cost of security? To answer this, we should look at the following two aspects: the information itself and the recipient of the information. This leads to the question: how detailed should that information be to be useful for the user? Letting users know that something is being done to protect the security of their data would suffice, however, overwhelming them with information that they do not understand because of its complexity and technicality, does not seem to serve its purpose.

Accommodating these value conflicts and tensions is not an easy task. Some cases require us to make trade-offs and prioritise. This is often a political decision when it comes to providing a legal framework as put forward in the General Data Protection Regulation (GDPR). What guides the normative decision-making on such trade-offs is the distinction between intrinsic values, which are not reducible to other values and are normally taken to be of utmost importance, and other values, which are often seen to be derivative, instrumental or of lesser importance. In situations of conflicting values, intrinsic values will normally take precedence over non-intrinsic values, implying that often the best choice is to opt for an action that least compromises intrinsic values.

Value conflicts can also occur between two or more intrinsic values. In such cases we can project our moral intuitions onto the situation. This would help us to decide which value seems more important in the particular situation. Even though the reasons or moral intuitions for giving priority to one value over another may often differ, employing moral reasoning allows us to explore the pros and cons for giving priority to one value over the other (Reijers, Brey and Jansen 2016: 43). In some cases, we may be able to attribute lexical or strict priority to the avoidance of the violation of certain values. However, lexical priority often leads to paradox outcomes, especially when safeguarding one value for some may result in the violation of other values for many. To make trade-offs possible we can use more complex models that attribute fixed or relative weights to certain values. Such models may also allow us to consider the extent to which a value may be violated if after weighing up the importance of all values the protection of another value (or set of values) has been given priority (Birnbacher 2003). For this we need to take into account the severity of the violation of certain values (this relates to the degree to which and scale at which a violation takes place). Weighing will therefore depend to a high degree on the information we have about the (expected) consequences of different options at hand. Even though there is no sure method for such a process, particular types of situations or contexts seem to favour some values more than others (Reijers, Brey and Jansen 2016: 43).

Nevertheless, we should be careful with value conflicts since they can easily lead to a misguided assessment of the situation. We talk about a value conflict when two things, A and B, stand in conflict with each other, so that both things could not be attained at the same time to the same extent. This means that having more of A directly implies having less of B. Even though there are situations that fit this line of reasoning, very often it may turn out that A and B do not necessarily exclude each other but rather serve as mutual control marks that prevent unjustified and premature trade-offs. In these cases, we avoid the value conflict by reconfiguring the situation in which it would otherwise occur. Here is the place for remedial actions and the co-design of solutions by including normative aspects at an early development stage.

Criteria for Normatively Permissible Employment of Big Data

Having mapped out the most important values in relation to big data and the possible ethical challenges that inevitably arise as a result thereof, in this section we provide an evaluative framework, an ethical compass, that can be used to assess the impact of big data activities on these values. As a starting point for our search for the criteria underlying such an evaluative framework we can take the six identified values as well as the analysed ethical challenges. For this let us first take a look at the underlying conditions that we think are important to fulfil the values to the best degree possible, also keeping in mind potential value conflicts as described above.

Without adequate information on data activities it seems impossible to fulfil not only transparency but any of the core values given above. For this first criterion it is important to ask questions about (a) what information is provided regarding practices and activities with personal data; (b) how comprehensive and concise the information is; (c) how understandable it is; (d) whether it can be easily located; and (e) how it is communicated to the user. Privacy policies are one tool that can empower users and also provide them with necessary and user-friendly information about their rights concerning their data.

Information is also crucial for a further criterion, users' control over their data. For that purpose, it is important that the user is given the possibility to access, restrict/object, amend or delete her or his data that has been collected, for instance, by a company as a result of using a service.

As pointed out in the section on privacy, data collection and use must be sensitive towards the context as well as the form of data. Data collection and use need to be limited and correspond to a previously defined purpose. A third criterion for the normatively permissible use of big data can therefore be found in the limitation of data collection and use.

Privacy also has a function in paving the way for autonomy. One way to make autonomous decisions is through informed consent. Informed consent itself allows users to voluntarily agree to the processing of certain data, and also gives them the possibility to opt-out from data collection and application or to withdraw previously given consent.

In relation to justice, anti-discrimination can be considered as a representative criterion. By including anti-discrimination, the idea is to fight any practices of data-based discrimination as well as decision-making based on biased algorithms which may unfairly disadvantage some individuals or groups in society.

Ensuring the protection of data, systems and networks where data are exchanged and stored is another criterion. One could not guarantee data privacy without providing a solid security infrastructure. It should, however, be emphasised that protection can be seen as a two-man job since it requires the efforts not only of the party collecting the data, but also of the user while moving around in cyberspace.

Finally, making sure that someone can be held accountable for unethical and impermissible activities with personal data comprises another criterion. It would need to address questions such as whether a party can justify and explain his or her past actions and, if necessary, deal with any negative judgements in the form of sanctions or liability issues.

Based on these considerations we can now provide a list of criteria that seem most relevant for the use of big data. To bring the criteria to a more concrete level corresponding indicators are assigned to each criterion. These indicators serve as tools which can measure whether the corresponding criteria have been met. The following table outlines a preliminary list of criteria and indicators that is readily applicable towards the collection and use of big data. It can therefore provide a compass for our orientation, but will need to be amended once the landscape changes and we are confronted with new challenges.

Information
- Users are informed:
  - when and what kind of their data are being processed;
  - how long their data are being stored;
  - about all the parties that will have access to their data.
- Information is comprehensive, concise, informative, easily understandable, clearly visible and easy to locate.
- Notice is provided regarding any changes to dealings with personal data.
- Users are informed about their rights regarding any personal data processing activities, including:
  - right of access;
  - right to rectification;
  - right to erasure ('right to be forgotten');
  - right to restriction of processing;
  - right to data portability;
  - right to object;
  - right not to be subject to a decision based solely on automated processing.

Limitation
- Data collection and use are limited to previously defined legitimate purposes.

Control
- Users can:
  - access all necessary information concerning their data and how they are processed;
  - access their personal data;

- have their data corrected in cases where they are incomplete or inaccurate;
- request the deletion of their personal data;
- restrict/object to the processing of their personal data.

Consent
- Users are given:
  - the possibility to voluntarily give (informed) consent for data processing;
  - the option to opt-in/out from data collection and application;
  - the option to withdraw previously given consent.
- The terms of use are unambiguous and easily understandable to the user.
- The silence or inaction of the user is not interpreted as consent.

Anti-discrimination
- Appropriate techniques are used for profiling.
- Algorithms are audited and reviewed in order to ensure no biases and discriminatory practices on the grounds of problematic parameters such as ethnic belonging, gender, religion.

Protection
- Users are informed about:
  - past security breaches;
  - potential cyber risks.
- Those collecting and storing personal data take care of the resilience and security of the systems and networks where the data reside.

Accountability
- Users are given the possibility to hold responsible those that collect, store or modify their personal data.
- Responsibilities for data activities are clearly stated.
- Work with law enforcement.

In order to better understand the relation between the values, criteria and indicators, it should be noted that the values stand on the top of the hierarchy in terms of abstractness and are followed by criteria and indicators, which operate at a more concrete level. Taking such an approach paves the way for the translation of the values, criteria and indicators into technical requirements. It is also important to emphasise that different criteria can be linked to more than one value, and that a value can be fulfilled (or partly fulfilled) by more than one criterion. One could describe the process as using the values to guide our search for criteria and indicators. There is no need to relate the values to the criteria as long as we can expect that using the criteria will lead us to the satisfying fulfilment of most of the values we have identified in the first part.

Conclusion

Based on the increased generation, collection and use of big data, as well as the opportunities and perils that go along with it, we have shown the need to establish an ethical framework that can guide decision-making concerning big data. Such a framework can contribute to the responsible and democratic employment of big data, also by indicating the limits regarding any big data processes and activities. We have provided the outline of such an ethical framework by: (1) identifying six core values (privacy, autonomy, transparency, responsibility, anti-discrimination and security); (2) looking for potential value conflicts; and (3) developing a set of ethical criteria and indicators. The values, criteria and indicators together could be used to guide the evaluation of big data activities. Of course, our ethical compass needs to be further activated by filling in some of the missing elements that we are not able to deliver in this context. It should then allow us to enhance our ability to manoeuvre the rocky coasts as well as the stormy high waters of the big data ocean.

Notes

1. This framework was proposed by Laney (2011). There are also attempts to enrich it by adding further dimensions, such as veracity, variability, complexity, value and decay. For more on this, see Lee (2017: 294–5).
2. A study by Christen et al. (2016) has identified 460 value terms in the context of cybersecurity.
3. This problem was initially used by Dennis Thompson (1980) who addressed the issue of moral responsibility of public officials. Later on, the notion was used in various other contexts.
4. Friedman and Nissenbaum (1996) distinguish three categories of bias in relation to computer systems: *pre-existing bias*, which stems from social institutions, practices and attitudes and exists prior to the design and development of a system; *technical bias*, which originates from technical constraints as part of the designing process; and *emergent bias*, which emerges after the design process and in the implementation phase due to the use of the created system in new contexts.
5. This is known as the CIA triangle and represents the industry standard for information security. For more, see Parker (1998).

References

Balboni, P. and T. Dragan, 'Big Data: Legal Compliance and Quality Management', in K. C. Li, H. Jiang and A. Y. Zomaya (eds), *Big Data Management and Processing* (Boca Raton, FL: CRC Press, 2017).

Birnbacher, D., *Analytische Einführung in die Ethik* (Berlin: Gruyter, 2003).

Brey, P., 'Ethical Aspects of Information Security and Privacy', in M. Petković and W. Jonker (eds), *Security, Privacy, and Trust in Modern Data Management* (Berlin: Springer, 2007).

Christen M., D. Narvaez, C. Tanner and T. Ott, 'Mapping Values: Using Thesauruses to Reveal Semantic Structures of Cultural Moral Differences', *Cognitive Systems Research* 40 (2016): 59–74.

Dean, M. D., D. M. Payne and B. J. L. Landry, 'Data Mining: An Ethical Baseline for Online Privacy Policies', *Journal of Enterprise Information Management* 29(4) (2016): 482–504.

Dhillon, G., T. Oliveira, S. Susarapu and M. Caldeira, 'Deciding between Information Security and Usability: Developing Value-based Objectives', *Computers in Human Behavior* 61 (2016): 656–66.

Donahue, J., N. Whittemore and A. Heerman, *Ethical Issues of Data Surveillance* (Ethica Publishing n.d.), available at: http://www.ethicapublishing.com/ethical/3CH20.pdf, last accessed 20 April 2018.

EGE, European Group on Ethics in Science and New Technologies to the EC (2012), *Opinion No. 26, Ethics of Information and Communication Technologies*, EU, Brussels, retrieved 20 February 2018, doi:10.2796/13541.

EGE, European Group on Ethics in Science and New Technologies to the EC, *Opinion No. 28, Ethics of Security and Surveillance Technologies*, EU, Brussels, 2014, doi:10.2796/22379.

Friedman, B. and H. Nissenbaum, 'Bias in Computer Systems', *ACM Transactions on Information Systems*, 14(3) (1996): 330–47.

Laney, D., '3D Data Management: Controlling Data Volume, Velocity, and Variety', *META Group*, 2001, available at: https://blogs.gartner.com/doug-laney/files/2012/01/ad949-3D-Data-Management-Controlling-Data-Volume-Velocity-and-Variety.pdf, last accessed 23 March 2018.

Lee, I., 'Big Data: Dimensions, Evolution, Impacts, and Challenges', *Business Horizons* 60(3) (2017): 293–303.

Mittelstadt, B. D., P. Allo, M. Taddeo, S. Wachter and L. Floridi, 'The Ethics of Algorithms: Mapping the Debate', *Big Data & Society* 3(2) (2016): 1–21.

Nissenbaum, H., 'Accountability in a Computerized Society', *Science & Engineering Ethics* 2(1) (1996): 25–42.

Nissenbaum, H., 'Privacy as Contextual Integrity', *Washington Law Review* 79(1) (2004): 119–57.

OECD, *Data-Driven Innovation: Big Data for Growth and Well-Being* (OECD Publishing, Paris, 2015).

Pariser, E., 'Beware Online "Filter Bubbles"', *TED2011*, 2011, available at: https://www.ted.com/talks/eli_pariser_beware_online_filter_bubbles/transcript, last accessed 10 May 2018.

Parker, D., *Fighting Computer Crime: a New Framework for Protecting Information* (New York: John Wiley, 1998).

Pipkin, D. (2000), *Information security: Protecting the global enterprise*, New York: Hewlett Packard Company.

Reidenberg, J. R., 'The Transparent Citizen', *Loyola University Chicago Law Journal* 47 (2015): 437–63.

Reijers, W., P. Brey and P. Jansen, *A Common Ethical Framework for Ethical Impact Assessment*, Deliverable D4.1, SATORI, 2016.

Rössler, B., *The Value of Privacy*, trans. R. D. V. Glasgow (Cambridge: Polity Press, 2005).

Spiekermann, S., *Ethical IT Innovation: a Value-based System Design Approach* (Boca Raton, FL: CRC Press, 2016).

Stelzer, H. and H. Veljanova, 'TRUESSEC.eu – Deliverable D4.2 Support Study: Ethical Issues', *TrueSec*, 2017, available at: https://truessec.eu/library, last accessed 27 September 2019.

Tavani, H., *Ethics and Technology: Controversies, Questions, and Strategies for Ethical Computing*, 3rd edn (New York: John Wiley, 2011).

Thompson, D., 'Moral Responsibility of Public Officials: the Problem of Many Hands', *American Political Science Review* 74(4) (1980): 905–16.

INDEX

EU representative:
Easy Access System Europe
Mustamäe tee 50, 10621 Tallinn, Estonia
Gpsr.requests@easproject.com

www.ingramcontent.com/pod-product-compliance
Lightning Source LLC
Chambersburg PA
CBHW051958270326
41929CB00015B/2706